THIS IS MY BODY

THE PRESENCE OF CHRIST in REFORMATION THOUGHT

THOMAS J. DAVIS

Baker Academic

a division of Baker Publishing Group
Grand Rapids, Michigan

Published by Baker Academic
a division of Baker Publishing Group
P.O. Box 6287, Grand Rapids, MI 49516-6287
www.bakeracademic.com

Printed in the United States of America

Library of Congress Cataloging-in-Publication Data
Davis, Thomas J. (Thomas Jeffery), 1958-
    This is my body : the presence of Christ in Reformation thought / Thomas J. Davis.
      p. cm.
    Several chapters that appear in this book were previously published as essays and some in substantially revised form.
    Includes bibliographical references and index.
    ISBN 978-0-8010-3245-5 (pbk.)
    1. Lord's Supper—Real presence. 2. Jesus Christ—Presence. I. Title.
BV823.D38 2008
234'.163—dc22   2008002964

In keeping with biblical principles of creation stewardship, Baker Publishing Group advocates the responsible use of our natural resources. As a member of the Green Press Initiative, our company uses recycled paper when possible. The text paper of this book is comprised of 30% post-consumer waste.

green
press
INITIATIVE

THIS IS
MY BODY

CONTENTS

DEDICATION

I have, in the past, thanked my graduate school professors, family, and friends for their help and support on various projects. Upon reflection, however, it struck me that I never said very much about those early educators who ignite the spark of learning that eventually becomes (some would say) a consuming fire. I would like to take this opportunity to thank those at each level of pre-PhD work who inspired me to a life of learning. Mrs. Y. A. Bailey taught me discipline (and English grammar) in fifth grade; may the soul of this wonderful teacher rest in peace. Jim Hagopian first opened my eyes to the realm of historical study in ninth-grade Western Civilization, for which I thank him. Carol Hagopian was my first foreign-language teacher; my French does not compare to John Calvin's, but insofar as I can read any French at all, I have her to thank. Y. Lynn Holmes first modeled for me what it meant to be a great college professor, and my recollection of his history classes inspires me still. David Buttrick stoked the desire within me not only to learn but also to lead a better life.

To these educators, I dedicate this book.

ACKNOWLEDGMENTS

Several chapters that appear in this book were previously published as essays. I gratefully acknowledge those venues of publication for allowing me to reprint them here, though (some) in (substantially) revised form.

"'His Completely Trustworthy Testament': The Development of Luther's Early Eucharistic Teaching, 1517–1521" appeared in *Fides et Historia* 25, no. 2 (Summer 1993): 4–22.

"'The Truth of the Divine Words': Luther's Sermons on the Eucharist, 1521–1528, and the Structure of Eucharistic Meaning" appeared in *The Sixteenth Century Journal* 30, no. 2 (Summer 1999): 323–42.

"'An Intermediate Brilliance': The Words of Institution and the Gift of Knowledge in Calvin's Eucharistic Theology" appeared in *Calvin Studies VI*, ed. John Leith (Davidson, NC: Davidson College, 1992), 77–86.

"Not 'Hidden and Far Off': The Bodily Aspect of Salvation and Its Implications for Understanding the Body in Calvin's Theology" appeared in *Calvin Theological Journal* 29, no. 2 (November 1994): 406–18.

"Preaching and Presence: Constructing Calvin's Homiletic Legacy" appeared in *The Legacy of John Calvin: Papers Presented at the Twelfth Colloquium of the Calvin Studies Society, 1999*, ed. David Foxgrover (Grand Rapids: Calvin Studies Society, 2000), 84–106.

"Discerning the Body: The Eucharist and the Christian Social Body in Sixteenth-Century Protestant Exegesis" appeared in *Fides et Historia* 37, no. 2 / 38, no. 1 combined issue (Summer–Fall 2005 / Winter–Spring 2006): 67–81.

"Hardened Hearts, Hardened Words: Calvin, Beza, and the Trajectory of Signification" appeared in *Calvin, Beza, and Later Calvinism: Papers Presented at the Fifteenth Colloquium of the Calvin Studies Society, 2005*, ed. David Foxgrover (Grand Rapids: Calvin Studies Society, 2006), 136–60.

While many of these chapters have previously appeared in scholarly journals or other venues, I should note that "An Intermediate Brilliance" and "Preaching and Presence" were originally presented with pastors in mind as well as scholars. In addition, I presented "The Communication of Efficacy" at the 2006 Sixteenth Century Society and Conference in a session that acknowledged and honored the work of Professor Elsie McKee of Princeton Theological Seminary; the chapter purposefully retains the flavor of a presentation.

Throughout this book, I have almost always used a standard and readily available translation when available. When this is the case, I cite the translation and then point the reader to where in one of the available critical editions the passage translated may be found. In those cases where I have translated material myself, I provide the appropriate citation along with the original language of the passage.

Abbreviations

CNTC   John Calvin, *Calvin's New Testament Commentaries*, ed. David W. Torrance and Thomas J. Torrance, 12 vols. (Grand Rapids: Eerdmans, 1959–72).

CO   John Calvin, *Ioannis Calvini opera quae supersunt omnia*, ed. Wilhelm Baum, Edward Cunitz, and Edward Reuss, 59 vols. (Braunschweig: C. A. Schwetscke, 1863–1900).

Inst.   John Calvin, *Institutes of the Christian Religion*, ed. John T. McNeill, trans. Ford Lewis Battles, 2 vols. (Philadelphia: Westminster, 1960). This is the standard English translation of the 1559 *Institutes*, Calvin's last Latin edition.

Inst, '36   John Calvin, *Institutes of the Christian Religion, 1536 Edition*, trans. and annotated by Ford Lewis Battles, rev. M. Howard Rienstra, rev. ed. (Atlanta: John Knox, 1975; repr., Grand Rapids: Eerdmans and the H. Henry Meeter Center for Calvin Studies, 1986).

Lenker   Martin Luther, *The Precious and Sacred Writings of Martin Luther*, ed. John Lenker, multiple volumes (Minneapolis: Lutherans in All Lands, 1903–).

LW   Martin Luther, *Luther's Works*, ed. Helmut T. Lehman and Jaroslav Pelikan, 55 vols. (Philadelphia: Fortress; St. Louis: Concordia, 1955–76).

Short Treatise   John Calvin, *Short Treatise on the Holy Supper*, in *John Calvin: Selections from His Writings*, ed. John Dillenberger (Missoula, MT: Scholar's Press, 1975).

SW   Huldreich Zwingli, *Huldreich Zwinglis Sämtliche Werke*, ed. Emil Egli, Georg Finsler, Walter Köhler et al. (Leipzig: M. Heinsius Nachfolger et al., 1905–66).

WA   Weimarer Ausgabe: Martin Luther, *D. Martin Luthers Werke*, Kritische Gesamtausgabe (Weimar: Hermann Böhlaus Nachfolger, 1883–).

11

INTRODUCTION

One Sunday morning many years ago, I was in a Presbyterian church. I had just decided to pursue Calvin's eucharistic teaching as the topic of my dissertation, so I anticipated the service with special eagerness that Sunday because we would be celebrating the Lord's Supper. We came to the part of the service where the elders moved down the center of the church with the broken loaf of home-baked bread on two plates (one for each side of the church). The elders would hand the plate to the person who sat nearest the aisle, who would then pass it to the next person. Each person would tear off a bit of bread from the loaf. As the plate moved along the row in front of me, one gentleman took a huge chunk of bread, elbowed his granddaughter, who was sitting next to him, and said in a whisper so loud that he must have thought he was on stage, "This is more than I had for breakfast."

I remember thinking that if he, like John Calvin, believed Christ to be offered in the Eucharist, then, indeed, it was more than he had had for breakfast. Given the laughter that erupted between grandfather and granddaughter, however, I quickly deduced that he did not, in fact, think anything like Calvin on the subject. He did not seem to take the Eucharist seriously at all.

How different than the sixteenth century, when conflicts over the celebration of the Eucharist, fights over its form, and polemics concerning the theology that underlay it were so prominent. From a modern point of view, the eucharistic controversies of the sixteenth century seem unchristian. Yet that is exactly part of the problematic: for the participants, those controversies were about what it meant to be a Christian, how to worship as a Christian, how to live in the world as a Christian. Indeed, what one finds is that eucharistic theology was not simply about church ritual but, rather, it was about who God is, how

God operates, how humanity is saved, where God might be found, what the Christian's duty is to others, and so forth. In other words, the Eucharist was a topic so wound up in Christian faith, doctrine, and practice that it impinged on all the important themes of Christianity. It thus was serious business—though, to the modern mind, perhaps, a seriousness gone mad, given the language that was often used toward one's opponents

Some of the language, as noted, was brutal, and it does (and should) repel us. Maybe this history is even why today we find believers who sit in churches and laugh in the face of the holy: they take things seriously, but not too seriously.

But some of the language was beautiful as well, and insightful, and through it the Reformers strove to express something of the true essence of Christianity. In regard to the Eucharist, they sometimes spoke with absolute certainty; sometimes the words they used carried a gentle tone of comfort and assurance; sometimes they stood in awe and humility as they tried to speak of the mysteries of God, knowing that something was lost between the experience of the presence of God and the way they tried to communicate that presence. So maybe the baby should not be thrown out with the bathwater: reject the ugly, yes, but take seriously that which deserves to be taken seriously. And maybe, in doing so, we can not only attend to the way the Reformers used language but also look at our own habits of speech, examining how we seek to express truth, beauty, and mystery while keeping an eye on the way that we, at times, use words as weapons to destroy rather than as building blocks to create and uplift. So, while it would be (and is, really) easy to criticize these sixteenth-century figures, I am willing to give them a break and focus on the good in them, and the good they sought to express, just as I hope that one day I will be judged mercifully as well.

Language. The American poet W. S. Merwin once wrote that "language is [a] vehicle of the unsayable."[1] What were the Reformers trying to put into human words about God? That God is good. That God saves. That God is present. Those are simple enough words until one asks "How?" How is God good? or at least, How do we know that God is good? How does God save? How is God present? The Reformers turned to Scripture, and therein they found Christ. God is good, yes, but that goodness is best understood in the way that Christ shows God to be good. God saves through Christ. God is present to humanity through Christ. At least, those are the answers given by Luther and Calvin. But then questions arise: But how do we know Christ? How does

---

1. W. S. Merwin, *Regions of Memory: Uncollected Prose, 1949–82*, ed. and introduced by Ed Folsom and Carey Nelson (Urbana: University of Illinois Press, 1987), 199.

God save through Christ? How is God present in Christ? Ask enough hows and finally language appears to fracture; more than that, it seems to dissolve before the mystery of God and God's revelation of God's goodness, intention, and Word.

Yet the Reformers thought it important to try to know about all these things, and they ended up basing their words, insofar as they were able, on God's Word understood preeminently in its expression in the incarnate Jesus Christ but also understood as Scripture, the substance of which, according to Luther and Calvin, was Christ himself. Their words were commentary on the divine Word, Christ, who became incarnate so that the divine Word would not only be heard but also be seen; indeed, not only be seen and heard but also be present.

So, what did Luther, Calvin, and others have to say on some of these issues? That is the substance of this book, which explores and analyzes ways in which Luther and Calvin understood the issue of Christ's presence (and all that entails and implies). Much of the discussion centers around the Eucharist, which means that the discussion will be wide ranging: we will look at the relationship of Word and Eucharist, examine the notion of body and presence (exhibited and offered in both Word and Sacrament), explore the issue of efficacious presence, and think about the use of language itself (this last will not center on the Eucharist as such but on the changing paradigm of signification, which does, as some of the illustrative material in the chapter shows, bear greatly on how body and presence are signified).

The book begins with chapters on Luther and the Eucharist, focusing on the development of Luther's understanding of the Word's role in the Eucharist (chaps. 1 and 2). Here, we look especially at his exegesis and sermons. I argue that the central issue in Luther's eucharistic teaching is not the ubiquity of Christ's body but the power of the Word. Luther certainly did vehemently defend the notion of Christ's ubiquitous body, but his real concern was the role of the Word in eucharistic celebration; indeed, the overriding concern of Luther altogether was the Word. In Luther's case, body and indeed presence had to do with the "truth of the divine words," the divine Word being the sine qua non that points to and reveals the hidden body of Christ, the incarnate Word necessary for salvation.[2]

Luther has often been thought of as one who focused on Christ's body because of the way he taught on the ubiquity issue. Calvin, because of the way

2. For an essay that emphasizes Luther's elevation of Word over the visible signs, see Randall C. Zachman, "Image and Word in the Theology of Martin Luther and John Calvin," chap. 8 in *John Calvin as Teacher, Pastor, and Theologian* (Grand Rapids: Baker Academic, 2006), 175–89.

he presented the issue of Christ's presence (not in any way given bodily "in, with, or under" the elements of bread and wine, to use Luther's terminology), has often been misread as a "spiritualizer," both in his own century and ever since. Yet every bit as much as Luther, Calvin tied the Christian's salvation to the presence of Christ's body, and he did so in a way thoroughly worked out in his commentary on the book of John. Though Calvin himself has often been characterized as a theologian of the Word, and he was, there was much more to Calvin's thought than some barren understanding of "Word." Indeed, Calvin thought that Christ, bodily, was given in the Word and the Sacrament; he believed that the bodily mediation of Christ was essential to the Christian's salvation, and he insisted that, to take advantage of that me-diation, the Christian must somehow or other participate in Christ's body and that such participation hinged, in large part, on *knowing* that such union with Christ was not simply a joining of the Christian's spirit to Christ's spirit but also to Christ's body. So, we have chapters on the role of knowledge in Calvin's eucharistic thought (chap. 3); on the importance of the human and divine body in Calvin's theology (chap. 4); on the part preaching has to play in Christian life, especially as it relates to Christ's presence (chaps. 5 and 6); the relationship of absence and presence when speaking of Christ's body (chap. 7); and on the proper understanding of power and efficaciousness in regard to the revelation of Christ through signs (chap. 8).

Finally, there are two chapters on exegesis and language. One chapter ex-plores the strategies that Luther, Zwingli, and Calvin employed to deal with Paul's injunction to "discern the body" in the midst of the eucharistic cel-ebration (chap. 9). What is meant there by "body," according to each? More than what people sometimes assume: we find a case where Luther reversed a position on how signs operate, where Zwingli paid more attention to the natural body than one might suppose, and where Calvin showed a flexibility in language that I think more and more Calvin scholars are recognizing as fundamental to Calvin's method of interpretation.

The final chapter (chap. 10) looks at the question of language in the early modern period. It suggests that there was a paradigm shift taking place es-pecially in the fifteenth and sixteenth centuries that pushed signs and the signifying of language toward the literal. Though the chapter itself is not directly about the Eucharist, it does carry implications for how we deal with the environment of the sixteenth century. Luther rejected the fourfold inter-pretation of Scripture that had served as the basis for medieval exegesis. In its place, he seemed to set a literal means of interpretation, wherein one sign (or word) could have only one meaning. Looking back, people might think that Luther and Zwingli, for example, were miles apart on the question of

Christ's presence in the Eucharist. But in at least one regard they absolutely agreed: the word "is" in the phrase "This is my body" could have only one meaning. This style of thinking carried over into their other disagreements as well: language was flattened out into a linear one-to-one correspondence between sign (and words are signs) and thing. Even if Luther thought something should be understood allegorically, for example, there was only one proper allegorical interpretation: all others were false. Perhaps it is helpful to know that, instead of being peculiar to these particular theological discussions among these theologians, this way of viewing language and signs was part of a larger cultural shift, one that required, in a sense, a literal reading of signs in order for that reading to be considered authoritative. There was, in other words, a *push* toward the literal in the world of the sixteenth century.

Which brings us back to our laughing grandfather. How seriously are we to take these Reformers, and studies such as this one that try to unpack their thought? Enough so that we may learn from them what it is we can learn, everything that is to our profit and edification; not so seriously that our studies become familiar diatribes, and we forget that even in the face of the holy there might be something to laugh about, the same as we laugh around a table laden with good food and surrounded by family and friends. After all, this study is about something that I always introduce in church by saying, "Friends, this is the joyful feast of the people of God."[3]

May it be so.

3. *The Worshipbook: Services and Hymns* (Philadelphia: Westminster, 1970), 34.

1

"HIS COMPLETELY TRUSTWORTHY TESTAMENT"

The Development of Luther's Early Eucharistic Teaching, 1517–1521

Luther's early eucharistic teaching, particularly from the years 1518–19, has been viewed favorably by some ecumenically minded Catholic scholars.[1] They characterize his thought from this period as both Catholic and pastoral: Catholic in the sense that he did not deviate from Catholic doctrine, and pastoral in the sense that he sought to address proper preparation for eucharistic participation without striving to overthrow Catholic doctrine. In large measure this assessment is based on the strong emphasis Luther placed on the communion of the saints, understood as the church, as the locus of belief that established the objectivity of the grace given in the Eucharist.

1. See, for example, Joseph Lortz's assessment of Luther's early sacramental thought in "Sakramentales Denken beim jungen Luther," in *Luther-Jahrbuch 1969*, ed. D. Franz Lau (Hamburg: Friedrich Wittig, 1969), 11. Lortz asserts that the early Luther bore witness to a Catholic conception of the Sacrament "that could have had its legitimate place in the Catholic church, to the church's continuing profit" ("das sie in der katholischen Kirche zu deren Nützen dauernd ihren legitimen Platz hätte haben können"). Others have lauded Luther's early eucharistic writings because they exhibited a genuine desire to reform the church along pastoral rather than dogmatic lines. In this regard, see, e.g., Frido Mann, *Das Abendmahl beim jungen Luther* (Munich: Max Hueber, 1971), esp. 144.

By 1520–21, however, Luther's understanding of the Lord's Supper, as revealed in his eucharistic writings, had undergone a noticeable shift. No longer willing to let the church be the deposit of faith for Christians, one that they could draw on without personal commitment, he insisted that the individual's faith played a much greater role—actually the *crucial* role—in the drama of proper eucharistic reception. Thus there appears to be a chasm that separates the two periods of Luther's thought on the Eucharist, one that sets apart the so-called Catholic and pastoral Luther from the evangelical and dogmatic Luther.

There is a bridge, however, that connects these two periods in Luther's thought: his *Lectures on Hebrews*. On the one hand, the style of commentary, along with many of its comments, is quite at odds with the commentaries Luther produced after having matured in his newfound faith. On the other hand, one finds in nascent form here two key components of Luther's most developed eucharistic thought: the importance of personal faith and the idea of the Eucharist as primarily the testament, the last will, of Jesus Christ. Moreover, the date of these lectures, from the spring of 1517 to the spring of 1518, locates the genesis of these ideas of personal faith and testament, as they relate to the Eucharist, in a period previous to the 1518–19 works.

Therefore, what one can argue is that an analysis of Luther's *Lectures on Hebrews* is essential to understanding how Luther developed his eucharistic teaching so as to be able to move from the emphases of the 1518–19 eucharistic work to those of his 1520–21 eucharistic writings. What one can conclude is that a neat distinction cannot be made between the 1518–19 Catholic and pastoral Luther and the 1520–21 evangelical and dogmatic Luther. Rather, Luther's concern for an evangelical doctrine of the Lord's Supper, based on his exegesis of Scripture, was already present by 1518.

This chapter, then, examines Luther's views on the role of faith in preparation for the reception of the Sacrament and the benefit that is then derived from the Sacrament, first as those views are expressed in the 1518–19 works and then how those views changed in the 1520–21 works. An analysis of the *Lectures on Hebrews* then follows.

The Communion of the Saints and the Faith of the Church in Luther's 1518–19 Eucharistic Writings

By 1518, the time of the Heidelberg Disputation, Luther had begun to garner the reputation of a pugnacious debater and fierce opponent. Yet his meditation on the Eucharist from that year breathed the spirit of humility one associates with the ideal monk. The title of the work bespoke Luther's concern that eucharistic participants examine themselves before Communion: "Sermon on the Proper Preparation of the Heart for the Sacramental Reception of the Eucharist." In a caring and gentle way, Luther sought to lead his readers through the appropriate mix of humility and confidence necessary to partake sacramentally of the Eucharist. He considered it the recipient's duty to cultivate a sense of true humility; faith, as we shall see, while necessary, was not particularly the individual's responsibility. In other words, Luther called on the individual to prepare for the Sacrament through humility; if the participant was humble, God through the church would grant the faith necessary for the Eucharist.

Luther made it clear that the confession of one's sins and a true sense of sorrow must precede the reception of the Sacrament. The sense of sorrow, however, must not be borne down by an overreliance on the individual's ability to confess all sin. Luther seemed to balance the notion of an engendered humility, which he thought to be absolutely necessary, with the church's wisdom of requiring that only plainly mortal sins need to be confessed in order properly to receive the Sacrament.[2]

Confession served to bring to recipients knowledge of themselves as sinners in need. Thus confession acted not only as a medium to clear the path for grace; it also functioned to ward off self-confidence. In many ways, for Luther, self-confidence was the major barrier to grace, for such an attitude brought only God's judgment, never God's grace.[3] A thorough, though not necessarily exhaustive, confession helped to bring about this proper preparation of the heart.

Such preparation was typified for Luther in this prayer that he offered as a model petition to God: "Here I am, Lord Jesus Christ. Look upon my wretchedness, for I am poor and needy. Yet, so far I have been disdainful of your remedy, so that I do not sigh for the riches of your grace. Awaken in me, O Lord, a longing for your grace, and enkindle faith in your promise that I

---

2. "First of all," Luther wrote, "it is necessary that you confess and grieve all plainly mortal sins." ("Primo, necessarium est, ut omnia peccata manifeste mortalia confitearis atque doleas," WA 1:329). Luther pulled on the psalmist for support as he asked, "Who knows his transgressions?" ("Delicta quis intelligit?" WA 1:329). Here Luther seems to support at least partially the late-medieval notion that mortal sin represented an obstacle (*obex*) to the grace of the Sacrament. Once the obstacle was removed through confession, the lesser sins could not stand in the way of the operation of grace.

3. "All these people eat and drink judgment to themselves, because they are not made worthy or pure by all these things; on the contrary, through this self-confidence the purulent are defiled even worse." ("Omnes hii iudicium sibi manducant et bibunt, quia hiis omnibus non fiunt digni neque puri, Immo per eam fiduciam puritates peius polluunter," WA 1:331).

may not offend you, my most excellent God, by my perversity, disbelief, and satiety."[4] Such a prayer, Luther thought, exuded both confidence in God's mercy and dread at one's own unworthiness. Such a mixture of confidence in God and humility, he believed, resulted in a purifying faith.[5]

Thus, according to Luther, the faith of the individual followed as a result of the Eucharist. It is portrayed as something bestowed on the sinner by the reception of the Sacrament. Indeed, there seems to be some sense in which Luther viewed the Eucharist as a finished work (*opus operatum*),[6] at least in the sense that he viewed the Sacrament as a work based not so much on the individual's faith and participation in the Eucharist but more on the communion of saints, the church. Luther thought the communion of saints could serve to mediate the benefits of the Sacrament through saintly sharing and participation. Certainly, faith is necessary, he thought, for the Sacrament to be efficacious;[7] however, Luther saw not Christ but the Mother Church as a refuge for those too timorous in faith to be able to partake of the Eucharist on their own. The church was the place where the infirm in faith could be nourished. Luther drew on Bernard of Clairvaux as an exemplar: "Thus, Saint Bernard once said to a brother who was so excessively fearful and anxious that he refused to celebrate: 'Go, my brother, and celebrate in my faith.' This brother benefited by obeying and was healed from all the weakness of his conscience."[8] The benefit of faith was available to the recipient through the Sacrament by means of another's faith because, according to this work, Luther believed the essence of the Supper, its primary benefit, to be the communion of saints.

For Luther, this meant that one was incorporated into the body of Christ through the means of the Eucharist and thereby shared the benefits of belonging

4. "Ecce me, domine Iesus Christe, miseriam meam respice, inops et pauper sum ego, et tamen adeo fastidiosus medicine tue, ut nec divitias gratie tue suspirem. Accende in me, domine, desyderium gratie tue et fidem promissionis tue, ut non offendam te optimum deum meum perversa mea et incredulitate et saturitate" (WA 1:331).

5. "Fiunt autem puri per fidem, ut sequitur" (WA 1:331).

6. As eucharistic theology developed in the church, by the late medieval period, the Eucharist was viewed as an *opus operatum*, meaning that it was a work that had been completed, a work already done. By participating in the Eucharist, the recipient reaped the benefits of a completed action: Christ's saving act. Luther rejected this notion of a completed or accomplished work and instead emphasized the personal faith necessary to derive benefit from the Sacrament: *opus operantis*, a work being done, in process, in which one is intimately involved.

7. "Fides enim est que iustificat, purificat, dignificat, ut Actu: 15. Fide purificans corda eorum, etc." (WA 1:331).

8. "Sic B. Bernhardus, quum aliquando haberet fratrem nimius timidum et scrupulosum, ita ut nollet celebrare, ait ad eum: 'Vade, mi frater et celebra in fide mea,' et ivit ille obediens et sanatus ab omni languore conscientie sue" (WA 1:333).

to that body; since the body, the church, had faith, then the recipient shared in that faith.[9] Luther drew on the ancient imagery of the church to underscore the unity the Sacrament created: "[The oneness of the saints] is figured in the elements of the sacrament, in which many grains, losing their individual diversity, are made into one bread; likewise with the grapes, which also lose their diversity and are made into one wine."[10]

It served as a great assurance to the young Luther that the entire body of the saints was so united and thus one. Such a situation, Luther thought, made the benefit of corporate faith available to the individual. Such a benefit, to Luther's mind, was truly necessary: one could never be certain of one's worthiness to partake.[11] Certainly, the need for faith in the Word of God was not absent,[12] but that faith appeared as something to be shared as one of the benefits of belonging to the communion of saints, the church. This comfortable and comforting notion was underscored by the fact that when Luther spoke about faith in the Word of God he did not mean the Word of promise as found in the testament of Christ, as he later would so strongly come to emphasize as the object of the individual's faith; rather, the Word he referred to here was Christ's word of comfort: "Come unto me, all you who are weary."[13] This word of comfort was important for Luther, who so strongly stressed that Christ's call came for sinners, not the just.[14]

When one moves to Luther's 1519 work "The Blessed Sacrament of the Holy and True Body of Christ, and the Brotherhoods," one finds the same combination of individual preparation and corporate faith as found in the "Sermon on the Proper Preparation of the Heart." The Supper is a balm for the sick, a hope for the hopeless and helpless. Proper preparation thus required self-knowledge of one's state before God as a sinner; indeed, it is that recognition, Luther thought, that enables the Sacrament to render its fullest effect. The rhetoric Luther used to evoke a personal sense of need is powerful: "For this reason, it thus happens that this holy sacrament is of no or little use to those

9. "The name is communion, a thing that means a unity of hearts, just as one faith, one baptism, one Lord, one hope, and, in short, everything is one and shared in common" ("Nomen est communio, res unitas cordium, sicut una fides, unum baptisma, unus dominus, una spes, ac prorsus omnia eadem et communion," WA 1:329).

10. "Quod et figuratur in speciebus sacramenti, in quibus multa grana, amissa singulorum differentia, in unum panem, Item uve multe, amissa sua quoque differentia, in unum vinum redacte sunt" (WA 1:329).

11. "At impossibile est ut ex se et suis viribus certus fiat" (WA 1:332).

12. "Hec itaque fides sola et summa ac proxima dispositio facit vere puros et dignos . . . in purissimo, piisimo firmissimoque verbo Christi dicentis: Venite ad me" (WA 1:331).

13. Ibid.

14. See esp. Luther's comments on Matt. 9:12 at WA 1:330.

who have no misfortune or are not in fear or do not feel their unhappiness. For it is only given to those who need comfort and strength, who have full hearts, who carry frightened consciences, who suffer from sin's temptation or who even have fallen into sin. What should it work for free and secure spirits, who neither need or require it? For as the Mother of God says, 'He fills only the hungry and consoles those who are oppressed.'"[15] To drive home his point, Luther further emphasized that it was only after Jesus had made his own disciples sad, sorrowful, and anxiety-ridden by the recognition of the sin of betrayal among them that he deemed them worthy to receive the Sacrament, for it was at that point that the disciples needed strength.[16]

Once again, as in the former work, Luther used the notion of preparation of the heart, a frank look at one's sinfulness, to gain a real sense of one's need for the Eucharist in order to declare its value as a remedy to the soul's distress. That remedy, however, comes in the form of a corporate faith, a sharing in the belief held by the communion of saints. Luther thought such a benefit to be the primary effect of the Eucharist. To go to the Sacrament, Luther observed, was to be in a community: thus the name "Communion." He elaborated by comparing participation in the Sacrament to being a member of a city, where each citizen is a member of each other and of the entire city. Luther thus concluded, "This sacrament, received in bread and wine, is nothing other than a sure sign of this community and incorporation with Christ and all saints."[17]

In this writing we find the same logic as in the 1518 sermon: Faith is required in order to receive the benefit of the Eucharist, but that faith does not necessarily have to be the individual's faith. The individual may draw on the faith of the community of saints so that one may receive the Sacrament's benefit. Again, preparation is personal and individual; reception takes place within the context of community via the community. Faith is seen as a common possession. Luther declared that "all the spiritual good

15. "Derhalben geschichts auch, das denen, die nit unfall haben odder an angist seyn odder yhr ungluck nit fülen, diss heylig sacrament nit nutz ist odder wenig, dan es nur den gebenn ist, die trost und sterck bedurffen, die blöd hertzen haben, die erschrocken gewissen tragen, die von sunden anfechtung leyden odder auch dreyn gefallen seyn. Was solt es bey den freyen sichernn geysten wircken, die seyn nit durffen noch begeren? Dan es spricht die Mutter gottis: Er erfullet nur die hungerigen und tröstet, die geengist seyn" (WA 2:746). I have preferred to give my own translation for this work; it has, however, been translated in LW 35:49–73. The editor of this volume of LW considered this work to be Luther's "first extended statement on the Lord's Supper" (LW 35:47). This assessment may be because the 1518 work is, in many aspects, so "Catholic" sounding.

16. WA 2:746.

17. "Ist diss sacrament yn brott und weyn empfahen nit anders dan eyn gewiss tzeichen empfahen disser gemeynschafft und eyn leybung mit Christo und allen heyligen" (WA 2:743).

things of Christ and his saints . . . [are] shared and common to him who receives this sacrament."[18] Luther concluded the sermon with an appeal to the Sacrament's unifying fruit: "The fruit of this sacrament is community and love, through which we are strengthened against death and all evil, . . . [so that] the particular self-serving love of self is uprooted by this sacrament and is replaced by a community-serving love of all people. Thus, through love, we are changed to one bread, one drink, one body, one community."[19] Fellowship, the communion of saints found within the church, is the benefit, therefore, of the Lord's Supper while at the same time serving as that which enables the participant to receive the benefit. In this treatise of Luther's, the eucharistic celebration is the visible sign of a fellowship that strengthens Christians in their need, serving as the vehicle through which faith and love are made possible.[20]

Luther's 1518 and 1519 writings on the Lord's Supper belong together for they share the same spirit. One sees in them a stress on the individual sinner's need to recognize the state of one's sinfulness before God, on the benefit of belonging to the communion of saints as both the means and fruit of true eucharistic Communion, and on the community's role in mediating both the faith that makes the Sacrament efficacious and the love that makes the Christian into Christ's likeness. There is, in short, nothing here that would set Luther apart from the church of his day; indeed, as Lortz and others have pointed out, Luther in eloquent fashion articulated emphases fully acceptable to the church.

18. "Das alle geystlich guter Christi unnd seyner heyligen mit geteyllet und gemeyn werden dem, der dyss sacrament empfeht" (WA 2:743). Luther emphasized the sharing; one grows in the community by sharing in its character, which is love. There actually seems to be some sense of the notion of infused love here: that one is Christlike not by imputation but by a growing uniformity with Christ through the love bestowed on the community and its Sacrament. The significance of the Sacrament, Luther declared, lies in the daily growth of love with which the believer is inflamed so as to take Christ's form ("davon wir ny lieb entzudet nemen sein gestalt"; see WA 2:748). What is more, it is that infusion of love that will eventually, in the last days, make Christians like Christ (see WA 2:749).

19. "Ist die frucht disses sacraments gemeynschafft und lieb, da durch wir gesterckt werden widder tod und alles ubell . . . das allso die eygen nutzige lieber seyns selbs durch diss sacrament auss gerodtet eyn lassed die gemeyn nutzige liebe aller menschen und allso durch die sacrament der liebe vorwandlung eyn brott, eyn tranck, eyn leyp, eyn gemeyn werde" (WA 2:754).

20. Though balanced by the community emphasis, the need for faith is not overlooked: it is necessary for the operation of the Sacrament (see WA 2:742). Still, it is the faith of the community of saints, not the individual, to which Luther referred. That seems to be the reason why, at this point in his career, Luther supported the church's celebration of the mass; since there is such a full sharing among the saints of the benefits of the Eucharist, it is not actually necessary that the laity, for example, commune under both kinds. Thus one reads as Luther opined that communion under one species was sufficient because that is the way the "Christian church orders and gives it" ("die Christenlich kirch ordenet und gibt," WA 2:743).

The Faith of the Individual and the Testament of Christ

Luther's 1520 "A Sermon on the New Testament, That Is, on the Holy Mass" signals a decided shift away from the accents found in Luther's 1518–19 eucharistic writings. Here, Luther explicitly moved to a consideration of the individual's personal faith in the role of eucharistic participation while also downplaying the notion of *communio sanctorum* in favor of accentuating the testamental character of the celebration. The implications of this shift are worked out more fully in *The Babylonian Captivity of the Church*, written within two months of the "Sermon on the New Testament," and in Luther's poignant farewell sermon to his fellow monks, given on Maundy Thursday of 1521 just days before Luther's trip to the Diet of Worms, a trip from which he did not expect to return.

In terms of preparation for Communion, Luther's 1520 "Sermon on the New Testament" still emphasized the need for the participant to recognize one's sins, which, Luther thought, would result in a "hungry soul."[21] What better preparation for the eucharistic meal than a spiritual appetite? However, in addition to this hunger, Luther now demanded that the participant bring to the Sacrament a "strong, joyful faith of the heart."[22] According to the Luther of 1520, this faith can no longer be "borrowed" from another but must reside in the individual believer's own heart. The difference in the matter of individual faith is obvious. Luther wrote: "Thus, you must here [at the table], above all things, look after your own heart, that you believe the words of Christ and take them to be true."[23] The believer must look after his or her own heart because it is only with a heart filled with personal faith that one can appropriate the words of Christ, such being now for Luther the essence of what makes one worthy and well prepared to receive the Eucharist.

This shift to the individual's faith is required by the shift in Luther's belief about what is received in the Sacrament. No longer is the communion of saints portrayed as the primary benefit of the Communion meal.[24] Instead, what one

21. "Ein hungerige seele" (WA 6:360). See LW 35:79–110 for an English translation of this work. Again, I prefer here to give my own translations.

22. "Ein fester frölicher glaube des hertzen" (WA 6:360). As Luther described the process later in the work, the soul is made hungry by the recognition of its sins, and thus the conviction of one's sins and a tormented conscience lead the Christian to this hunger. Once at the table, however, the horror of one's sins should give way to a joyful faith in the forgiveness Christ offers (see WA 6:376–77).

23. "Alßo mustu hie fur allen dingen deyniss hertzen warnhemen, das du den worten Christi glaubist und lassist sie war seyn" (WA 6:360).

24. Luther does not simply discard the concept. See Dennis Alan Laskey, "In Faith and Fervent Love: The Concept of *Communio* in Luther's Understanding of the Lord's Supper" (PhD diss., Lutheran School of Theology at Chicago, 1983). The communion of the saints is, however, placed

receives from God in the Supper is a testament, Christ's Word of promise. Luther averred that the words of testament constituted the whole of the mass, "with all its essence, work, use, and fruit, without which nothing is received in the mass."[25] The Christian therefore must keep the words of the testament in sight, depend on them as the chief thing, so that the "correct, basic, and proper preparation for the mass is learned."[26]

It is in the testamental words of Christ at the Last Supper that the Christian finds God's promise, Luther believed. Moreover, trust in this promise constitutes salvation, according to Luther. What does one take from the Sacrament? In this 1520 work, it is the Word of divine promise, which must be trustingly believed; there must be faith that God does as God promises. As Luther would more and more emphasize in his theology, here he affirmed that "this trust and faith is the beginning, middle, and end of every work and righteousness."[27] It thus is through belief in the testamental promise of Christ that the Christian is made "pious and blessed."[28]

Therefore, to benefit from the Sacrament of the altar, the Christian must receive Christ's promise, trusting Christ to keep his word. One could not benefit, Luther thought, from a testament that was not believed; indeed, not only must the testament be believed, it must also be claimed as one's own. Thus Luther here asserted that the Eucharist is not an *opus operatum*, a completed work, but an *opus operantis*, a work that requires the active presence of personal faith for it to be completed. Luther had said as much in 1519, but with a difference; the active agent could be the church as a whole, not just the individual. In this 1520 context, however, it is not enough for the corporate faith of the church to be present; the individual must have faith in order for the benefit to work in oneself. Luther underscored the necessity of personal faith in the way he talked of Christ the Testator, who sealed

---

within a different hierarchy of meaning so that its significance is apparent and valid only within that hierarchy. The controlling element in that hierarchy is the concept of testament as a word of promise. I expand on this hierarchy of meaning in the next chapter.

25. "Mit all yhrem wessen, werck, nutz und frucht, on wilche nichts von der mess empfangen wirt" (WA 6:355).

26. "Die recht grund gutte bereytung zur mess und dem sacrament gelernt wirt" (WA 6:357). Specifically, Luther considered these to be the words of testament: "Take it and eat, this is my body, which is given for you. Take it and drink from it one and all, this is the cup of the new and eternal testament in my blood, which is poured out for you and for many for the forgiveness of sin" ("Nemet yhn und esset, das ist mein leychnam, der fur euch geben wirt. Nemet yhn und trinkt darauss allesampt, das ist der kilch des newen und ewigen Testaments yn meynem bluet, das fur euch und fur viele vorgossen wirt zuvorgebung der sund," WA 6:356).

27. "Disse trew und glaub ist der anfang, mittell und end aller werck und gerechtickeit" (WA 6:356).

28. "Frum und selig" (WA 6:357). The testamental promise is the promise to forgive sins.

his Word of promise with his own blood, thus making it sure for his heirs. Indeed, it is Christ who assures the individual's faith, as is apparent in how Luther wrote out the intent of Christ's testament and death: "That you are sure and know that such a vow remains irrevocably for you, so I will die for it and give my body and blood for it; and both—body and blood—I leave to you as a sign and a signal that, by them, you should remember me."[29] God became human and died to seal for eternity the testament for the Christian. For Luther, the only appropriate response was faith and trust in so great a promise and truly to believe Christ when he says to the Christian that the testament is "fur euch." What the Lord's Supper brings to the Christian, then, is a reminder and guarantee of God's testamental Word of promise sealed with the body and blood of the Savior.[30] It is the Christian's duty, through faith, to prepare to receive that Word.

Luther's "Sermon on the New Testament" was written in July 1520. The papal bull Exsurge Domine (June 15, 1520; cf. Ps. 7:6) had not yet reached him, but he had begun to hear rumors of its coming. However, by September 1520, Luther knew the bull was well on its way. With this situation in mind, we turn to *The Babylonian Captivity of the Church*, Luther's first full-scale attack on the sacramental system of the Catholic Church.

In *Babylonian Captivity*, Luther built on his July work. The change in emphasis that one can recognize between the "Sermon on the New Testament" and Luther's 1518–19 writings crescendoed in *Babylonian Captivity*. Consistent with what he had written just a few months earlier, Luther started by showing how a human stands before God as a sinner; thus there can be no notion that one prepares for the Eucharist by works.[31] What a sinner needs before God is

29. "Das du gewiss seyest und wissest, das solch gelubd dir unwidderrüfflich bleib, ßo will ich drauss sterben und meyn leyb und bluet dafur geben, und beydes dir zum zeychen und sigell hynder mir lassen, da bey du meyn gedencken solt" (WA 6:358).

30. Though the sacramental sign is important, it amounts to nothing, in Luther's opinion, without the Word of promise. What constitutes the Sacrament, purely and simply, is the Word and vow of God. On this, see WA 6:363; see also the discussion at WA 6:373–74. Here, then, is why Luther started his demand for liturgical reform: the mass should be read loudly and in German and in accord more with the first mass, that of Christ, because by these reforms Luther believed the Word of promise would be stressed; moreover, it is the Word of promise that constitutes the mass, not any notion of priestly sacrifice or good work (see WA 6:362, 355, 364). If the hearing and believing of the Word of promise, then, constitutes the true mass, then faith becomes the only true priestly office (see WA 6:370). Luther developed his notion of real presence in relation to the emphasis on the Word of promise; the body of Christ is not given in, with, and under the bread in order to be sacrificed again or in order for the Christian to partake of his substance so that there may take place a transfusion of substance; rather, the body and blood are present as the surest and best sign that God keeps God's Word.

31. LW 36:38–39 (WA 6:514).

faith in God's divine promise. Self-preparation for the mass consists of nothing other than faith.[32] This faith, Luther proclaimed, consists of laying "hold of the word of Christ, and fix[ing] our gaze much more steadfastly on it than on these thoughts of our own weakness."[33] Thus faith as the proper preparation for eucharistic participation was underscored by Luther.

Moreover, the new emphasis on the individual's faith, versus the corporate faith of the church, is again very pronounced. Indeed, the individual's responsibility for oneself in matters of faith before the Lord's altar now stands in bold contrast to Luther's earlier thoughts from 1519, when he had held out the possibility of relying on the corporate faith of the church. Instead, Luther heartily affirmed in *Babylonian Captivity*: "Therefore, let this irrefutable truth stand fast: where there is a divine promise, there every one must stand on his own feet; his own personal faith is demanded, he will give an account for himself and bear his own load. . . . Each one can derive personal benefit from the mass only by his own personal faith. It is absolutely impossible to commune on behalf of anyone else."[34] Once again, in line with the July sermon, Luther propounded the necessity of personal faith as the only proper preparation of the heart for the eucharistic celebration because of his conviction concerning what the Christian receives from the Lord's Supper. What is given is the promise of God. In the Word of testament, God speaks the Word of forgiveness, which itself speaks of the promise of eternal life.[35] But for whom is the promise? Luther bluntly wrote that it "is received only by the person who believes for himself, and only to the extent that he believes."[36]

The rest of *Babylonian Captivity*, with what seems to be its sweeping call for reform of the eucharistic rite itself (a call much at odds with his defense, for example, of Communion under one species [bread but no wine for the people] in the 1518–19 works), simply follows from Luther's analysis of the full implications of what he had, so to speak, laid out on the table: faith as the only proper preparation of the heart for the Eucharist, and the Word of testament received by the properly prepared heart. Based on the faith/testament schema Luther proposed, he attacked Communion under one species, transubstantiation, and the concept of *opus operatum*. On the same basis, he advocated celebrating the Eucharist in the vernacular and stripping away all

32. LW 36:39, 43, 46 (WA 6:514, 517, 520).

33. LW 36:45 (WA 6:519).

34. LW 36:49 (WA 6:521). The word "personal" is used twice in this translation, but it is not present in the original. However, given Luther's stress on the personal throughout the treatise, the word does give the appropriate flavor to what Luther was trying to say.

35. LW 36:38 (WA 6:513).

36. LW 36:51 (WA 6:522).

parts of the rite that stood in the way of the clear proclamation of the Word of promise.[37]

I say "faith/testament schema" because by the time he wrote the *Babylonian Captivity* Luther had in a real sense moved beyond the notion of preparation and reception as completely separate entities, or linear realties: first comes faith, then the reception of the Word of promise. Rather, as he tried to safeguard the objectivity of the Sacrament, Luther located the objective nature of sacramental grace in the Word of promise itself. Salvation and grace are given by God in the Sacrament, according to Luther, but they are given in the Word rather than in the eucharistic elements. Faith is necessary to obtain the benefit of the words, but the faith that an individual has comes from God and is prompted by the Word of promise itself. Luther explained: "It is plain, therefore, that the beginning of our salvation is a faith which clings to the Word of the promising God, who, without any effort on our part, in free and unmerited mercy takes the initiative and offers us the Word of his promise."[38] Thus, by the end of the *Babylonian Captivity*, Luther had developed a eucharistic theory centered completely around the *verba testamenti*. In this theory, the Word of testament is that which is received in the Eucharist (the benefit) and is also that which instills the faith necessary to receive the benefit (the preparation).

Finally, we turn to Luther's "Sermon on the Worthy Reception of the Sacrament," delivered on Maundy Thursday, March 28, 1521, less than a week before his departure for Worms. The mood of the work is subdued, with an almost total lack of polemic. Luther's pastoral intent is clear.

Luther's notions of faith as preparation and Word of promise as the benefit of the Eucharist are well in place by this time. He again points to the need for sinners to recognize their sin so that they may cultivate a true hunger for the benefit of the Supper;[39] knowing their sin thoroughly, they are famished for the Word that promises forgiveness. Though this all sounds familiar from previous

37. See LW 36:27–34, 36–37 (WA 6:507–13).
38. LW 36:39 (WA 6:514).
39. See, for example, the beautiful passage in LW 42:172 (WA 7:693), where Luther describes the pathway to the beginning of true hunger and thirst for the gospel: "Such hunger and thirst are created not by compelling a man, but by showing him his frailty and need so that he will see his wretched condition and feel the desire to be delivered from it. This happens, for instance, when you recognize that you are weak in faith, cold in love, and faint in hope. You will find that you are disposed toward hatred, impatience, impurity, greed, and whatever other vice there is. This you will undoubtedly find and feel if you really look at yourself. All the saints have found this to be true about themselves. You must also see whether you have weakly yielded or would have fallen to one or the other. To know and understand your sin and to be willing to resolve to get rid of such vice and evil and to long to become pure, modest, gentle, mild, humble, believing, loving, etc.—that is the beginning of such thirst."

texts, there is a new element: for the first time in a eucharistic text, Luther rooted the knowledge and burden of self-sin in the law of God. "God has given his commandment so that you may thereby know your sin," Luther wrote.[40] Indeed, it is this commandment of God that spurs humility, which is requisite for the proper reception of the Sacrament. Faith, Luther argued, worked in a person who recognized one's own unworthiness but who, at the same time, recognized the truth of God's promises. Both are rooted in the Word of God. A feeling of unworthiness makes one ready because it engenders a desire to be relieved of the burden of unworthiness. Then, when true faith is added to the formula, one is able to grasp the Word of promise as an anchor. "If you believe," Luther counseled, "the sacrament gives you everything you need."[41]

How, then, may Luther be characterized in terms of his thought on the proper reception of the Eucharist? Three words serve the purpose: recognition, desire, and faith. But what Luther so strongly advocated was not that the individual was left to oneself to properly prepare for Communion; rather, God beforehand prepared everything for the believer: the law to help one recognize one's need, burdens that heighten one's desire for relief, and the promise of Christ's Word to engender faith. Luther reminded his audience, "Worthy reception, however, is not based on our diligence and effort, our work and prayers, or our fasting, but on the truth of the divine words."[42] Luther taught that these words come to the Christian as judgment on the old self, slaying of the old self, and resurrection to new life.

The law condemns and slays; the Gospel raises to new life. The life-giving words of Christ pour forth from his testament. And they *are* life-giving. In this sermon, Luther falls back on the traditional idiom for the mass, calling it the "medicine for the soul."[43] It is clear, however, that Luther does not mean what had traditionally been regarded as the medicinal power of the Sacrament: the objective infusion of grace by the elements themselves. Rather, the Eucharist is medicine for the soul, in Luther's mind, because it presents the healing Word of Christ, the Gospel Word of forgiveness, which alone remits sin, gives grace, lends help, and finally enkindles the faith that gives "strength in everything good against sin, death, and hell."[44] The essence of that faith is one that, even in the face of sin, prays, "Dear Lord, I do not doubt the truth of your words."[45]

40. LW 42:173 (WA 7:693).
41. LW 42:177 (WA 7:697).
42. LW 42:174 (WA 7:695).
43. LW 42:177 (WA 7:697).
44. LW 42:175 (WA 7:695).
45. LW 42:174 (WA 7:695).

There is, then, an obvious history of development in Luther's teaching on the Eucharist. In regard to proper reception, Luther began with the notion of recognition of sin, added the concept of a fervent desire for the Eucharist, and finally brought in and fully incorporated the notion of individual faith as the only truly appropriate preparation of the heart for eucharistic feasting. By 1521, moreover, all three aspects of proper reception are grounded in Luther's understanding of the Word of God as law and as Gospel.

Luther's position on the benefit of the Eucharist also underwent an evident transformation. In 1518 he began with an understanding of the communion of saints that entailed the possibility of sharing in a common faith; in other words, he indicated that, for the weak person, the church's faith was sufficient. Other Christians could believe for the individual, and that individual might thus reap the benefit of such belief. By 1520, however, Luther had shifted to an understanding of the words of divine promise as the primary benefit of the Eucharist. The Eucharist became primarily, for Luther, a declaration of the testament of Christ.[46] Moreover, these words of the New Testament must be believed; the individual must respond in faith for his or herself. Furthermore, Luther came to emphasize that it was the testament itself, not the community, that begat such faith. Forgiveness of sin and eternal life, Luther asserted, belonged to those who claimed the promises of the testament as their own.

"His Completely Trustworthy Testament": Luther's *Lectures on Hebrews* and the Eucharist

Luther began his lectures on the letter to the Hebrews in April 1517. In the lecture are elements that appear to be quite "un-Lutheran" when compared to the mature Luther.[47] It is clear here, however, that Luther began to work

46. Thus the Word, not the elements, becomes the unifying factor in the Eucharist. The elements are, in a real way, secondary in the sense that they are present only as a sign and assurance that the Word of promise is true. The true Sacrament that all Christians partake, therefore, is the divine Word of Christ, presented through the proclaimed Word and sealed visibly for the Christian's benefit by Christ's body in the eucharistic elements, which (body) assures Christians of God's nearness as God makes promises.

47. See, for example, Luther's comments on the Christian making "constant progress" at LW 29:139, 179 (WA 57.3:132–33, 179); the notion of progress in the Christian life becomes much more ambiguous in the mature Luther. Luther still, at this time, made distinctions along the medieval fourfold method of exegesis; see his remarks on tropological meaning at LW 29:161 (WA 57.3:158). The distinction between "formed" and "unformed" faith has not been totally discarded (see LW 29:188 [WA 57.3:187]). Finally, and most surprisingly for both Catholic and Protestant opponents of Luther's eucharistic teaching, we find Luther seeming to endorse the traditional view that John 6 actually does have something to do with eucharistic life (see LW 29:201 [WA

extensively through the concepts of personal faith and the Word of testament (the promise) and how the two are related in such a way as to portend his mature beliefs. In this work the foundations are laid for the emphases of his later eucharistic writings.[48]

In a rather remarkable passage, Luther observed that repentance, though necessary, does not serve to clear the path for God's salvation. Luther declared, "Before we repent, our sins have already been forgiven by God."[49] Thus nothing the individual can do prepares the Christian for grace. Rather, those who repent are those whose old natures have already been destroyed. The Gospel "preserves nothing of the old man." God "kills in order to make alive."[50] The only preparation for this process is faith in God's Word of promise, and the Word itself evokes faith.

Faith is a clinging to the Word of God for Luther. It is the *only* work of the Gospel, and it is internal.[51] In a telling passage, Luther declared, "Without faith it is impossible for God to be with us." Why is this so? Because God "does everything through the Word."[52] For that Word to bear fruit for the believer, there must be faith. One can tie this arrangement to the incarnation. If Christ is God incarnate, as Luther certainly affirmed, the way one possesses that incarnate Word is through faith. The union of believers with the incarnate Word, a union so real that Luther speaks of Christ as the Christian's substance, is achieved only through faith.[53] If the Sacrament is a visible word, as Augustine of Hippo taught and Luther accepted, then the Word itself is an audible body, Christ's substance, possessed through the hearing and believing of it—through faith.

57.3:199]), where Luther cites John 6:35 ("I am the bread of life") and then immediately says, "For we receive him [Christ] in the sacrament and feast ourselves on him in this life."

48. Luther worked on other things as well during the time he was lecturing on Hebrews. The famous Ninety-Five Theses came when Luther was more than halfway through his lectures on Hebrews; the Heidelberg Disputation, held in 1518, is rife with the fruit of Luther's exegetical labors. It seems to me, however, that the fullest explication of the themes of faith and testament during the 1517–19 period come from the lectures. The material from the disputation is the reflection, not the foundation, of Luther's exegetical work. With the Hebrews commentary, Luther first began to deal exegetically and at some length with questions surrounding eucharistic faith and practice. On this point, and for a summary of Luther's (sparse) exegetical work on the sacrifice of the mass before the Hebrews work, see Carl F. Wisløff, *The Gift of Communion: Luther's Controversy with Rome on Eucharistic Sacrifice* (Minneapolis: Augsburg, 1964), 12–13.

49. LW 29:112 (WA 57.3:101).

50. LW 29:119, 130 (WA 57.3:109, 122).

51. LW 29:123 (WA 57.3:113).

52. LW 29:148 (WA 57.3:143).

53. LW 29:157 (WA 57.3:153); see also LW 29:156 (WA 57.3:152), where Luther speaks of faith as the means of possessing Christ.

Still, the question remains: what does Luther mean by this faith? It is not a substance added to the substance of the individual, nor is it properly a work of the individual, an act of the will or intellect. Rather, it is that which is evoked by the Word itself: faith is what "causes the heart to cling fast to celestial things and to be carried away and to dwell in things that are invisible."[54] With such an emphasis on heart religion, it is no surprise, then, that when Luther specifically addresses sacraments he is bold to say, "It is not the sacrament but faith in the sacrament that makes righteous."[55] Such is the case because, for Luther, the essence of a sacrament is the Word of God that it proclaims. Thus the only preparation for such a gift is the faith that is evoked by the Word and that then clings to the Word as true.

If one is properly prepared for the Word, then, the sacramental participant can expect, indeed, to receive God through the Sacrament—not in the elements, however, but in the Word of testament. For not only does Christ rule in power over his church through the Word,[56] but the whole notion of presence also is wrapped up in a proper understanding of the Word. Again, in a remarkable passage that presages Luther as, above all, a theologian of the Word, he declared, "For one falls away from the living God when one falls away from His Word, which is alive and gives life to all things, yes, is God Himself."[57] Through no other medium than the Word, the Christian has God and all that God promises through Christ Jesus.[58] And when Luther spoke of

54. LW 29:185 (WA 57.3:185).
55. LW 29:207 (WA 57.3:206).
56. LW 29:118 (WA 57.3:108–9).
57. LW 29:153 (WA 57.3:148).
58. In discussing Luther's ideas about the presence of Christ in the Eucharist, one must move from talking solely about the Word as presence to a discussion of the true body and blood of Christ present in, with, and under the elements as Luther propounded in his theory of presence. This cannot be directly addressed here: Luther had not yet fully developed this notion by 1517–18. Yet there are clues in the Hebrews lectures that point to why ubiquity would become important to Luther; moreover, the lectures provide a context that may better explain what Luther was trying to protect by using that concept. Luther stated that it is only through the humanity of Christ that the Christian can know God; indeed, Christ's humanity is that "holy ladder" by which the Christian climbs to a proper knowledge of God. There follows a section, reminiscent of Luther's speaking of the Word as God's "baby talk," where Luther spoke of the incarnation as a humiliation of God as necessary for God to "become recognizable" (LW 29:111 [WA 57.3:99]). Thus knowledge and recognition of God are both tied to the humanity of Christ. What is more, to be sure of God's promises presented in the Word, Luther stated that it is not enough even that the Christian believes Christ has done things "fur euch," though that is essential. The Christian must also believe that such a promise is played out "before our eyes" (LW 29:123 [WA 57.3:114]). With the sense of almost physically palpable presence, Luther affirmed that Christ, as the Christian's brother in the flesh, is both like and near to believers (LW 29:134 [WA 57.3:126–27]). Indeed, it is through that humanity, that nearness and likeness, that the Christian is saved: "In [Christ's] humanity alone we are protected and saved from . . . judgment"

that Word, he meant, as the entire Hebrews work makes clear, the testament of Christ that promises forgiveness of sins and life eternal. Faith receives the Word and is aroused and supported by it.

For this truly to be the case, however, the faith that receives the gift of the Word must be a personal faith. Even though these lectures were given before Luther's "Sermon on the Proper Preparation of the Heart," in which the faith required for the Eucharist was not personal faith but the corporate faith of the church, the lectures already place a strong emphasis on personal faith.[59]

(LW 29:167 [WA 57.3:164]). Thus the notion of ubiquity is developed to maintain and preserve the Christian's central way of knowing God: the flesh of Christ, without which everything goes up in a cloud of uncertainty. What is more, it is exactly the presence of that human Christ as guarantor of the testament that lends the Word of testament its surest foundation. In other words, Luther was developing a type of religious epistemology: one can know that the words are true and trust in them because Christ is actually present to make them sure.

59. Though the accent on personal faith is strong, the notion of a corporate faith is not completely discarded; it is even lauded to a degree. See Luther's remarks at LW 29:150 (WA 57.3:145), where he talks of the faith of the fathers as "gain and strength of faith for those who come later." This is not surprising since Hebrews speaks of the "cloud of witnesses" to the faith (Heb. 12:1). Yet Luther qualified even this statement in later lectures, I believe, when what he seems to have given with one hand he takes back with the other in discussing why faith cannot be simply believing because other people believe. If that were so, then Adam and Abel (and Eve, I assume) had no faith at all. Luther stated, "For this way faith would be nothing else than one person's credulity that has been established and proved by means of the credulity of another person" (LW 29:229 [WA 57.3:227]). In light of this statement, despite what he has said about the fathers, it is hard to fathom how Luther could write so passionately in the 1518–19 works about how exactly it was possible to commune under another person's faith. In the Hebrews lectures, Noah and Abraham are specifically commended because they believed on their own, relying on the Word of God alone, apart from the words or testimonies of others. See LW 29:237–38 (WA 57.3:235–36); see also Luther's comments on Abraham and the necessity that the children of Abraham believe for themselves the promise made to Abraham, so that Abraham could not believe for them (LW 36:48–49 [WA 6:521]). For a fuller exposition of the role of faith in the Hebrews commentary, especially as opposed to the notion of ex opere operato and the *obex* (hindrance, obstacle) teaching, see Wisløff, *Gift of Communion*, 49–51. It had become commonplace to think that the Eucharist conferred grace as long as the communicant did not put an obstacle in the way of grace, such as coming to receive the elements while knowingly in a state of mortal sin (itself usually thought of as a sin of grave matter, one that the sinner recognizes to be a grave sin and understands its magnitude and consequences, yet commits the sin anyway). The reception of the Eucharist, because of the understanding of its objective nature (ex opere operato), was seen to confer grace and nullify venial sins because of its status as a good work. Luther's emphasis on personal faith can be seen in contrast to the "ecclesiastical model" described by Gary Macy, who says of what becomes the dominant (though not the only) strand of eucharistic thought: "The basic metaphor upon which the ecclesiological approach to the Eucharist rests is . . . the notion of the community as the chosen people of God. The community as such is saved; the individual appropriates salvation through membership in the community as saved. In the twelfth and early thirteenth centuries, membership in the community of the saved tended to be defined in increasingly juridical fashion. . . . Not surprisingly, theologies of the Eucharist were affected by this move towards institutionalization. . . . The question of worthy reception tended to become a question of juridical standing rather than a question of spiritual intent"

Luther more fully fleshed out the notion of corporate faith in 1518–19, only to discard it within a few years.

The best way to describe this personal faith, perhaps, is to think of it as "glue" or "cement," as something that binds together two different things. Luther's language is replete with words that evoke this sort of image. In talking of justification, Luther wrote that it is faith in the Word of God that makes one pure: since the Word is pure and good, "so it makes him who adheres to it pure and good like itself."[60] The adhesive is personal faith. Elsewhere, Luther spoke even more explicitly about the adhesive nature of faith: "For these three—faith, the Word, and the heart—become one. Faith is the glue or the bond. The Word is on one side; the heart is on the other side. But through faith they become one spirit, just as man and wife become 'one flesh.' Therefore it is true that the heart is combined with the Word through faith and that the Word is combined with the heart through the same faith."[61] Thus Luther has begun here to flesh out his understanding of Word, faith, and the heart. Christianity works for Luther only when these three are completely united. The Word comes; it is received by the hearing of it, by faith;[62] and faith unites that Word to the heart.

If faith is a trust in the promise of God, and if the Word is primarily God's Word of forgiveness given in the testament of God's Son, Christ Jesus, "heart" is Luther's word for the person. When Luther spoke of uniting heart to the Word through faith, he meant the Christian in one's individual, personal self. It is only the one who personally *believes* who is a child of God.[63] And not just believe about God, but believe *in* God. "It is not enough," Luther wrote, "for a Christian to believe that Christ was appointed to act on behalf of men unless he believes that he, too, is one of those men."[64]

A personal faith, then, or a heart faith, is one that hears the promises and applies them to oneself. It is this heart-faith combination that enables a person

---

(Macy, *The Theologies of the Eucharist in the Early Scholastic Period: A Study of the Salvific Function of the Sacrament according to the Theologians, c. 1080–c. 1220* [Oxford: Clarendon, 1984], 129–30). Elsewhere Macy summarizes Thomas Aquinas's last writings on the Eucharist: "Thomas . . . would merely repeat his insistence that the metaphysics of the sacrament outweigh the importance of the intentionality of the believer" (Gary Macy, *Treasures from the Storeroom: Medieval Religion and the Eucharist* [Collegeville, MN: Liturgical Press, 1999], 45). Here Macy has in mind Thomas's *Summa*, part 3, question 80.

60. LW 29:152 (WA 57.3:147–48).

61. LW 29:160 (WA 57.3:156–57).

62. "The characteristic of a *testimonium* is that it is *audible*. It can only be grasped by the ear, that is, by faith" (Kenneth Hagen, *A Theology of Testament in the Young Luther* [Leiden: Brill, 1974], 73).

63. LW 29:155 (WA 57.3:151).

64. LW 29:171 (WA 57.3:169).

to approach the Sacrament with confidence—believing that the promises are not only true in the abstract but also true concretely "for us."[65] Indeed, Luther stated that it is such heartfelt *faith* in the Sacrament, and not the Sacrament itself, that justifies.[66] There is an objective grace given in the Sacrament, and it is always given: the Word of promise. Moreover, it is that objective grace that enables faith to grow and the heart to believe. Yet the fulfillment of the promise is believing it for oneself. Luther himself said that to be "valid" means to be fulfilled; something is invalid if it is not fulfilled.[67] The Sacrament is valid for a person when the promises it carries are fulfilled; it is invalid for those who do not bring faith to it, for the fulfillment of promises is only for those who believe. Valid preparation and reception of the Eucharist occur when the point of the Eucharist, the forgiveness of sins, takes place. Within the confines of the individual heart, and there alone, such validation takes place through faith and the power of the Word.[68]

Conclusion

This analysis of the Hebrews lectures shows how the key concepts of Luther's eucharistic writings from the 1520–21 period are in place, at least exegetically, by early 1518. There is a small time lapse between the explication of the theological themes and their application in works dealing specifically with the Eucharist. One sees this, for example, in Luther's explanation of the importance of the testamental Word of promise in his Hebrews commentary of 1517–18, a theological schema of promise/faith that is not applied to a eucharistic context until 1520.

It is fair to say, then, that the 1518–19 works on the Eucharist do not reflect Luther's developing theology of the Word. When one considers that the sacramental system of the church was the support structure for a Christian's

65. LW 29:209, 210 (WA 57.3:208–9).

66. LW 29:172 (WA 57.3:170).

67. LW 29:122 (WA 57.3:112). The words translated as "valid" and "invalid" are "firmari" and "infirmari." Thus valid is meant as "strength" to accomplish.

68. In another writing of roughly the same period, the 1519 *Exposition on the Lord's Prayer*, Luther commented that God offers "no other consolation than his holy Word" (LW 42:50 [WA 2:106]). For Luther, that Word sufficed. If some see Luther's stress on the importance of the individual's faith as too subjective a basis for the reality of the Eucharist as an objective force, they have missed the point: though the individual person is thoroughly implicated in the process of grace, it is the Word in all of its objective power that brings the promise of testament, calls forth faith, and prepares the human heart. After all, it is the testament, and not the human heart, that is "completely trustworthy."

entire life, from birth to death, it is not surprising that one would hesitate before restructuring the entire conception of the Eucharist.

Still, in this light, one must at least qualify the view that Luther's earliest eucharistic writings carry a Catholic tone and exhibit a pastoral aura.[69] From that point of view, the stress is often laid on the errors of practice;[70] the assumption is that, if the errors had not been there, Luther would not have been driven to dogmatic extremes. This is not to say that ecumenically minded Catholics agree with Luther; all decry his stress on the individual, for instance. But all in all, they approve of the 1518–19 writings and see Luther's work as that of a religiously motivated man working for legitimate reform.

Yet attempts at reading Luther in such a manner, however well intentioned, are ultimately misleading. Certainly, Luther had a strong pastoral concern, but his reform worked along the lines of a developing train of thought that was to emerge as an honest-to-goodness "theological reality."[71] To deal with Luther's reaction only in terms of a pastoral problem does not do justice to what Luther thought undergirded all proper pastoral practice: sound doctrine.

What is more, I think it is a mistake to think of Luther's 1518–19 eucharistic writings as "most Catholic." Such an assessment can occur only outside a fuller consideration of what is taking place in Luther's thought during these years. It is better instead to think of Luther, even at this early stage in his career (and it was a career with stages) as a reformer, as a biblical theologian, one who considered it his primary task to expound Scripture.[72] Certainly, there

69. In addition to Lortz and Mann, cited in note 1 above, consider the following: "[Luther's] first texts and sermons on the eucharistic sacrament are classics. They speak of our union with Christ in a perspective more moral and personal than dogmatic" ("Ses prémiers textes et sermons sur le sacrement eucharistique sont classiques. Il y parle de notre union au Christ, dans une perspective plus morale et personnelle que dogmatique"; Yves M. J. Congar, "Lutherana: Théologie de l'eucharistie et christologie chez Luther," *Revue des sciences philosophiques et théologiques* 66, no. 2 [April 1982]: 170).

70. "The picture of the practice was, in part, very dark and had changed from the mystery of the Sacrament to grimacing superstitions and sinful distortions" ("Das Bild der Praxis war zum Teil sehr dunkel und hatte sich vom Mysterium der Eucharistie zum Fratzenhaften abergläubisher und sünd haften Verzerrungen hin verändert," Rudolf Padberg, "Luther und der Canon Missae," *Catholica* 37, no. 4 [1983]: 293).

71. Robin Leaver, "'Verbi Testamenti' versus Canon: The Radical Nature of Luther's Liturgical Reform," *Churchman* 97, no. 2 (1983): 125.

72. Kenneth Hagen makes a point that supports my contention about studying the "exegetical" Luther: "One of the by-products of this study is that such denominational determinants are largely non-existent because of the control of the text (Hebrews). Interpretations differ. Polemics enter in. But in large areas, e.g., authorship, authority of the epistle, Christology, even soteriology, Old Testament hermeneutic, interpretations are not along confessional lines" (Kenneth Hagen, *Hebrews Commenting from Erasmus to Bèze, 1516–1598* [Tübingen: Mohr Siebeck, 1981], 3). There *is* a hermeneutical circle: Luther brought things to the text. But his theology, though not purely exegetical, was surely driven by exegetical concerns. This realization should help one

are Catholic elements in his thought in 1518–19 and later; he was a son of the Catholic Church. But the work that would so shape his life and thought was the Bible. After all, this is the man who claimed that his conscience was held captive by the Word of God.

It is in studying Luther, who saw himself as a servant under the authority of the Word, that one gets at the heart of what Luther offers. The question is not, then, was Luther more Catholic or more Protestant here or there. Rather, the question is, how did Luther interpret Scripture? If one seeks an answer to that question, one is driven to review Luther's study of the Bible. Reference to that study of the Bible enables one to say that, despite appearances given by the 1518–19 eucharistic works, the notion of Word that was going to direct Luther's thought on the Eucharist had already, in 1517, begun to create the path that would become characteristic of Luther's theological journey.

---

recognize that to apply the terms "Catholic" and "Lutheran" to Luther's thought in any particular period can be misleading, especially when those terms are reified. Perhaps the best way to use the designations is not to see them as absolute categories but as labels by which one can chart the movement in Luther's thought. If the emphasis is placed on the movement of that thought rather than the markers by which it is charted, the engine that drives the motion—the Bible and its exegesis—takes center stage. This approach takes Luther's own concerns seriously.

2

"THE TRUTH
OF THE DIVINE WORDS"

Luther's Sermons on the Eucharist, 1521–1528,
and the Structure of Eucharistic Meaning

For many, Luther's teaching on the Eucharist is epitomized by two images: his stance on the real presence of Christ in the Eucharist at the Marburg Colloquy of 1529 and his vitriolic rhetoric as it was aimed at those he called "sacramentarian." The most memorable scene at Marburg came when Luther chalked out on the table, "Hoc est corpus meum [This is my body]." By such maneuvering, Luther thought to underscore his insistence on heeding the words of Christ spoken at the Last Supper. Christ's body, Luther averred, had to be present in the Eucharist because Christ had said so: "The devil cannot get around that," Luther claimed. Thus he argued for Christ's presence in the eucharistic celebration through an appeal to the divine Word.[1]

The rhetoric was inflammatory. When preaching against the "fanatics," those who scorned Luther's position on the true presence of Christ in the Eucharist, Luther responded in a way that would more and more characterize how he dealt with opponents on this issue: "For this is what they say: If I

1. For an account of the events at Marburg, see G. May, ed., *Das Marburger Religionsgespräch 1529* (Gütersloh: Gütersloh/Mohn, 1970), 23, 36.

believe in Jesus Christ, who died for me, what need is there for me to believe in a baked God? Wait and see, he will bake them when the time comes, so that their hides will sizzle."[2] The fat hit the fire, so to speak, when it came to those who questioned Luther's view on the presence of Christ in the Eucharist, especially when they impugned the notion of the ubiquity of Christ's body that, in Luther's opinion, served as explanation for such a presence.

Given these images, it is not surprising that some scholars have focused on the troublesome ubiquity issue: the explanation for *how* Christ is present in the Eucharist is seen as one of Luther's most distinctive teachings. In one of the standard treatments of Luther's eucharistic thought, Hermann Sasse asserts that in the 1520s (especially up to the Marburg Colloquy of 1529) the real presence controversy and the ubiquity issue so consumed Luther that it became the center of his theological thought.[3] Yet as Brian Gerrish has pointed out, what is most distinctive about a theology and what is central to it may well be two different things.[4] In terms of Luther's eucharistic teaching, then, what is *central*? It is the hierarchy, or order, of eucharistic meaning, and within that order the how of the real presence is not the glue that holds the parts together: the Word is the glue.[5]

2. LW 36:344 (WA 19:494).

3. Hermann Sasse, *This Is My Body: Luther's Contention for the Real Presence in the Sacrament of the Altar* (Minneapolis: Augsburg, 1959), 104. Sasse is not alone on this point. See also, among others, Karl Barth, "Luther's Doctrine of the Eucharist: Its Basis and Purpose," in *Theology and Church: Shorter Writings, 1920–1928*, trans. Louise Pettibone Smith (New York: Harper & Row, 1962), 76–77; and Robert C. Croken, *Luther's First Front: The Eucharist as Sacrifice* (Ottawa: University of Ottawa Press, 1990), 48. The notion of Christ's presence and Luther's defense of it is important for Luther: it is significant, and Luther is unwilling to have it discarded *because* of the way he understood the Word. Without the Word, presence is, quite literally, a nonissue. In the end, Luther's defense of real presence is a defense of his understanding of the Word of God.

4. Brian A. Gerrish, *Grace and Gratitude: The Eucharistic Theology of John Calvin* (Minneapolis: Fortress, 1993), 2.

5. In terms of the importance of the proper ordering of elements of meaning, Luther himself explicitly set up an order that this chapter duplicates with a bit of expansion and explanation. See Luther's 1528 work *Vom Abendmahl Christi: Bekenntnis*, wherein Luther states that the Word is first; and because the Word is present, Christ is present as Testator, proclaiming the forgiveness of sins; and following forgiveness of sins, there is life and salvation (because of the way the sermons present the material, I speak of use and fruit); LW 37:338 (WA 26:478–79). A fine entry into the importance of taking into account the order of elements in Luther's eucharistic thought can be found in Kyle A. Pasewark, *A Theology of Power: Being beyond Domination* (Minneapolis: Fortress, 1993), 60 and 60n15.

In a very detailed article, Ralph Quere analyzes Luther's understanding of the real presence in the 1520s: "Changes and Constants: Structure in Luther's Understanding of the Real Presence in the 1520s," *Sixteenth Century Journal* 16, no. 1 (1985): 45–78. In many ways, Quere agrees with those in note 3 above who see presence as what becomes the controlling idea in Luther's eucharistic thought. Indeed, Quere holds that ubiquity—Luther's explanation of Christ's real

I will unearth Luther's hierarchy of eucharistic meaning through an examination of his sermons from the years 1521–28.[6] These dates run from the time when Luther's eucharistic teaching was more or less settled[7] to the time of his last major set of sermons on the Eucharist before the Marburg Colloquy. What we find in the sermons is an insistence on the proper ordering of eucharistic meaning; ubiquity, rather than being the cornerstone of that thought, simply serves as a way for Luther to protect elements of that hierarchy of meaning. In other words, rather than being part and parcel of eucharistic meaning, ubiquity stands as a guarantee and explanation for that meaning. What we can say is that the notion of ubiquity is part of the way Luther theologically explained his eucharistic teaching, but it was not an integral part of the structure itself.

In a way that treatises do not, the sermons reveal what Luther considered to be of primary importance as one sought to understand the Eucharist. In these sermons, Luther is generally nonpolemic in his approach (the exception being what was published as "The Sacrament of the Body and Blood of Christ—against the Fanatics"). As a pastor, he tried to lay out for the people how they should come to the Sacrament and with what understanding. What emerges from these sermons is a hierarchy of meaning, with the elements of

---

presence—is the "ontological substratum" of the Word (66). In speaking of ubiquity as the "new structural dimension" in Luther's eucharistic thought, Quere indicates that ubiquity causes the Word to be repositioned in Luther's eucharistic structure, though the Word retains its function and power (75). This chapter argues that the position of the Word in Luther's eucharistic doctrine, once it is established (see chap. 1 of this book), remains constant in the structure of his thought and that ubiquity as an explanation of presence is not so much part of the structure of meaning as much as it is a defense of the Word's position as the first and controlling element in eucharistic meaning. This has to do with Luther's understanding of the incarnational nature of the Word, which is discussed near the end of this chapter.

6. That Luther's sermons can profitably be used as a means to explicate his theology is nicely demonstrated in Ulrich Asendorf, *Die Theologie Martin Luthers nach seinen Predigten* (Göttingen: Vandenhoeck & Ruprecht, 1988).

7. The basic outline of Luther's maturing eucharistic thought is laid out in his 1520 works: *A Treatise on the New Testament, That Is, the Holy Mass*, LW 35:79–111 (WA 6:353–78); and *The Babylonian Captivity of the Church*, LW 36:11–126 (WA 6:497–573). In these two treatises, Luther makes the theological move from the mass as a sacrifice and a good work to the position that a proper and Christian mass is the proclamation of Christ's testament (the forgiveness of sins) by means of the Words of Institution. In many ways, the biblical rationale for such a view is worked out in Luther's *Lectures on Hebrews*, LW 29:109–241 (WA 57.3:97–238). Kyle Pasewark suggests that a further and more elaborate development is at work in Luther's eucharistic teaching (see his *Theology of Power*, esp. chap. 2). Pasewark's nuanced analysis of the development in Luther's teaching is tied to concerns of the movement of power. Relating to analysis of the sermons I herein examine and the hierarchy of meaning centering around the Word that develops in them, the main watershed in Luther's eucharistic thought came when Luther, in 1520, began to emphasize the function of the Word in the eucharistic celebration, based on his understanding of testament and Testator that is worked out in his *Hebrews* lectures (see chap. 1 above).

greater significance controlling the interpretation of parts of lesser significance (which does *not* translate into "unimportant" for Luther). Even the notion of the communion of saints, so prominent in Luther's earliest eucharistic writings, does not simply disappear as an element of meaning (as some suggest)[8] but finds its niche in a new ordering of meaning in which it functions in relation to other parts. What one finds is that these elements can be understood and related apart from the ubiquity concept. In other words, something stands behind the ubiquity concept and is the thing of ultimate importance for Luther, not ubiquity itself.[9]

An Appeal to the Words of Institution: The Word of Power

In March 1522, Luther made his dramatic return to Wittenberg. For almost a year he had been holed up in Wartburg Castle, with only one short, secret trip to Wittenberg punctuating what he generally considered to be his captivity. By March, however, he could no longer stay away; the cause of reform seemed to be threatened in its birthplace. Luther mounted the pulpit on Sunday, March 9, and preached the first of a series of eight sermons, seeking to restore order to church and town.[10] Three of these sermons (on March 13, 14, 15) concerned the Lord's Supper; here I will examine the first of these.

Throughout the sermon, Luther emphasized the primacy of the Word of God. As had become characteristic in his thought, the Word was the instrument by which God effectively ruled God's church. To stand in the way of that Word was to try to obstruct God's purpose. Preaching was to be the weapon of choice; explication of Scripture, a laying bare of the power-laden Word, was sufficient. The Word itself would work the results. Luther's belief in the effective power of the Word is clear in these sermons.

One of the reforms initiated by the Zwickau prophets was Communion in both kinds (bread and wine). Luther himself had advocated such, and in

8. One can find this point of view represented, for example, in Paul Althaus, *The Theology of Martin Luther*, trans. Robert C. Schultz (Philadelphia: Fortress, 1966), 321–22. Althaus speaks of how the battle over real presence restricted and impoverished Luther's teaching on the *communio sanctorum*. What actually happens, as will be shown, is that the concept takes up a new place in the order of eucharistic meaning. If anything, because of that new position, the *communio sanctorum* becomes a stronger theological concept because of Luther's reformulation of that doctrine in relation to the Word.

9. In other words, I am arguing against Quere's notion that ubiquity serves as "ontological substratum."

10. A good introduction to these sermons is provided by Jane E. Strohl in, "Luther's Invocavit Sermons," in *Freiheit als Liebe bei Martin Luther*, ed. Dennis D. Bielfeldt and Klaus Schwarzwäller (Frankfurt: Peter Lang, 1995), 159–66.

preaching he affirmed that the layperson who partook of the cup committed no sin.[11] However, the practice as it had been set up in Wittenberg drew Luther's fire on two accounts. First, although partaking of both kinds was not a sin, Luther thought, neither should it be made into a new law; it should be left to the decision of a free conscience. Indeed, by making reception in both kinds compulsory, God had been offended.[12]

Second, Luther spoke with concern about the "weaker brother." What the Wittenbergers had done, in Luther's view, actually "caused offense everywhere." Indeed, people had been driven away from the cause of reform. He considered such a situation worse than anything his enemies had done to him.[13]

Luther presented what to his mind was the simple and only true solution to the problem: that the Word be preached. Rather than turning the reception of the Sacrament in both kinds into a new law for the laity, Luther claimed, "we must rather promote and practice and preach the Word, and then afterwards leave the result and execution of it entirely to the Word."[14] Luther then appealed to his congregation to give up the practice until "the gospel has first been thoroughly preached and understood."[15] The Word, then, controlled the eucharistic celebration.

A year or so later, having grown somewhat impatient with his flock, Luther again preached on the Sacrament, reversing his earlier outlook on those he had spoken of as weaker; in his opinion, it was time to overcome the imperfections.[16] In his Maundy Thursday oration of 1523, however, the solution was the same as preached in 1522: the Word must be preached.

When Luther spoke of the Word in relation to the Eucharist, he explicitly meant the Words of Institution, the Word spoken by Christ at his Last Supper. The words spoken by Christ on this occasion *constituted* the Sacrament; and the bread and wine, his body and blood, were instituted by these words as "a token and seal that his words are true."[17]

Though the bread and wine that carry Christ's body and blood are tokens of the Word, it is the Word itself that creates a true presence of Christ in the Sacrament. This became more and more an emphasis in Luther's sermons: the Word is always a Word of power, and the Words of Institution by their

---

11. LW 51:89 (WA 10.3:41–42). One of Luther's earliest calls for at least the option of Communion under both kinds for the laity is found in *The Babylonian Captivity of the Church*, LW 36:27–28 (WA 6:506–7).

12. LW 51:89 (WA 10.3:42).

13. Quoting LW 51:90 (WA 10.3:44); LW 51:91 (WA 10.3:47).

14. LW 51:90 (WA 10.3:45).

15. LW 51:90 (WA 10.3:45).

16. Lenker 11:225 (WA 12:478).

17. Lenker 11:226 (WA 12:479).

utterance create presence, evoke faith, and prepare believers for worthy reception. One sees this clearly in a sermon preached four days after the Maundy Thursday sermon, on Easter Monday 1523. Who is worthy to receive the Sacrament? Those who are "moved in their hearts to believe" the Sacrament's promises—and this work is done by God's Word alone, which comes, according to Luther, "without any of my preparing or doing."[18]

For Luther, the whole issue of Christ's presence in the Eucharist was controlled by his view of the Words of Institution as God's Word of power. In 1526, preaching against the fanatics, Luther spoke at length about the power of the Word to effect what it proclaimed. If it were not for the Word, he said, there would be no need to pay attention to the bread whatsoever.[19] But the Word is present, and as present, it is powerful.[20]

Luther made explicit the connection between the Word of power and Christ's presence in the Eucharist. The Word and what it teaches is absolutely reliable. Is the body and blood of Christ present in the Sacrament? Yes. How so? Luther responded, "For as soon as Christ says: 'This is my Body,' his body is present through the Word and the power of the Holy Spirit."[21] The power of the Word itself actually derives from the presence of Christ; Luther teaches that Christ "has put himself into the Word, and through the Word he puts himself into the bread also."[22] Though bread may be the vehicle, it is the Word that makes the body of Christ present, just as it makes God's promises present and real.

This emphasis on the power of the Words of Institution and their ability to make present Christ in body and blood was most fully laid out in Luther's catechetical preaching from the year 1528. In a mixture of German and Latin, given to theological students, Luther preached on the Eucharist three times—in May, September, and December.

18. Lenker 11:269–70 (WA 12:496–97).

19. LW 36:346 (WA 19:499). These 1526 sermons were published together to form the well-known sermon "The Sacrament of the Body and Blood of Christ—against the Fanatics," LW 36:335–61 (WA 19:482–523).

20. As Pasework points out, "Luther identifies the power-word as the distinctive feature of God's Word compared with our words" (Pasework, *Theology of Power*, 87n135). Jaroslav Pelikan is helpful on the general point of the powerful nature of God's Word in Luther's theology. In his discussion of the Hebrew word *dābār* (which may be translated as "word"), Pelikan explains that Luther interpreted "word" to mean both the spoken word and also that to which the spoken word refers. Thus, according to Pelikan, Luther interpreted the Word of God as a concrete action of God, specifically, a redemptive action. See Pelikan, *Luther the Expositor: Introduction to the Reformer's Exegetical Writings* (St. Louis: Concordia Publishing House, 1959), 54–55.

21. LW 36:341 (WA 19:491).

22. LW 36:343 (WA 19:493). It is well known that Luther followed Augustine of Hippo in calling the Sacrament a *verbum visibile*, a visible word. Given the way Luther here describes the operation of the Sacrament, it might be well to think of his description of the Word of the Sacrament as an audible body, as was suggested in chap. 1 above.

The May sermon dealt primarily with what the Eucharist is and who it is that works it. The Sacrament is Christ's body and blood by means of Christ's Word. Many times Luther thus asserts: "It is not his body and blood except by his Word." "It is his body and blood through his Word, promise, command and order."[23]

Luther clarified that it is not a human work that makes the bread and wine the body and blood of Christ.[24] It is not the spoken word of the priest that works the miraculous change; it is the Word of promise himself—Christ—who speaks. The objective ground of the Eucharist is not the faith of the participant (which would be too individualistic and subjective) nor the speaking of the priest to God (which implied to Luther an offering up to God rather than God's gracious act of giving). Rather, it is Christ himself, who instituted the Supper and continues to institute it by his Word, who is the unshakable ground on which the Eucharist is founded. "You see," Luther preached, "the one who institutes [the Eucharist] shall accomplish it."[25] Thus the one who instituted the Supper, Christ, is the one who causes his body and blood to join with the bread and wine in the eucharistic celebration by means of the same Word by which he instituted it.

In Luther's September catechetical preaching, one finds much the same emphasis as in the May sermon. Everything in the Sacrament is dependent on the Word. In speaking of the Words of Institution, which contain the promises of God, Luther emphasized that it is only by those Words that the body of Christ is handed to partakers through the bread.[26] For that reason, Luther instructed his listeners, "You must depend on the Word and consider it more than the bread."[27] Indeed, the Word is the Christian's bulwark against the heretics. Luther taught his flock that, in dealing with the fanatics' appeal to reason, they should respond, "It is proper that I hear what my God says, not my reason."[28]

With the proper emphasis given to the Word and its place of primacy—the Word is the first thing to consider in the Eucharist, and it controls the proper understanding of everything that follows—Luther reminded his listeners that the bread is necessary for the very reason that the Word speaks of bread.[29] As

---

23. WA 30.1:23.34–35, "non esset corups et sanquis, nisi verba"; WA 30.1:24.1–2, "Es ist sein leib und blut durch sein wort, herheissung, befehl und ordenung."

24. "Non sunt humanum opus," WA 30.1:24.8.

25. Ibid., "Vide, quis instituat, faciat."

26. "Ibi verba faciunt panem zum leib Christi traditum pro nobis," WA 30.1:53.23–24.

27. WA 30.1:53, "Du must dich an die wort hengen et ea plus considerare quam panem."

28. Ibid., "Tu dicas: oportet audiam, quid deus meus dicat, no mea ratio."

29. It is the application of the divine Word that creates the correspondence between the bread and the body of Christ, not natural analogy; Luther rejected, at this time, all attempts at such

Kyle Pasewark has shown, when God speaks God's Word, it is incumbent on Christians to obey, in Luther's opinion.[30] The bread thus becomes important, not in and of itself, even as a vehicle of Christ's presence, but because God's Word directs the Christian's attention to it as Christ's body. Luther thus concludes his sermon, "I say, however, that the bread and the Word of God, the two things belong together; so let the sacrament remain whole."[31] Indeed, it is the Word of power in the Words of Institution that makes the Sacrament. And it is this Word of power that binds bread and wine to body and blood, for the Word is Christ himself. This category—word of power—sits at the top of Luther's hierarchy of eucharistic meaning. It relates and controls the proper working of everything that follows.

Declaring the Words of Benefit: The Word of Forgiveness

The Word of power, in its proper working,[32] carries a benefit: the forgiveness of sins. The benefit of the Eucharist—the forgiveness of sins—does not come through the elements of bread and wine / body and blood, but through the Word attached to the elements. The elements that present the body and blood of Christ serve only as a guarantee of the proclaimed Word of forgiveness. This is why Luther can attack the Catholic notion of transubstantiation, though the concern of the doctrine to make present Christ's body looks to be similar to Luther's doctrine of ubiquity. For Luther, it made no sense to have the seal of forgiveness without the proclamation of that forgiveness. In other words, for there to be an effectual seal, there must be something to seal. According to Luther, that something was God's promise of forgiveness.

Luther's view of the Lord's Supper as a last testament of Christ was a concept that had its roots in his exposition of the book of Hebrews, a work he had undertaken in 1517–18.[33] It is in the Supper that the Testator, Christ, bespoke the inheritance to his heirs, the testament. By his Word (the Word of power) and by his seal (his body present to believers in the bread by virtue of

---

analogies because then the logic of the Eucharist would depend on human insight instead of divine Word (but see the second half of note 13 in chapter 9). Also, Luther's experience was that those who used such analogies were the very ones who robbed the Eucharist of the real presence.

30. Pasewark, *Theology of Power*, 78.

31. WA 30.1:55, "Ich sage aber, das das brod und verbum dei, die zwei stucke zusamen gehorn, Lasse das Sacrament ganz bleiben."

32. For Luther, there is also an "alien" work that accompanies the Word of power; this is not dissimilar to the idea of the proper and alien works of the law.

33. On the relationship between Luther's work on Hebrews and the development of his eucharistic theology, see chap. 1 above. Gerrish has remarked on the peculiarity of this relationship in his *Grace and Gratitude*, 104n77; see also 146–47.

the Word of power), he bequeathed the benefit of his life's work: the forgiveness of sins. The Supper declares the inheritance.

Yet the proper hearing of the Word of forgiveness does depend on a proper understanding of the hierarchy of meaning that Luther established. The Words of Institution as a Word of power—as Christ himself presented in Word—must be understood as holding first place in this system of the Word preached at the table. It is only the absolute certainty of that Word that makes the hearing of the Word of forgiveness possible. Christ as Word of power comes first; then the declaration of the benefit of Christ, the forgiveness of sins, can be heard with the assurance necessary to strengthen Christian faith.

In a number of places in his sermons, Luther explicitly linked Word of power with Word of forgiveness. Thus in the Maundy Thursday 1523 sermon, Luther argued that the Word is so arranged that (as power) it tells one that Christ is in the bread and wine; the purpose is the remission of sins.[34] Indeed, the benefit of forgiveness that properly works from the Word of power (Words of Institution) is termed the "great treasure of the gospel."[35]

In the third of the 1528 catechetical sermons, Luther laid out this hierarchy of eucharistic meaning in one-two order. It is such an important point that Luther actually made it twice, once in the body of the sermon and again at the end, where he summed up his teaching: "If the sacrament is rightly administered, one should preach that the sacrament is the body and blood of Christ, as the words say. Secondly, the benefit: it effects the forgiveness of sins, as the words say, 'which is shed for the remission of sins.'"[36] "First, the sacrament is Christ's body and blood in bread and wine comprehended in the Word. Secondly, the benefit is the forgiveness of sins."[37]

In these passages one can see why the proper understanding of the order of meaning in the Eucharist is important for Luther, and how that relates to his insistence on the Real Presence of Christ in the Eucharist. Put simply, the Testator and the testament are two different things, and it is only by the power of the first that the second can be accomplished. Christ is the Testator. It is by his Word that the testament and its words are enacted.

Scholars have often remarked that Luther rejected the notion of the bread and wine in the Eucharist as signs:[38] in his mind the word "sign," when applied to bread and wine, was meant to bespeak the absence of Christ's body in the

34. Lenker 11:204 (WA 15:492). This sermon was repreached by Luther on Palm Sunday 1524.

35. Lenker 11:206 (WA 15:494).

36. LW 51:190 (WA 30.1:119).

37. LW 51:193 (WA 30.1:122).

38. See note 29 above.

eucharistic celebration. But in Luther's understanding, the body and blood are truly present by the Word. That is why the Word is powerful: it effects what it says. And it is only this power, Luther thought, that protected what is dependent on it: the forgiveness of sins. The Christian knows that the Word is powerful because it effects Christ's true presence. And here is where sign came in for Luther. Even though the bread and wine cannot be reduced to signs of Christ's absent body and blood, the body and blood themselves—because of the power that guarantees their presence—serve as signs that the promise of forgiveness is true and unalterable. The expression of power in the Eucharist, shown or signified by the real presence comprehended in the Word, is the guarantee that God's Word is reliable.

At each and every Supper, the Testator is there to bespeak the testament. Thus the bedrock of salvation—its certainty—is God's Word, not the human ability to work by analogy from bread and wine to body and blood to promise of forgiveness. This schema was how Luther protected the objectivity of the Eucharist; subjectivity can in no way invalidate what is truly offered. "Our unbelief does not alter God's word," Luther declared.[39] And it is by the sign of powerful presence, which is the seal of the Testator, that the inheritance, the testament left to believers, the forgiveness of sins, is made sure.[40]

Heeding the Words of Comfort: The Command of Right Use

On Maundy Thursday, March 28, 1521—less than a week before the Diet of Worms—Luther preached a sermon on the Eucharist that in many ways summed up his thought on the Christian life. In preparing to receive the Eucharist, Luther reminded the monks that "worthy reception, however, is not based on our diligence and effort, our work and our prayers, on our fasting, but on the truth of the divine words."[41] In other words, it is not human effort but God's Word that is paramount, not only in the constitution and proclamation of the Eucharist, but also in its very reception.

The category of right use of the Sacrament has to do with the application of the Word of power and the proclamation of the testament as they relate

---

39. LW 51:189 (WA 30.1:118).

40. Another way to discuss this relationship and its inherent logic is to speak of gift and giver. Luther made the distinction between Christ and what he offers when he spoke about how union with Christ is the step from which forgiveness proceeds—for example, when Luther asserted that, to receive the benefit of Christ, one must first become one bread with Christ, because only in that case does "his innocence and my sins, my weakness and his strength, . . . all become one" (Lenker 11:232 [WA 12:487]).

41. LW 42:174 (WA 7:695).

to the individual. Though Luther would not, I think, have wanted for this to be called the "subjective" side of the Eucharist, it is certainly the personal side of the Eucharist since the grace of God is applied to the individual.[42] In this category and for the first time, there is the notion of personal interaction between the Word of God exhibited in power and benefit and the soul of the participant. Yet the ability of the Word of God to serve as a comfort to the soul rests on understanding the right use of function within a hierarchy of meaning that places the soul under the control of the Word of God in its objective power and objective promise. Thus what is explored by Luther is how, given this hierarchy, the Word interacts with the soul and its condition. First, then, we shall examine what Luther said in regard to the Word's role in proper reception, meaning proper use, of the Eucharist. Once that role is established, it will become clear what effect that Word works on the soul so that the "subjective" characteristics of the worthy participant become clear.

From the early 1522 sermons, it is clear from Luther's perspective that all aspects of the Eucharist—including its proper use and reception—are controlled by the Word. "We must . . . promote and practice and preach the Word, and then afterwards leave the result and execution of it entirely to the Word," Luther proclaimed to his congregation on March 13.[43] Let us look at the role of the Word in regard to use and then look at the result, as Luther suggests.

The function of the Word is twofold in terms of its role in preparation and use: it underscores the participant's need and highlights God's will to meet that need. What is more, the bridge that unites the two—need and fulfillment—is the faith that the Word itself creates in the believer. In other words, the Word makes clear the believer's need, the Word makes clear God's power and promise to fulfill that need, and the Word creates the faith that enables the participant to acknowledge one's need and trust God to meet it.

Luther's favorite image for the Christian's need for what the Eucharist gives was that of the hungry and terrified soul. The need for both nourishment and assurance is apparent when he used these words, such as in the 1522 sermons, when he proclaimed that "this bread is a comfort for

42. From this time period, Luther actually made the distinction in his sermons that preaching is for the multitudes while the Sacrament is for individual believers, offered to them personally. See Lenker 11:199 (WA 15:486). The reason for the personal aspect will become clear in what follows.

43. LW 51:90 (WA 10.3:45). Though this statement refers to the problem of forcing reception in both kinds onto the Wittenberg congregation before they were ready for such a practice (it is clear he expected the eventual establishment of such a practice once "the gospel has been thoroughly preached and understood" [ibid.]), the principle applies to the category of use, for part of proper use is proper celebration.

the sorrowing, a healing for the sick, a life for the dying, a food for all the hungry, and a rich treasure for all the poor and needy."[44] But how does that state of hunger—which sounds so much a part of the subjective state of the believer—come about? Is it purely a matter of introspection? No. For such a state—even within the context of exhortation to believers—finally relies on the Word. How did Luther connect this interior state to the Word in his 1523 Easter Monday preaching? "Humble yourselves, and abide in fear so as to feel your struggles and weaknesses, and desire faith. If you experience that, then thank God, for that is a sure sign the Word has struck and moved you, and exercises, constrains and impels you."[45] Obviously, it is the Word that prepares the heart.[46] The religious "feelings" to which Luther refers are not conditions the soul creates to receive the Word; rather, these feelings are the sign that the Word has been at work.

If, in Luther's mind, the Word makes clear to the participant one's need, it is also the Word that fills that need. For it is the Word of comfort contained in the eucharistic celebration that seals to the participant the Word of benefit, and the power behind it is spoken personally to the participant. The whole action and power of God unto salvation is held out in the eucharistic Word, as Luther explained: "How does the Father draw us? Through Christ. How through Christ? By the Word. But leave it to God, how you may remain steadfast, and go [to the Sacrament] now, while you have the Word and feel your misery. Then the Word itself will teach you how to prepare yourself aright, . . . for it must be something great for God to give me his Word and cause it to be pleasing and attractive to me."[47] What is it that is pleasing and attractive in the Word? What is the comfort it holds out? Two words from Christ's testament constitute the Word of comfort: "for you." The Words of Institution reveal the Word of power, exhibited by the real presence of Christ in the Eucharist; the power of the Testator is necessary for the testament—the forgiveness of sins—to be accomplished. Yet one can believe all of that to be true and still stand outside the proffered salvation unless the Word of comfort is spoken, heard, and believed—that the power, the forgiveness, is "for you."

The "for you" aspect of the entire of Luther's theology has been well remarked: it stands as a standard heading in the study of Luther's theology.[48]

44. LW 51:95 (WA 10.3:54).
45. Lenker 11:273 (WA 12:499).
46. See Lenker 11:270 (WA 12:497).
47. Lenker 11:279 (WA 12:504).
48. As an example, see Timothy George, *The Theology of the Reformers* (Nashville: Broadman, 1988), 59–60.

Yet it is especially clear in the celebration of the Eucharist, for it is from the eucharistic language of Jesus that the phrase is taken. On Palm Sunday 1524, Luther preached a sermon on confession and the Eucharist. He delineated three types of confession: that before God, which is absolutely necessary; that before one's neighbor, which is a fruit of love; and that before a priest. How does that last—and traditional—confession relate to the Eucharist? Luther claimed that this type of confession is neither necessary nor commanded in order to receive the holy Sacrament, but that it can be helpful. One is to go to confession, not so much to enumerate sin, but rather to hear the Word of comfort, the declaration that "God is merciful to you." Indeed, this confession can be a great comfort, for the promise of forgiveness the priest speaks is not his own word but God's Word. Luther even pointed out that the excellence of confession lies not in a Christian's confession but in God's "Word and how you believe it."[49]

To stress inclusion, Luther often changed the language from second person to first person. What is it that the words of the Eucharist accomplish? "Here the words make the bread into the body of Christ given for us."[50] And it is this change of person that, for Luther, in a real sense constituted the change in personhood. In a sermon wholly about the words "which is given for you" as part of God's Word, Luther distinguished between believer and unbeliever on this basis: believers are those who remember to include themselves in the little phrase "for you."[51] When "for you" becomes "for me," then the word of comfort has been rightly used.

It is this right use, controlled at every step by the Word, that constitutes faith. And it is at this point, and at this point in the hierarchy of meaning, that Luther would make a "big distinction between outward reception and inner and spiritual reception." Faith is the distinction. Faith is "a firm trust that Christ, the Son of God, stands in our place and has taken all our sins upon his shoulders and that he is the eternal satisfaction for our sin and reconciles us with God the Father." One who has such faith "has his rightful place here and receives the sacrament as an assurance, or seal, or sign to assure him of God's promise and grace."[52] In other words, those worthy to receive the Sacrament have faith that they are included in "for you" and thus receive the benefits of

49. Lenker 11:195–201, quotes on 201 (WA 15:482–89).
50. WA 30.1:53, "Ibi verba faciunt panem zum leib Christi traditum pro nobis." This comes from the September 1528 catechetical sermon.
51. LW 51:191 (WA 30.1:120). This is taken from the final of the three catechetical sermons on the Eucharist, December 1528. Immediately after the words "for you," Luther continued, "Therefore let each one see to it that he comes to the sacrament himself and his family, if they want to be Christians."
52. LW 51:92–93 (WA 10.3:48–52).

forgiveness Luther listed (above) through the power of God's Word.[53] When Jesus commands, "Take, eat," it is in heeding the command of right use that one is able to hear the word of comfort: for you.

The Fruit of Communion: The Word of Love

In his earliest eucharistic sermons, Luther was very concerned with the communion of saints. In these early sermons he was eager to show that the Eucharist itself proceeded from a communion by which even faith itself became a common possession of the participants; thus one could commune in the faith of another. In a 1518 sermon, Luther wholeheartedly endorsed the advice that Bernard of Clairvaux gave to a brother so anxious that he refused to participate in the Eucharist: "Go, my brother, celebrate in my faith."[54]

By 1522 this approach was no longer possible, in Luther's opinion. As shown above, Luther had come to think of the Eucharist as something applied to the individual; one could not commune in the faith of another. Yet the notion of the communion of saints did not disappear from Luther's theology; its place and function changed.[55]

53. It cannot be emphasized enough that such a faith is personal but not subjective: the faith that appropriates the promise of the Sacrament, stands under "for you," is a faith that God makes. "For it must be a faith that God makes, you must know and feel that God works this in you" (Luther's 1523 Maundy Thursday sermon, Lenker 11:230 [WA 12:484]). Moreover, this category of right use, controlled by the notion of faith that bridges need and fulfillment, is part of the structure of Luther's hierarchy of eucharistic meaning, but right use is not in and of itself a formal part of the Sacrament. In other words, Luther made a distinction between the Sacrament and its use, between what he calls the external and the internal. The Sacrament consists of the body and blood of Christ comprehended in bread and wine by the Word—the objective power of God to do what God promises and the promise attached to the Sacrament, which is that of forgiveness. Faith is what enables a personal appropriation of that power and promise, which enables proper use and which will, we shall see in the next section, empower the fruit of love in the individual. For this distinction, see Luther's "The Sacrament of the Body and Blood of Christ—against the Fanatics," LW 36:335, 342, 350, 352 (WA 19:482, 492, 507, 509). Finally, to show that Luther really was interested in the order of how things were to be understood, Luther's December 1528 catechetical sermon, the text quoted at note 37 above, continues: "Thirdly, those who believe [those with faith, those who make right use] should come."

54. "Sermon on the Proper Preparation of the Heart for the Sacramental Reception of the Eucharist" ("Vade, mi frater et celebra in fide mea," WA 1:333). For a brief analysis of the communion of saints theme in Luther's early eucharistic teaching and the change that takes place in it due to the development of his notion of the Supper as a testament, see chap. 1 above.

55. On this, see Dennis Alan Laskey, "In Faith and Fervent Love: The Concept of *Communio* in Luther's Understanding of the Lord's Supper" (PhD diss., Lutheran School of Theology at Chicago, 1983). See note 8 above for citation for Althaus, a representative figure of those who have argued that the concept of "communio" disappeared because of Luther's concern over real presence.

In brief, the change in place is this: the Word of Communion follows and is dependent on the three preceding Words of power, benefit, and comfort. In the Christian's life it is the result of the proper working of God's Word as it unfolds. This is why Luther often spoke about Communion either toward the end of an individual sermon or at the end of a series of sermons: the first three Words had to be comprehended before the final one (Communion) could be effective.

The change of function has to do with a change in the direction of a person's attention. In the earliest eucharistic sermons—before his work on Hebrews had been incorporated into his theology of the Supper, a process that took a few years—the notion of Communion had much to do with faith as a communal property that could be shared with the individual partaker. In his new schema, Communion has to do with love as a property that the individual shares with the community. It is the faith-strengthened individual who has made proper use of the Sacrament, who by faith is empowered to hear the Word of forgiveness comprehended in the Word of power that makes present Christ's body and blood, who then is empowered to turn from the Communion table to the community. What God has done for the individual in eucharistic celebration then becomes the model for how the believer acts toward others. Examples from the 1522–28 sermons will illustrate how Luther understood this.

In the 1522 sermons, upon his return to Wittenberg, Luther saved discussion of the fruit of the Sacrament for the last sermon—after he had discussed the Word's power, promise, and use. He declared that the fruit of the Sacrament is love, defined as acting so that "we should treat our neighbor as God has treated us."[56] Luther made clear, however, that only as the Christian grows in faith through the assurance received in the Eucharist will love as a fruit be exhibited. In other words, only proper relationship to God through faith in God's Word enables a proper relationship of the Christian to his or her community.

The Maundy Thursday 1523 sermon followed much the same structure. After discussing the Words of Institution as power words, the blessing that comes when the promise is believed to be true, and the use one makes of the Sacrament in faith,[57] Luther moved to the category of fruit, which follows from right use.

Luther explained that, even in this category, the results of love are given by grace, not human action. For true communion to take place between believers, the Eucharist first enables believers to become one bread with Christ.[58] The

56. LW 51:95 (WA 10.3:55).
57. See Lenker 11:226–30 (WA 12:479–85).
58. Lenker 11:231, 232 (WA 12:485–86, 487).

basis for unity is not, according to Luther, that Christians fellowship together in the Sacrament and thus become one (remember: by this time, Luther thought that the Sacrament in its celebration was addressed to the individual); rather, the unity resides in Christ and his benefits. Christians are one bread because Christians "receive all that Christ has and is."[59]

Once Christians become this spiritual body, however, through the power of Christ exhibited by the presence of his true body,[60] the power he shares is turned to the neighbor. The partaking of Christ's true body and blood enables a symbolic eating; as a result of worthy reception, Christians eat one another, in the sense that what one has all have. To illustrate this concept, Luther added, "When I become a public servant and serve you so that you enjoy my service whenever you need me, then I am thus your food."[61] It is this partaking of one another that proves whether or not, for Luther, right use has been made of the Sacrament. When this fruit of love does not follow, Luther told his flock, "we can excommunicate [that one] from the congregation."[62] How could Luther say this? In a sermon preached four days later, on Easter Monday 1523, Luther declared, "It is impossible for God's Word not to produce fruit and be a blessing."[63]

One finds the same structure and emphasis in Luther's 1524 Palm Sunday sermon on confession and the Sacrament. Again, following an exposition of the Words of Institution, promise, and use,[64] Luther turned to the notion that proper use of the Sacrament bears fruit, and that fruit is love: love in the sense that Christians serve one another as Christ has served them, giving of himself in the Eucharist. As Luther phrased it: "Now this is the fruit, that even as we have eaten and drunk the body and blood of Christ the Lord, we in turn permit ourselves to be eaten and drunk, and say the same words to our neighbor, Take, eat, and drink, . . . meaning to offer yourself with all your life, even as Christ did with all that he had."[65] By means of the outward form of the Sacrament, the bread and the wine, Luther explained

---

59. Lenker 11:231 (WA 12:486).

60. "Luther's position is not just that the natural body of Christ *is* the precondition for the spiritual body [of the church]; more than that, it *must* mediate the spiritual. Otherwise, spirit and spiritual body are lost" (Kyle A. Pasewark, "The Body in Ecstasy: Love, Difference, and the Social Organism in Luther's Theory of the Lord's Supper," *Journal of Religion* 77, no. 4 [October 1997]: 529).

61. Lenker 11:234 (WA 12:489).

62. Lenker 11:235 (WA 12:491).

63. Lenker 11:275 (WA 10.1.2:227).

64. Lenker 11:201–7 (WA 15:490–97).

65. Lenker 11:208 (WA 15:498).

how it is that Christ has displayed for Christians what love should be like among them.[66]

Luther's 1528 catechetical sermons on the Eucharist concentrate on the order of power, forgiveness, and use. He does not deal with the fruit of Communion: love. Yet in 1528 in the context of catechetical sermons on the Eucharist that do not explore the communion-of-saints component, Luther repreached a sermon from 1519: "The Blessed Sacrament of the Holy and True Body of Christ, and the Brotherhoods." This is significant, especially since the issue of communion of saints does not appear in the catechetical sermons. For, at a time when Luther was preoccupied with the problem of the real presence of Christ in the Supper, Luther repreached this sermon, dealing chiefly with the communion of saints as a primary concern of the Eucharist, which expresses itself in the growth of love.[67]

Structure and Content: Eucharistic Meaning and Incarnational Theology

This rendering of the hierarchy of meaning in Luther's eucharistic sermons from the 1521–28 period seems not only plausible; it is also consistent with the overall structure of Luther's thought. There is the same connection between word, faith, and love in his eucharistic hierarchy as in his broader theology. This, I think, lends credence to using this hierarchy of meaning to get at what is central to Luther's eucharistic teaching.

God's grace, for Luther, is mediated through the Word: the Word is God's power unto salvation. It always works what it says. Indeed, the Word's objective power is what, in Luther's opinion, worked the work of Reformation while he and "Amsdorf drank beer."

The Word that God speaks to Christians is the Word of promise of the forgiveness of sins. For Luther, this is the Gospel and the benefit of Christ's work on earth and intercession in heaven.

Moreover, it is the Word that prepares Christian hearts to receive and believe the word of forgiveness. Faith is not subjective feeling or human-wrought belief; it is God's making of new ears so that the Gospel message can be heard. The good word of salvation, the Christian's comfort, can be received only by

66. Lenker 11:212–13 (WA 15:503).
67. "Die bedeutung odder das werck disses sacraments ist gemeinshafft aller heyligen" (WA 2:743). For the notion of this work (or fruit, the way Luther more consistently characterized it) as expressing itself primarily in the growth of love (which means becoming one—one bread, one body, one drink, sharing all things), see WA 2:748.

a heart created anew by God. The Word, all-powerful in its effect and salvific in its benefit, creates the faith that receives it. This is why, for Luther, there could be no talk of merit or good works earning salvation; grace is a gift effected, presented, and received by the Word. This schema is matched by the eucharistic structure of power, benefit, and use.

And just as in the sermons outlined above, so also in his general theology, Luther did not do away with the notion of good works, works of love; he repositioned good works so that they follow necessarily from the working of the Word. Good works do not effect salvation; they are its flowering. The *communio sanctorum*, the community of love, is thus a *necessary* result of the Word.

Therefore, the structure of eucharistic meaning exhibited in these sermons of Luther mirrors the structure of his broader theology. Eucharistic meaning does not, however, simply mirror the *structure* of Luther's theology; it also reflects the foundation, the heart, of this theology. For at the heart of all theology for Luther is God and how one knows God; or perhaps better said, one must start all theology with understanding how it is that God reveals Godself.

In Luther's thought, it is simply impossible to know God in and of Godself. The "naked" God is hidden, inaccessible to human reason. Therefore, God must take action to reveal Godself to humanity.[68] That action is God's Word.

God's Word as revelation, however, is not vocalization or a spirit's voice or a disembodied will; it is Jesus Christ. So, by God's design the Word of God as the revelation of God and God's will is an embodied Word, because of God's willingness to stoop to accommodate that revelation to human nature.[69] If one would know God, one must know Christ; what is more, one must know

68. The hidden and revealed God in Luther's thought has received much attention in the study of Luther's theology. See, among others, Althaus, "God in Himself and God as He Reveals Himself," chap. 4 in *Theology of Martin Luther*; Heinrich Bornkamm, *Luther's World of Thought*, trans. Martin H. Bertram (St. Louis: Concordia, 1958), 88, 98; Brian A. Gerrish, "'To the Unknown God': Luther and Calvin on the Hiddenness of God," chap. 8 in *The Old Protestantism and the New: Essays on the Reformation Heritage* (Chicago: University of Chicago Press, 1982); and David C. Steinmetz, "Luther and the Hidden God," chap. 3 in *Luther in Context* (Bloomington: Indiana University Press, 1986), who states, "The center of Luther's understanding of Christianity is the proclamation of a God who is both hidden and revealed" (23).

69. In other words, there is a principle of accommodation at work in Luther's theology. As Althaus summarizes Luther, "[God] adjusts himself to our human ability to comprehend him" (Althaus, *Theology of Martin Luther*, 22); see also Steinmetz, "Luther and the Hidden God," 25. This is certainly one area where Calvin's thought clearly is quite close to Luther's, and also one in which it is clear that Zwingli stands at the other end of the spectrum. More will be made of this in the conclusion of the chapter.

Christ in his humanity. There is no other God for us, Luther stated, than the one who comes in "swaddling clothes."[70] Luther's theology is incarnational, and that is certainly reflected in his eucharistic thought.[71]

To speak of Luther's theology as incarnational carries with it a number of implications because of Luther's understanding of incarnation. The most important implication is that, when the Bible speaks of the Spirit as over against the flesh, this cannot mean the Spirit over against the body. Since Christ came to reveal God in a body, it is clear that the bodily can serve as the means by which the spiritual—meaning the things of God—is revealed. The spiritual has to do with the execution of God's will; the flesh is the totality of sinful impulses that turn one away from God's will to one's own selfish will. Thus, flesh and spirit have to do with one's basic disposition in life, not with materiality and nonmateriality. In Luther's understanding, the incarnation means that God's Word truly is a concrete, visible, bodily word.[72]

70. As Althaus nicely states it, "[Christ's] humanity is the place to which God summons us" (Althaus, *Theology of Martin Luther*, 22); Althaus also points out that God and salvation are mediated specifically through the humanity of Christ (idid., 183); see Steinmetz, "Luther and the Hidden God," 27. Luther and Calvin have much in common on this point; indeed, in his commentary on John, Calvin works out a schema for how the righteousness of God is finally mediated to human beings through the body of Christ (see CNTC 4:167–68 [CO 47:153]). Both Calvin's and Luther's notion of the humanity of Christ, in its bodily aspect, as being the instrument by which God mediates salvation, it seems to me, echoes Augustine's opinion when he says of Jesus, "For how far forth he was a man, so far forth he was mediator" (Augustine, *Confessions*, 2 vols. [Cambridge, MA: Harvard University Press, 1970], 2:203).

71. The connection between incarnation and Eucharist in Luther's thought has long been recognized. The question is, however, whether that connection is proper to Luther's theology or an alien element. Harnack, for example, saw that for Luther "the Eucharist must be conceived of as the parallel to and guarantee for the Incarnation" (Adolf von Harnack, *History of Dogma*, trans. Neil Buchanan from the 3rd German ed., in 7 vols. bound as 4 [Gloucester, MA: Peter Smith, 1976], 7:263). Harnack sees this eucharistic parallel to the incarnation, however, as a "Catholic holdover" in Luther's theology (ibid., 2:267). A more appreciative view of the relationship of Eucharist to incarnation can be found in Pascwark, "Body in Ecstasy," 531.

72. On the notion of the "spiritual," Ebeling reminds us that for Luther, "The spiritual is not a special realm of being, a sphere of spirituality, inwardness and invisibility. Instead, the spiritual is a category of understanding. Whoever exists spiritually exists in the visible realm, but he exists in it not as manifest but as hidden" (Gerhard Ebeling, "The Beginnings of Luther's Hermeneutics," *Lutheran Quarterly* 7, no. 3 [Autumn 1993]: 317). On the meaning of the incarnate Word for Luther, Asendorf writes, "Wenn Luther also sagt, es gehe ihm im Abendmahl um den schlichten Glauben an Gottes Wort, so ist das gerade nicht biblizistisch gemeint, sondern Wort Gottes ist immer konkretes, leiblich gefasstes Wort, sei es durch den Predigen oder vermittels der Elemente im Sakrament. Luther meint also das Wort als ganzheitliche, leibliche, vermittelte, inkarnierte Wirklichkeit. . . . Wort als Wort Gottes ist in diesem Sinne inkarniertes Wort" (Ulrich Asendorf, "Das Wort Gottes bei Luther im sakramentalen Zusammenhang patristischer Theologie: Systematische und ökumenische Überlegungen zu Luthers Schrift, 'Dass diese Worte Christi' (1527)," *Kerygma und Dogma* 39, no. 1 [January–March 1993]: 45).

Second, because Luther's theology is a theology of the cross, God's Word is embodied in unexpected places—indeed, in hidden places, or under "contraries"—so that not only is God in Godself hidden, but God in God's revelation is also hidden to some extent.[73] Thus even if God's Word is primarily an incarnate Word embodied in concrete things, that Word is not self-evident; it requires a further working of the Word to point to the revelation. Hence, the Word of God as revelation has a dual function: both to embody God's revelation (the *content* of God's Word) and to point out God's revelation in its embodied hiddenness (the signifying function of God's Word).

Third, the embodied Word that is hidden and must be pointed out carries consequences for how Luther understands the notion of God's transcendence, as David Steinmetz has demonstrated.[74] If some people thought of transcendence as a God above human and material existence, Luther did not. Because of the embodied nature of the Word, God is, in Luther's thought, in all God's works because God's works are simply a function of God's Word.[75] God, in a sense, is all around; though not contained by creation, God certainly permeates it. The question, then, is one of knowledge, or one of accessibility to God. God is present in everything created, so God's presence is not a question of distance; it is a question of knowing where and how to look for God. Part of the revelatory function of the incarnate Word is to point out the God who is near. God's Word, in a sense, does not make God present; it simply points to a place where God already is and to a place where God is to be accessible to humanity, a place that God has designated.[76]

73. See Bornkamm, *Luther's World of Thought*, 88. See also Ebeling, "Beginnings of Luther's Hermeneutics," 315–17; "The spiritual is everything in light of the cross of Christ, in light of God's revelation, hidden under its contrary" (317).

74. Steinmetz, "Luther and the Hidden God," 24: "The doctrine of divine transcendence does not mean that God is removed from creation. . . . God is not merely present in eucharistic bread; he is present in all common bread and the wheat from which bread is made. The transcendence of God is not equivalent to his absence. On the contrary, transcendence means that, while God is present in every creature that surrounds me, his presence is inaccessible to me apart from his Word."

75. See Pelikan, *Luther the Expositor*, 54–55.

76. As Althaus says concerning this point in Luther's theology, "God enters into a saving encounter with man only by 'clothing' himself and causing himself to be found at a place he himself has designated" (Althaus, *Theology of Martin Luther*, 35). What is more, the "place" God designates does not require a miracle to "bring" God to that place, God is already there; only the Word is needed to point out the presence. God, by nature, is near unto humanity, and Christ, even in his humanity, shares that characteristic. Luther uses Occamist categories to speak of modes of presence; the way God and Christ are present, according to Luther, is "repletively," a category that Luther wrote about in these terms: "This mode of existence belongs to God alone, as he says in the prophet Jeremiah [23:23–24], 'I am a God at hand

One sees, then, a high degree of consistency between Luther's eucharistic preaching and his theology as a whole in terms of content. In the Eucharist, Christ's body reveals the divine; the revelation itself, however, is hidden to some extent, so that the bodily mediation of divine grace is not readily apparent to human senses or reason. One sees that the Word directs the believer to that hidden bodily mediation as the place of encounter with God: in a sense, the spoken Word points to the bodily Word. Whether one likes this way of looking at the Eucharist[77] is less the point than the fact that it is thoroughly consistent with Luther's broader theology in both structure and content.

Conclusion

The importance of examining Luther's eucharistic preaching during this period leading up to Marburg (1529) and analyzing the structure of eucharistic meaning found therein lies in the way such an examination counters a misreading of Luther's intent and rhetoric at Marburg. An analysis of the structure of these sermons also points to ways in which Luther's thought may be more thoughtfully compared to other Reformers.

The issues that separated Luther and Zwingli at Marburg lay deeper than a disagreement on how Christ can be present in the Eucharist (Luther's concern) or how best to read John 6 (Zwingli's concern). As far as Zwingli was concerned, as Carl Leth has pointed out, materiality versus Spirit was not the main issue; rather, it was the deeper issue of a proper doctrine of God and

---

and not afar off. I fill heaven and earth.' This mode is altogether incomprehensible, beyond our reason, and can be maintained only with faith, in the Word" (cited in Steinmetz, *Luther in Context*, 79). Cf. what Calvin has to say on nearness in chap. 4.

77. Thus one has to assume that both Harnack and Althaus, though critical of Luther's eucharistic thought in different ways, have both essentially missed the way Luther's eucharistic thought—even in the period of Luther's fight on a "second front" of the eucharistic conflict—really is quite in harmony with his thought as a whole. Understood as I have outlined it in this chapter, Luther's work on presence did not "impoverish" his teaching (Althaus, *Theology of Martin Luther*, 322), because the idea of the community of saints is still as much present in his eucharistic structure as in 1519, as the Word of Love. Yet now the community of saints is grounded differently than before and in a eucharistic structure that reflects Luther's theological structure since *communio sanctorum* follows from the Word understood in a hierarchy of meaning, just as good works flow from the Christian as a result of the Word's work, thus placing works in their appropriate place in a theological hierarchy of meaning. Neither did Luther's work on presence bring in a "host of evils" dependent on Catholic nominalist thought that needed to be corrected by Luther's "original" ideas (Harnack, *History of Dogma*, 7:260–61), because presence, for Luther, had to do with the very nature of the Word itself.

how God's providence relates to the Eucharist, thus making causality, not materiality, the real issue for Zwingli.[78]

For Luther as well, the deeper issue is the nature of God and God's revelation, not *how* Christ is present in the Eucharist.[79] For Zwingli, God's nature is simple and undeceptive;[80] for Luther, that nature is hidden, as we have seen, and its revelation has to be accommodated through concrete, bodily means. For Luther, the very nature of the Word itself, as incarnate in Christ Jesus, was the issue. And thus central to Luther's understanding of the Eucharist was the truth of the Divine Word: the truth of its power to do as it says, because that truth is tied to *who* the Divine Word is. Then, if the Word is true in power, it can be true in its promise of forgiveness. If the promise of forgiveness is true, then the word of comfort is true and can be used by God to construct faith in the believer. And following from that flow of power through the forgiveness that comforts and upbuilds the Christian, the Word's truth is finally sealed as love permeates the community of saints. God's Word indeed is true for it has remade the Christian into a little Christ, one who is able to spend oneself on others in a communion created by the Word. The Word of power incarnated in Christ ends as power to do good in the Christian.[81]

What one can thus say is that, in Luther's mind, Zwingli's *basic* theological mistake was not a denial of bodily presence: it was the denial of God's Word and how to properly understand its ordering and meaning.[82]

78. Carl M. Leth, "Signs and Providence: A Study of Ulrich Zwingli's Sacramental Theology" (PhD diss., Duke University, 1992), 1, 159, 178.

79. As Leth notes, there was an offer by the Lutherans at Marburg that, if Zwingli's side would accept that the body of Christ was somehow present in the Eucharist and not solely in memory, then the Lutherans would not force discussion on matters such as the manner of presence. As Leth says, this was an offer that "almost certainly [came] from Luther himself" (ibid., 176). This should not be surprising, given the fact that in *The Babylonian Captivity of the Church* Luther had stated that the how of presence should not be a matter of strict doctrine but that some room should be given for various ways of understanding how Christ could be present; see LW 36:35 (WA 6:512).

80. "Zwingli findet den für Erwählte fasslichen, unparadoxen und eindeutig erfahrbaren Gott" (Christof Gestrich, *Zwingli als Theologe: Glaube und Geist beim Zürcher Reformator* [Zurich: Zwingli-Verlag, 1967], 38; cited in Leth, "Signs and Providence," 30).

81. This, really, is the point of Pasewark's *Theology of Power*. Though the book is subtitled *Being beyond Domination*, the real gist of the book is captured in the phrase from the title of the dissertation on which the book is based: "The Communication of Efficacy."

82. I argue that the development in Luther's eucharistic thought is not a shift from (1) body pointing to Word, to (2) Word pointing to body (articulated by Friedrich Graebke, *Die Konstruktion der Abendmahlslehre Luthers in ihrer Entwicklung dargestellt* [Leipzig: Deichert, 1908], 72, and followed or modified by many since); rather, I say that it is in the fact that, for Luther, there was a growing understanding of an inherent "bodiliness" to the Word when spoken as incarnate Word to humanity for its salvation. Thus Luther came to understand that bodiliness

Other errors, such as the denial of the bodily presence or the elevation of the memorial function of the Eucharist to a controlling place within the hierarchy of meaning, followed from this first and basic mistake, as Luther saw it.[83]

Much has been made of the way Luther understood Christ's presence in the Eucharist and the how of it all. I suggest that if one focuses instead on what I argue is actually prior and primary—the Word, its character, its promises, and its levels of meaning—one can begin to compare Luther's thought to others in a new and fruitful way. This way of reading Luther might actually lend insight to the story of Luther's reading of John Calvin's *Short Treatise on the Holy Supper*, one that relates Luther's favorable comments about Calvin and the spirit of the 1545 Latin edition of that work.[84] In a comparison of Calvin and Luther, if one focuses on the how of presence, one ends up in the morass of the Calvin/Gnesio-Lutheran diatribes, such as the bitter exchanges between Calvin and Joachim Westphal (1510–74), which characterize for many the ugliness of Reformation debates on the Eucharist. As stressed here, Luther was willing, at least in early works such as the *Babylonian Captivity*, to suggest that the how did not have to be a matter of doctrine. But if one focuses instead on the order of eucharistic meaning by seeing how levels of the Word are related and how Christ's body is related to an undergirding of that Word's power and work, one might see some remarkable similarities that would explain Luther's praise for the Word's work. Hence, in reading Calvin's *Short Treatise*, Luther might have seen someone at work concerned with the Word in its expression of power, forgiveness, comfort, and love—someone who saw the body of Christ as a seal and guarantee as well of the truth of the divine words.[85]

---

as characteristic of the Word itself, not something alien or added, something for which I have argued in this and chap. 1 above.

83. Remembrance, for Luther, is the result of eucharistic celebration rather than its foundation. It falls under the fourth order of the Word, the Word of Love, because for Luther, remembrance is not an internal act of the mind but an external proclamation for the benefit of the other. On this, see Pascwark, "Body in Ecstasy," 533.

84. See the account given by Christoph Pezel, translated into French, in Émile Doumergue, *Jean Calvin: Les hommes et les choses de son temps*, 7 vols. (Lausanne: Georges Bridel, 1899–1927), 2:572–73.

85. On many of the issues presented in this chapter, Calvin actually stood much closer to Luther than to Zwingli. Some of these include the hiddenness of God, the need for accommodation of God's Word, and the importance not only of the sensible but also of the bodily as such as a means of grace (we will explore Calvin's teaching on the bodily as a means of grace below in chap. 4, "Not 'Hidden and Far Off': The Bodily Aspect of Salvation and Its Implications for Understanding the Body in Calvin's Theology"). This is not to say that there were not differences between Luther and Calvin: there were. But the approach suggested here opens a way to fruitfully explore the relation of Calvin's eucharistic thought to Luther's without getting caught up in the differences before it is necessary to do so.

3

"AN INTERMEDIATE BRILLIANCE"

The Words of Institution and the Gift of Knowledge
in Calvin's Eucharistic Theology

One thing is certain about Calvin's view of the Eucharist. Without the Words of Institution, the rite makes no sense. Such a situation Calvin considered tragic, for according to Calvin, it is the special function of the Eucharist to make sense of—indeed, to make *sensible*—Christ's union with believers. For the Eucharist to function properly, however, the Words of Institution must precede the fraction in an understandable manner, meaning both that the words must be proclaimed loudly and in the native tongue and that, once pronounced, the Words be properly interpreted. When such clear proclamation and exposition of the Words of Institution take place, the eucharistic action involving bread and wine presents to believers what Calvin characterized as the clearest promises of God.[1]

The chapter proceeds as follows: after a brief discussion of Calvin's "Manner of Celebrating the Lord's Supper," found in the liturgies of 1542 (Geneva)

1. On this, see Thomas J. Davis, *The Clearest Promises of God: The Development of Calvin's Eucharistic Teaching* (New York: AMS Press, 1995). On the emphasis on eucharistic action in Calvin's teaching (that Calvin's concern with the eucharistic sign was, if you like, with the entirety of the celebration, Word and sign joined in worship rather than on the elements themselves and considered apart from this action), see Brian A. Gerrish, *Grace and Gratitude: The Eucharist Theology of John Calvin* (Minneapolis: Fortress, 1993), 13n55.

and 1545 (Strassburg), we will examine Calvin's ideas on the function of the Words of Institution as they relate to eucharistic doctrine. Next, we will look at the function of the eucharistic signs in Calvin's thought. Then, we will explore how the proper use of the Words of Institution enables the eucharistic signs to serve as an accommodated instrument of knowledge that gives to believers the greatest humanly possible certainty of their union with Christ. This knowledge, I suggest, is the special gift or grace of the Eucharist, one that enhances enjoyment of the more general gift of bodily communion with Christ. Finally, we will conclude by seeing how the proper use of the Words of Institution distinguishes praise from abomination in the eucharistic celebration.

Calvin's "Manner of Celebrating the Lord's Supper"

As one reads the eucharistic portion of Calvin's liturgies,[2] one finds a strong emphasis on the assurance and confidence that the Sacrament imparts to believers. In the prayer before the Words of Institution,[3] the faithful hear that they should be "assured that it is [God's] good pleasure" to be to them a "gracious Father forever."[4] The prayer ends with the request that, in their eucharistic celebration, God grant the faithful "much greater confidence" in order to proclaim God as Father and to glory in God.[5]

In the liturgy, the minister then moves to a proclamation of the Words of Institution as found in 1 Corinthians 11. There follows an exposition of those words, which includes: (1) an excommunication of the unworthy; (2) a call to examination of conscience; (3) a proclamation of the Supper's benefit to sinners who know themselves as such but who rely on Christ for their righteousness; (4) an exposition of the promises of Christ pledged by the Sacrament; and (5) the Sursum Corda, with its appeal to lift hearts and minds on high.[6] Again, Calvin's liturgy brings to the fore the belief that the Eucharist should be seen as a source of assurance and confidence. The truly penitent should never doubt

2. The "Manner of Celebrating the Lord's Supper" constitutes the eucharistic portion of Calvin's "Form of Church Prayers." For an English translation, see Bard Thompson, ed., *Liturgies of the Western Church* (New York: Meridian Books, 1961), 197–203, "Form of Church Prayers"; 203–8, "Manner"; for the original, see CO 6:172–84, "Form"; CO 6:192–202, "Manner."

3. The prayer comes before the confession of faith in the Genevan liturgy and after the confession in the Strassburg liturgy. See Thompson, *Liturgies*, 202–5 (CO 6:179–80 [Geneva], 197 [Strassburg]).

4. Thompson, *Liturgies*, 202 (Geneva) and 205 (Strassburg) (CO 6:179 [Geneva] and 197 [Strassburg]).

5. Thompson, *Liturgies*, 203 (Geneva) and 205 (Strassburg) (CO 6:180 [Geneva] and 197 [Strassburg]).

6. Thompson, *Liturgies*, 205–7 (CO 6:197–200).

that they are God's own children. That assurance extends even to those who recognize their imperfections, for the Sacrament is a medicine for sick souls; believers are assured that they receive Christ despite imperfections. Christians are exhorted to believe that they partake of Christ and his benefits. In giving himself, Christ gives testimony that all he has belongs to the faithful, and the Eucharist is a further pledge of that exchange. Finally, the bread and wine are invoked as signs and witnesses, revealing that Christ is indeed the true and only nourishment of his people.[7]

At the end of the eucharistic service stands a prayer of thanksgiving. Here I point out that Calvin's liturgy speaks of two benefits connected with the Holy Supper. The first is communion with Christ, whose body serves as the food of immortality.[8] The second benefit mentioned has to do with the recognition of that communion as the basis for Christian life. Calvin stated it in the negative: "Now grant us this other benefit: that thou wilt never let us forget these things."[9] The Eucharist imprints that communion on the hearts and minds of participants so that, growing in faith, they might praise God and edify neighbors. Yet we have a question to answer: how, according to Calvin, does the Eucharist imprint the Christian's communion with Christ on faithful hearts and minds? To answer that question, we must discuss the Words of Institution as the basis for correct eucharistic doctrine, and then examine how the signs, guided by that doctrine, work to help the believer understand and appropriate union with Christ.

The Words of Institution: The Lens of Meaning

Calvin's view of Scripture as a lens that brings creation into focus is well known.[10] I think the concept applies equally well to the relationship between the Words of Institution and the signs of the Eucharist: the words bring the signs into focus, making them clear and sharp. Even more, the words give meaning to the signs. By themselves, bread and wine are mute; joined to the Words of Institution, they speak God's truth and promise; indeed, they point to where God may be found and experienced. What is certain is that, to derive benefit from the eucharistic celebration, the Christian must hear the Words of Institution and understand them.

7. Thompson, *Liturgies*, 206–7 (CO 6:198–200).
8. "Whom thou givest as the meat and drink of life eternal" (Thompson, *Liturgies*, 203 and 208 [CO 6:180]).
9. Thompson, *Liturgies*, 203 and 208 (CO 6:180).
10. *Inst.* 1.6.1 (CO 2:53).

The importance of knowing true doctrine was underscored by Calvin in his commentary on Galatians. In his discussion of Galatians 1:8, Calvin said that "with Christians there is no faith where there is no knowledge." He then tied knowledge to worship: "The legitimate worship of God . . . must be preceded by sure knowledge."[11]

We can apply this insistence on the importance of knowledge to the Eucharist. Indeed, Calvin himself did so. In his commentary on the Words of Institution in 1 Corinthians 11, Calvin underscored the role that the Words and their proper interpretation (true doctrine) play in the eucharistic celebration: "You see bread, and nothing else, but you hear that it is a sign of the body of Christ. Be quite sure that the Lord will carry out what you understand the words to mean: that his body, which you do not see at all, is spiritual food for you."[12] What this passage reveals is that, for Calvin, the benefit of the eucharistic signs is made clear only in the hearing of the words and in the understanding of the words. That is why in his liturgy Calvin not only proclaimed "This is my body" over the bread, but he also explained the meaning. Only by such a procedure, in Calvin's mind, could the body of the Lord be discerned in the rite.

For Calvin, the entire eucharistic celebration served as a source of knowledge about the Christian's union with Christ. But in connection with the Words of Institution, the Eucharist, as a specially accommodated source of knowledge about communion with Christ, depended on correct knowledge *about the Eucharist*. According to Calvin, for the Lord's Supper to fulfill its function as the instrument that most clearly shows forth God's promises, proper doctrine must frame the celebration.

Calvin addressed just this concern in his *Short Treatise on the Holy Supper*. In the first paragraph of the work, Calvin voiced his concern over the "errors," "divergent opinions," and "contentious disputes" to which the Eucharist had been subjected.[13] Such an environment, Calvin indicated, worked to the detriment of "many weak consciences" who, because of the controversy surrounding the Eucharist, could not "fairly resolve what view they ought to take of it."[14] Calvin then asserted that "it is a very perilous thing to have no certainty on an ordinance, the *understanding* of which is so *requisite* for our salvation."[15]

It was Calvin's objective to supply just this requisite understanding. However, he saw himself not acting on his own but following the intentions of

11. CNTC 11:14 (CO 50:173).
12. CNTC 9:24 (CO 49:488).
13. *Short Treatise*, 507 (CO 5:433).
14. *Short Treatise*, 508 (CO 5:433).
15. *Short Treatise*, 508 (CO 5:433), with emphases added.

Jesus Christ himself. As Calvin explained, "The principal thing recommended by our Lord is to celebrate with true understanding. From this it follows that the essential part lies in the doctrine."[16] For Calvin, this meant that the whole should be referred to the Word, specifically, to the Words of Institution, from which the Sacrament derived its virtue, he believed.[17] The Words fully explain the Eucharist, and by them the promises are clearly proclaimed. In other words, through the reading and exposition of the Words of Institution, the Eucharist can be understood for what it is supposed to do: show forth, present, and seal to the believer the true communion that one has with the body and blood of Christ.

In his commentaries, Calvin continued his emphasis on the necessity for a proper understanding (true doctrine) of the Eucharist so that its witness could be appropriated by believers. It can be seen, for example, in his commentary on the Words of Institution as found in the Gospels. The Words are to awaken eucharistic participants to the mystery at hand in the Supper and to make it clear that there is a focused picture of the reality of that mystery, which is true communion with the body and blood of Christ. At the time of the original institution, Calvin explained, Christ aroused his disciples "from their inertia, that they should be attentive to such a sublime mystery."[18] Likewise, the Words of Institution serve the same purpose for all who partake of the Holy Meal: they awaken weak human consciences to the nature of the divine mystery. Besides alerting weak souls to the mystery, the Words also clarify the rite. Calvin related Jesus's action to the Passover: "Reason itself demands that this clear testimony of the life of the Spirit should be distinct from the old shadow."[19] If the Passover, as Calvin thought, related to the Eucharist as shadow to the brilliance of sunlight, it is certainly the Words of Institution that serve to cast the fullness of day on the signs of bread and wine.

The clarity that the Words bring to the celebration *is* the consecration, or eucharistic conversion, in Calvin's opinion. The emphasis on the Words as true doctrine is again unmistakable. "But we must hold at the same time," Calvin explained, "that the bread is not consecrated by whispering and blowing, but by the clear teaching of faith."[20] Calvin understood consecration or conversion to indicate a change in the use, not in the substance, of the elements of bread and wine within the context of eucharistic celebration. It is the appointment of an earthly sign to serve a heavenly purpose. Thus, according to

16. *Short Treatise*, 533 (CO 5:454).
17. *Short Treatise*, 534 (CO 5:454–55).
18. Comment on Matt. 26:26, CNTC 3:132 (CO 45:704).
19. Ibid.
20. Comment on Matt. 26:26, CNTC 3:134 (CO 45:706).

Calvin, the consecration of the bread and wine, accomplished by the Words of Institution, is nothing other than God's testimony that such an earthly sign is put to heavenly use. That being so, it is logical to assert, as Calvin did, that consecration cannot take place unless God's "command and promise are heard clearly for the upbuilding of faith."[21] Thus any real celebration of the Lord's Supper depends completely on the Words of Institution, without which there is no consecration or conversion.

The proper use of the Words of Institution was twofold, according to Calvin: first, the Words must be proclaimed; second, they must be interpreted. In Calvin's view, that interpretation took place not only in the explication he gave in the "Manner of Celebrating the Lord's Supper" but also in the preaching, the sermon.[22] In a line new with the 1543 *Institutes*, Calvin claimed the importance of such preaching for the proper functioning of the signs: "Therefore, when we hear mention made of the sacramental word, let us understand the promise, which, preached with a clear voice by the minister, leads the people by the hand where the sign aims and directs us."[23]

This emphasis was underlined in the 1545 liturgy prepared for use in Strassburg. There, in his instructions for the use of the "Manner of Celebrating the Lord's Supper," Calvin explicitly detailed how people were to be led by the hand. He wrote that the people should be instructed about four things. The first is that human beings are sinful by nature, heirs to Adam's sin, and therefore unable, because of "being in the flesh," to inherit the kingdom of God. Second, Calvin asserted that the people should be taught that only Christ and his death can bring about remission of sin. Third, Calvin said, the people should be instructed to know that Christ gives himself in the Sacrament of the Supper and that, by partaking of him, the Christian gains all Christ's benefits. Fourth, the people should be taught to give thanks for God's great gifts.[24] These four points can all be derived, Calvin thought, from the Institution of the Supper itself.

21. CNTC 3:134 (CO 45:706).

22. Thompson, *Liturgies*, 204 (CO 6:197).

23. "Ergo quum de verbo sacramenti fieri mentionem audimus, promissionem intelligamus, quae clara voce a ministro praedicata plebem eo man ducat, quo signum tendit ac nos dirigit" (CO 1:940).

24. CO 6:195–96. The text of the instructions runs as follows: "Pour ceste cause, quand nous admonnestons le peuple de se preparer devant que venir a ce sacré banquet, nous l'enseignons et admonnestons tousiours de ces quatre choses.

"Premierement que nous summes tellement perduz par le peché d'Adam, et les propres, qu'il n'y a aucun bien de soy en toute nostre nature ny en notre chair. Pourtant nostre chair et nostre sang ne peuvent aquerir en heritage le Royaume de Dieu. . . .

"Secondement, que Iesus Christ est seul lequel nous a merité la remission de noz pechez. . . .

"Tiercement que Christ se communiquer en ce Sacrement de la Cene. . . . que par ce Sacrement Iesus nous donne son corps et son sang pour vivre en luy, et qu'il vive en nous, en nous

These four points of instruction are important, in Calvin's opinion, because they provide the proper understanding and context for the celebration of the Eucharist. With proper eucharistic doctrine fully explained, the Eucharist can then serve its chief end and goal: to proclaim and exhibit the forgiveness of sins that results from communion with Christ. The Words of Institution are preached, then, "in order that we know how much it is necessary that Christ live in us, and we in him."[25] They are the lenses that clarify and give meaning to the signs.

Bread and Wine: Earthly Mirrors of Divine Truth

A question arises (and did arise): If the Word makes plain the meaning of the eucharistic signs, are the signs at all necessary? Some in Calvin's time (and ours) thought not. Calvin, however, considered the signs essential. To refer back to the prayer of thanksgiving in Calvin's "Manner of Celebrating the Lord's Supper," it is the special function of the signs to imprint on the believer's heart one's communion with Christ. The imprinting process requires that physical signs accompany the word for two reasons: the necessity of God's condescension because of human weakness and the requirement that Christians follow God's commands. We will examine the issue of human weakness first.

Calvin explained the necessity of the eucharistic signs at length in his *Short Treatise on the Holy Supper.* He began the work with a concern over weak consciences. Though the phrasing may sound as if Calvin were addressing certain individuals who had problems of understanding that others did not have, it soon becomes clear, from Calvin's viewpoint, that human nature in its fallen state is weak and incapable of understanding what it should about things divine. This viewpoint stands at the center of Calvin's eucharistic thought; it is what requires that there be a Eucharist. "For seeing we are so weak that we cannot receive him [Christ] with true heartfelt trust," Calvin wrote, "when he is presented to us by simple doctrine and preaching, the

---

asseurant que par luy nous avons l'entiere abolition de noz pechez et la confirmation de grace due pere celeste, et l'alliance eternelle, que nous summes enfants de Dieu, qu'il est nostre pere, et qu'il nous donne tous biens. . . .

"Finallement nous enseignons, qu'il faut rendre graces au Seigneur Iesus pour ces grans benefices icy de cueur, de parolles, et de fait."

25. "Afin que nous congnoissons combien il est necessaire que Christ vive en nous, et nous en luy" (CO 6:196). Calvin continued, "Afin aussi que nous croyons qu'il se donne soymesme en ce Sacrement icy à nous, pour vivre en luy, et luy en nous, pour obtenir remission de noz pechez et accomplir la lie de Dieu en nous."

father of mercy, disdaining not to condescend in this matter to our infirmity, has been pleased to add to his word a visible sign by which he might represent the substance of his promises, to confirm and fortify us by delivering us from doubt and uncertainty."[26] The Eucharist is to take care of doubt and uncertainty that arise because Christians by nature cannot be sure that they have communion with Christ, body and blood. Even to the Christian mind, Calvin thought such communion to be "mysterious" and "incomprehensible." The faith of the Christian is such that it is always in need of help.[27] Calvin clearly believed that it was because of this weakness in the Christian believer that God in mercy instituted the Sacrament. The Eucharist is, therefore, that "special remedy,"[28] as Calvin called it, that human nature requires to better grasp that communion with the body and blood of Christ is the source of salvation.[29]

The bread and wine are, therefore, accommodated instruments that God uses to help Christians grasp the essentials of their salvation. This accommodation is to human understanding: "We are on our part so rude and gross that we cannot understand the least things of God," Calvin claimed, and so "it is important that we should be given to understand it [communion with the body and blood of Christ] as far as our capacity would admit."[30]

Calvin used the metaphor of mirror to describe this accommodative process.[31] He believed that God employs earthly signs to reflect divine truth. These signs are used because the human is an earthly creature, and the signs are earthly and easily comprehended; there is a continuity between the perceiver and the perceived. Earthly existence depends on the senses; with great emphasis on those senses, Calvin described the mirrors of bread and wine: "Now there cannot be a spur which can pierce us more to the quick than when he [God] makes us, so to speak, see with the eye, touch with the hand, and distinctively perceive this inestimable blessing of feeding on his own substance."[32] Inasmuch as human understanding at least starts with human perception, God has come down to the level of humanity in the way God presents the truth of the Christian's communication with the body and blood of Christ. Calvin surely believed that the purpose of those earthly signs is to move the believer beyond the earthly to the divine, so there can be no preoccupation with the

26. *Short Treatise*, 510 (CO 5:435).
27. *Short Treatise*, 510, 514, 515 (CO 5:435, 439).
28. *Short Treatise*, 522 (CO 5:445).
29. For the reason Calvin considered the body and blood of Christ to be the (accommodated) source of salvation, see the discussion of John 6 on pages 84–87 in the next chapter.
30. *Short Treatise*, 511 (CO 5:435).
31. *Short Treatise*, 511 (CO 5:437).
32. *Short Treatise*, 516–17 (CO 5:440).

material signs. However, they serve as the first rung on a ladder of ascension to communion with Christ in heaven.[33]

This notion of the need for the external means to mediate God's presence was not peculiar to Calvin's view of the sacramental signs; rather, he thought that God always comes in mediated form, whether to the Old Testament patriarchs or to the disciples in Jesus Christ, the accommodation par excellence of God, or to the church. There is no direct communication with God—it is always mediated.[34] The use of earthly signs has always been God's modus operandi. Calvin said, "God from the first manifested himself by visible symbols [so] that he might gradually raise believers to himself, and conduct them by earthly rudiments to spiritual knowledge."[35] To speak of the bread and wine, then, as accommodated instruments that convey knowledge of God and God's presence was, for Calvin, to speak of God's usual way of communicating God's self to the elect. Thus such an accommodation is a gift and vitally necessary for Christian life. After all, it is God who has decreed that the Eucharist is the best means to convey knowledge of communion with the body and blood of Christ. It is also one of the ways God has chosen effectively to exhibit and give that communion to believers.

Therefore, as shown above, one of the reasons the external signs are necessary is that they are required by the weakness of humankind. However, along with this reason stands another, which Calvin also considered very important: God commands their use. Moreover, though they can be distinguished, this command cannot be separated from God's promise. Calvin makes this clear in his commentaries.

In his comments on Matthew 26:27, Calvin addressed those who claimed they could be partakers of Christ without external means. He labeled such persons "impious" and stated, "Nothing is more odd than for the faithful freely to do without the assistance handed down by the Lord or allow themselves to be deprived, and nothing is more intolerable than to tear

---

33. On the notion of ascent in Calvin's theology, see Randall C. Zachman, *Image and Word in the Theology of John Calvin* (Notre Dame, IN: University of Notre Dame Press, 2007), 339–42; on Calvin's relation to the broader Christian tradition, Christopher Kaiser notes, "Far from being an esoteric idea, the presence of which in Calvin's writings requires special explanation, the idea of our ascent in the sacrament, was well entrenched in Calvin's patristic sources. . . . The eucharistic ascent can be viewed as a widespread Catholic teaching that goes back to the early church" (Christopher B. Kaiser, "Climbing Jacob's Ladder: John Calvin and the Early Church on Our Eucharistic Ascent to Heaven," *Scottish Journal of Theology* 56, no. 3 [2003]: 265).

34. See H. Jackson Forstman, *Word and Spirit: Calvin's Doctrine of Biblical Authority* (Stanford, CA: Stanford University Press, 1962), 9.

35. This statement is found in Calvin's second treatise against Westphal ("Deum se ab initio visibilibus symbolis patefecisse, ut gradation ad se fideles eveheret, ac terrenis rudimentis ad spirtualem notitiam perduceret," CO 9:84).

apart the mystery in this way."[36] Thus Calvin clearly thought that sign must accompany word.

If we move to Calvin's commentary on 1 Corinthians, the relationship between the Word of promise and the sacramental signs as external means to appropriate that Word is even more explicit. First, Christians cannot dispense with the sacramental signs because God commands that they be used. Calvin was clear about what this meant: "If we do not obey this commandment of his, all our boasting about having His promise is to no avail." Second, Calvin explained that "the promise is bound up with the commandment, as if the latter were a condition; the promise therefore only becomes effective if the condition is fulfilled. . . . What we have to do is to obey God's commandment so that He may carry out what He has promised us; otherwise we deprive ourselves of its fulfillment."[37] Obedience to God's commands is part of the Christian's faithful response to God. If the command is dismissed, there is a lack of faith, which precludes reception of what God offers.

Having established that the eucharistic signs are necessary for the Christian believer[38] because of human need and God's command, still the question remains: what heavenly reality do the earthly mirrors reflect?

The bread and the wine were, for Calvin, figures of the body and blood of Christ; they exhibit on a natural plane what is given through the power of the Holy Spirit: Christ's true body. As the earthly elements sustain physical life, so Christ's body sustains spiritual life.

In his John commentary, Calvin stated that everything relating to the new life of the Christian is called "food." Moreover, he explained that when Jesus used the word "bread," what he meant to convey was the notion of "nourishment." Therefore, when Christ spoke of his flesh as meat, according to Calvin, he meant "that souls are starved if they lack that food. You will only find life in Christ when you seek the substance of life in His flesh."[39] The whole of salvation is accomplished in union with the flesh of the Mediator. That union is symbolized in the eating of eucharistic bread and wine. Therefore, because of the scriptural principle of metonymy, Christians call bread and wine the body and blood of Christ. Look into those mirrors, and there exhibited is the true Christ.

36. CNTC 3:138 (CO 45:710).

37. Comment on 1 Cor. 11:24, CNTC 9:244 (CO 49:485).

38. Just because the eucharistic signs are indispensable for the believer does not mean that God cannot work without them. From the human perspective, they are necessary; from the divine perspective, they are not.

39. Comment on John 6:55, CNTC 4:170 (CO 47:155).

Such a clear exhibition of the flesh of Christ works to take the Christian's spirit literally out of this world and into the kingdom of heaven, where union with Christ is enjoyed. The sign is imperative for that ascension. Calvin said, "This [ascension] can never take place apart from the help of a figure or sign."[40] Thus the name of body is transferred to the bread so that the figure may work to bring about the transition from the earthly to the heavenly.[41] Bread and wine are true mirrors of Christ; but it is important, in Calvin's opinion, to understand that they are mirrors that reflect upward.[42]

The Clearest Promises of God: The Eucharistic Gift of Knowledge

There appeared in the 1539 *Institutes* a new emphasis on the intellectual nature of faith, and that emphasis was applied to the sacraments. Calvin wrote, "It is certain that whatever is more evident, accordingly, it is more capable of sustaining faith. And, in truth, the sacraments convey the clearest promises."[43] By "intellectual" I mean an emphasis on *intellectus*, understanding. It is the special gift of the Eucharist, with the Word and sacramental signs working in tandem, to increase the Christian's understanding of life in Christ in a way not otherwise possible.

We can look at the issues by briefly referring to Calvin's Genevan Catechism. Calvin certainly taught that communion with Christ comes through

40. This statement is found in Calvin's third treatise against Westphal, the "Last Admonition" ("Hoc quando nisi figurae vel signi adminiculo fieri nequit," CO 9:162).

41. Such a transfer of name, however, requires that the believer be clearly taught that it is the function of such signs to raise the believer to God's presence. Therefore, the sign must retain its own nature rather than having its reality collapsed into the divine nature. Otherwise, according to Calvin, Christ is brought down rather than the soul being elevated.

42. In his comments on Matt. 26:29, Calvin was explicit in his use of the mirror image and its function to lead upward. It is, however, the crucified Christ who is mirrored. Calvin stated that Jesus "set His death before their eyes as in a mirror." If it is the Supper that mirrors Christ, the image of Christ reflected is that of Jesus on the cross. Here, Calvin switched metaphors to get across the ascension function of such an image: "They had to be guided to Christ's death that they might use it as a ladder to ascend into heaven" (CNTC 3:136–37 [CO 45:709]).

43. CO 1:941, "Nempe ut quaeque est manifestior, ita est ad fulciendam fidem magis idonea. Sacramenta vero, promissiones afferunt clarissimas." Calvin goes on to say, "Et hoc habent prae verbo peculiare, quod eas velut in tabula depictas nobis ad vivum repraesentant." Thus, once again, it is clear that Calvin considered the human senses to be indispensable in making *sensible* the eucharistic celebration, though Word frames and directs the work of the senses. Jean-Daniel Benoit has shown that the 1539 *Institutes* makes more of the intellectual nature of faith (Benoit, "The History of the Development of the *Institutio*: How Calvin Worked," in *John Calvin*, ed. G. E. Duffield [Appleford, UK: Sutton Courtenay, 1966], 104). Though I believe this is true, it should not lead one to believe that Calvin discarded the use of the bodily senses as a source of understanding. See Zachman, *Image and Word*.

the Gospel as well as the Supper. Thus why is the Eucharist necessary?[44] It is necessary because communion with Christ, offered through the Gospel, is "confirmed and increased" in the Supper. This meant, for Calvin, that the Eucharist functions in such a way that "we may certainly know that reconciliation belongs to us."[45] It is important, therefore, not only for Christ to dwell in the Christian, united as one flesh, but it is also important for the believer's growth in the Christian life to "recognize that he [Christ] dwells in us, and that we are united to him, . . . [and] that, by virtue of this union, we may become partakers of all his blessings."[46] In other words, proper knowledge and recognition of the source of salvation, according to Calvin, is a constituent part of growth into that salvation. The Eucharist helps piety grow; growth in piety enables a better grasp of doctrine; a better grasp of doctrine enables greater understanding of the sacramental signs; a heightened awareness of the signs leads to greater recognition of union with Christ, which leads to increased piety. Word and Sacrament work together, each building up the other, to accomplish growth in the Christian life. The Words of Institution that enliven the sacramental signs give a special understanding, assurance, and certainty to Christians, serving to establish the meaning of the eucharistic action and signs, which in turn imprint on the senses the nature of the Christian's union with Christ, so that the Words are fully grasped and indeed experienced.

One of Calvin's comments on baptism reinforces this view of the sacraments as especially geared to provide certainty through the knowledge it brings to believers. In his Acts commentary, Calvin wrote about how the sacrament of baptism can be called the laver of the soul at Paul's baptism, when plainly the Spirit serves as the formal cause of regeneration. Calvin

44. This certainly is a real question. There is a tradition of Calvin scholarship that thinks Calvin's eucharistic teaching—and the role he assigned the Eucharist in Christian life—is actually unnecessary. Such thought is best epitomized by François Wendel's famous questioning of Calvin's eucharistic theology: "What exactly does the Supper give us that we cannot obtain otherwise?" (Wendel, *Calvin: The Origins and Development of His Religious Thought*, trans. Philip Mairet [London: Collins, 1963], 353).

45. CO 6:125 (French) / 126 (Latin). Actually, the French and Latin vary slightly; the first quote is taken from the Latin, "confirmatur et augetur," where the French has "confermeé en nous, et comme ratifée." For the second quote, the French has "Pour nous certifier que nous avons part en ceste reconciliation," whereas the Latin reads, "Ut certo sciamus, reconcilationem ad nos pertinere."

46. CO 6:125 (French) / 126 (Latin). Again, the French and the Latin vary slightly; in the Latin we read, "Sed in nobis quoque habitare agnoscimus, nosque illa coniuntos esse eo unitatis genere, quo membra cum capite suo cohaerent: ut huius unitatis beneficio omnium eius bonorum participes fiamus." The French reads, "Mais aussi qui'il habite en nous, et est conioinet avec nous en telle union que le chef avec ses membres, afin de nous faire participans de toutes ses graces, en vertu de ceste conionction."

stated that when Luke speaks of washing, he "is not describing the cause, but is referring to Paul's understanding, for, by receiving the symbol, he grasped better that his sins were expiated."[47] If we work by analogy to the Holy Supper, we can say that the Spirit effects union with Christ, and that the presentation of Christ's body and blood through bread and wine refers to the Christian's understanding. The symbols enable the faithful to better grasp and understand the reality.

In the 1559 *Institutes*, Calvin added a most enlightening line that seems to sum up much of his life's thought on what happens when the Word is added to a visible sign: in our case, when the Words of Institution are appropriately joined to the sacramental signs. He declared, "The Father of lights cannot be hindered from illumining our minds with a sort of intermediate brilliance through the sacraments, just as he illumines our bodily eyes by the rays of the sun."[48] Such a statement emphasizes the gift of knowledge and its mediated nature.

It may be appropriate to ask if this emphasis on knowledge in the Eucharist does not overshadow what Calvin considered to be the substantial gift given there: Christ himself. I do not think so. I suggest that the specific gift of knowledge in the Eucharist leads to a greater delight in the more general gift: Christ himself. Heightened recognition of union enhances the actual Communion itself. It is a matter of knowing what one has.

And here we are back to the Words of Institution. They tell the believer what the signs mirror. They enable the signs to serve their function. They work with the signs to display graphically, in the most humanly comprehensible way, the mystery of Christ's union with his elect. Thus without the Words and their explication, as found in Calvin's liturgy, Calvin believed that the rite yielded no edification; this was his complaint against the Roman mass.[49] If the Words are not clearly proclaimed and explained, there is no lens of meaning for the signs; without their proper meaning, the signs cannot serve as mirrors; therefore, the rite cannot convey knowledge, leaving the participant with no assurance of salvation. Because of this situation, Calvin considered the mass an abomination.

However, when the Supper is appropriately celebrated, with Word and sign held together, and when the Eucharist truly mediates union with Christ and knowledge thereof, it leads the Christian believer to "praise [God] openly, so as to let men know, when we are in their company, what we are aware of

47. Comment on Acts 22:16, CNTC 7:218 (CO 48:496–97).
48. *Inst.* 4.14.10 (CO 2:949).
49. *Short Treatise*, 535 (CO 5:456).

within ourselves in the presence of God."[50] In other words, a proper Eucharist evokes gratitude, which is, according to Calvin, the chief end of human existence. Since the Supper provides the clearest expression of the mystical union, it should evoke the clearest expression of gratitude, which results in thankfulness to God and love toward neighbors.[51]

50. Comment on 1 Cor. 11:26, CNTC 9:250 (CO 49:490).
51. Comment on 1 Cor. 11:24, CNTC 9:243 (CO 49:485).

4

NOT "HIDDEN AND FAR OFF"

*The Bodily Aspect of Salvation and Its Implications
for Understanding the Body in Calvin's Theology*

The title for an obituary from the December 4, 1993, Saturday edition of the Indianapolis *Star* reads, "Lewis Thomas, 80, had won acclaim as 'poet laureate of medical science.'" The man who had served as the head of the Memorial Sloan-Kettering Cancer Center and as dean of the Yale University Medical School died of a rare form of cancer. At one point, when asked about his illness, Mr. Thomas said, "I'm beginning to lose all respect for my body." This from a physician/writer who had spent his life exploring the wonders of the human body.[1]

Another writer who has been accused, in a variety of ways, of having no respect for the human body is John Calvin. His anthropology has been characterized as dim in its view of the body because, the argument goes, it emphasized the soul as *the only* important aspect of the human being. Certain passages from Calvin's works lend some credence to this viewpoint. The most-cited phrase is the one in which Calvin referred to the body as a "prison."[2]

---

1. *Indianapolis Star*, December 4, 1993.
2. References to the body as a prison can be found at *Inst.* 1.15.2; 3.2.19; 3.6.5; 3.9.4; 4.1.1; 4.16.19; and 4.17.30 (CO 2:136, 413, 505, 526, 745, 990, and 1032). The Latin terms translated as "prison" are *ergastulum* and *carcer*; also *carcero* (to imprison) is used. Calvin used both

79

Thus one finds titles such as "The Persistent Dualism in Calvin's Theology";[3] statements by scholars claiming that, if not dualistic in his thinking, Calvin's thought was certainly spiritualizing in its tendencies;[4] and finally, the best that can be said, some think, is that Calvin betrayed a curious ambivalence toward the human body.[5]

Explanations for Calvin's view of the human body tend toward the philosophical: Calvin was a Platonist in the way he treated the body, unable to box his way out of the corner that philosophy forced him into, unable to appreciate the more biblical view of the body.[6] And to be sure, the notion of the body as a prison for the soul is found in Plato.[7] Therefore, the appeal to the philosophical basis of Calvin's body-view is assumed to stand as the best way to lay bare Calvin's corporeal conceptions. This despite the fact that Calvin consistently criticized vain philosophy enough that one might, with justification, look elsewhere. The point is, where? Where might one more profitably look for Calvin's view of the body, at least in order to give the question a different spin so that the answer might come out looking differently—and not philosophically based?

corpus (body) and caro (flesh) to denote what imprisons the soul. Caro means more than body in some places in Calvin's thought, such as those times when he used it to denote the unregenerate human being, as in the Romans commentary and various places in the Institutes. However, in the above-cited places, "body" and "flesh" are synonyms.

3. S. Fowler, "The Persistent Dualism in Calvin's Theology," in Our Reformational Heritage: A Rich Heritage and Lasting Vocation, ed. T. Van der Walt et al. (Potchefstroom, South Africa: Potchefstroom University for Christian Higher Education, 1984).

4. Mary Potter Engel, John Calvin's Perspectival Anthropology (Atlanta: Scholars Press, 1988), 169; see chap. 5 for a fine summary of opinions of Calvin as a spiritualist and a dualist in his thinking on the body.

5. Margaret R. Miles, "Theology, Anthropology, and the Human Body in Calvin's Institutes of the Christian Religion," Harvard Theological Review 72, no. 3 (1981): 311.

6. Some of these points of view are cited and analyzed in Charles Partee, "Soul and Body in Anthropology," chap. 5 in Calvin and Classical Philosophy (Leiden: Brill, 1977). Partee makes the entirely sane observation that, whereas Platonism tinted Calvin's view, Scripture was its source (65). What is more, "Calvin's anthropology could, and does, contain a distinction between body and soul without the Platonic division." This is certainly true, and furthermore it is part of the deeply rooted principle in Calvin that things can (and should) be distinguished without being separated as one thinks about them. From the first edition of the Institutes, Calvin explicitly linked his christologically understood "distinction without separation" principle to anthropology: the notion of Christ's human and divine natures, distinguished as two things yet united and not separated, was applied directly to and is used as the model for the relationship between body and soul in his anthropology. See Inst. '36, 52 (CO 1:66).

7. See editor's note at Inst. 3.6.9n9. I think it begs the question to assert that, simply because Calvin used Platonic language, he was a Platonist. The Platonic language, though the coin of the realm in much of the thought world of the sixteenth century (not to mention much of the history of Western Christian thought), cannot simply be equated with Platonic philosophy, in my opinion. The closest I can come to explaining this position is to say that in our own culture, where the psychotherapeutic reigns supreme and its language peppers the discourse of the culture, the simple use of psychotherapeutic language does not make one a psychotherapist.

I will offer a suggestion after I have laid bare another modern assumption that one often encounters when dealing with Calvin and the body: that Calvin was obviously wrong when he, at times, expressed negative statements concerning the body.[8] Calvin is seen as extreme, Protestantly ascetic, when it comes to the body: he is stereotypically painted as a man who inherently disliked bodily pleasures, hated them, and wished to suppress the body in all its natural beauty. His dourness is seen in contrast to the festive celebration of the body in much Renaissance art.[9] For the all-too-cursory look backward, Calvin is seen as a throwback when compared to the artists who obviously saw much more beauty in the body—certainly more sensuousness—than the Genevan reformer did.

Yet the point I want to make here is that it was the Renaissance painters who portrayed unreality: the unblemished, healthy, young body eternally captured on canvas in its state of exuberance.[10] Calvin had to deal with the much more realistic problem that besets humanity: bodies are not unblemished, healthy, and young forever. The canvas lies: bodies decay. And it is from the *experience* of the decaying body that Calvin wrote.[11] I add that if one purviews the death-

8. Miles is an example of this sentiment when she speaks about "modern people who *want* our life 'tied to the body'" (Miles, "Theology, Anthropology, and the Human Body," 323).

9. The notion that Calvin was a dour person who disliked bodily pleasures (or pleasures of any kind) was established firmly in the American consciousness by the stereotypes of Calvin that began to appear in America in nineteenth-century world history textbooks. See Thomas J. Davis, "Images of Intolerance: John Calvin in Nineteenth-Century History Textbooks," *Church History* 65, no. 2 (Summer 1996): 234–48. This is not to say that negative stereotypes of Calvin did not exist before this time; they obviously did. However, it was through nineteenth-century world history textbooks that Calvin's negative stereotype took on the air of established "historical fact" for the general American populace. Add to this the cultural work of certain American fiction writers, who were trying to displace what they saw as the "Calvinist" culture, and the negative stereotypes were reinforced in pleasure reading as well as the school textbooks. See Thomas J. Davis, "Rhetorical War and Reflex: Calvin and Calvinism in Nineteenth-Century Fiction and Twentieth-Century Criticism," *Calvin Theological Journal* 33, no. 2 (November 1998): 443–56. For more context on negative images of Calvin, historically and geographically, see Johan de Niet, Herman Paul, and Bart Wallet, eds., *Sober, Strict, and Scriptural: Collective Memories of John Calvin, 1800–2000* (Leiden: Brill, 2008).

10. Indeed, if one looks at what became the standard textbook for painting during the Renaissance, Leone Battista Alberti's *On Painting*, one finds this advice to painters, despite previous appeals to take nature as one's master: "It will please him [the painter] not only to make all the parts true to this model but also to add beauty there; because in painting, loveliness is not less pleasing than richness. Demetrius, an antique painter, failed to obtain the ultimate praise because he was much more careful to make things similar to the natural than to the lovely. For this reason it is useful to take from every beautiful body each one of the praised parts and always strive by your diligence and study to understand and express much loveliness" (Leone Battista Alberti, *On Painting*, trans. John R. Spencer [New Haven: Yale University Press, 1956], 92).

11. From such an experiential viewpoint, one sees in Calvin's writings a "logic of life," as it has been called by Doumergue, cited in Partee, *Calvin and Classical Philosophy*, 35.

and-dying literature in just a cursory manner, our culture does not deal well with the dying and decaying body. With illness hidden away and the modern celebration of the body taken as a norm, the tendency is to shake our heads a bit and ask, "Why did Calvin say negative things about the body?" Many take it almost as an insult that he would do so. Thus interpreters are backed into philosophical philanderings to dig up an explanation for Calvin's insult to the modern consciousness of body.

But in proceeding this way, I suggest that most interpreters have left out consideration of an obvious point, which leads them to incomplete answers. Let us try a different tack, taking as our cue Lewis Thomas's statement about how, as a sick person, he had lost respect for his body.

Calvin lived in pain, and he saw death all around him. People he knew suffered and died. This may not sound like a startling discovery. However, it is essential to underscore this point to get at the right question.[12]

It is from this perspective that, I think, it is helpful to view Calvin. He himself at times endured exquisite pain: chronic and acute suffering plagued him. One can simply list the problems he probably had: chronic tophaceous gout, kidney stones, chronic pulmonary tuberculosis, pleurisy, hemotypsis, tertiary and quartan fevers, intestinal parasites, thrombosed hemorrhoids, and migraine headaches. Calvin died of septicemia: toxic shock ended his life. According to a twentieth-century physician who has studied his medical problems, Calvin's latter years (the last ten, at least), healthwise, were marked by severe pain and extreme difficulty in breathing. A painful existence devoid of many of the pleasures Calvin enjoyed as a youth characterized his middle and old ages.[13]

From this experiential jumping-off place, then, the question should not be, "Why did Calvin say negative things about the human body?" No, given

12. What started me thinking in this direction was my own experience with my first wife's suffering and death. She lived with acute lymphoblastic leukemia for a year and a half. During much of that time, she lived in extreme pain. Her body was a source of grief and suffering. More than once, she voiced her wish that she could just leave her body behind and soar above and beyond it. She fantasized about having an existence without being weighed down by her body. This came from a person who before had always had a healthy appreciation for the body and its appetites. But the pain at times changed her view of the body, at least in the way she talked of it. Her rhetoric betrayed what would have been, in healthier times, her true view of the body. One could argue that, unless the body, and life itself, is viewed from the perspective of death, it is always an unrealistic view. For an interesting literary development of this theme, see Harriet Beecher Stowe, "The Mourning Veil," *Atlantic Monthly* 1 (1858): 63–70. As Henry F. May has summarized the point, "Until one has seen the world through . . . [a black] mourning veil, he has not truly lived" (introduction to Harriet Beecher Stowe, *Oldtown Folks* [Cambridge, MA: Belknap Press of Harvard University, 1966], 24).

13. This paragraph is based on Charles L. Cooke, MD, "Calvin's Illnesses and Their Relation to Christian Vocation," in *Calvin Studies IV*, ed. John Leith and W. Stacy Johnson (Davidson, NC: Davidson College, 1988), 41–52.

his pain, what is remarkable is not what negative statements he pronounced but the good things he maintained about the body. It is astonishing, not that Calvin might have had dualistic or spiritualizing tendencies, but that Calvin did not become a full-fledged dualist. He certainly had reason to be one. One may start to question Calvin regarding the body by asking, "Why did Calvin say anything *good* about the body?" He had little reason to do so.

For Calvin did, indeed, say good things about the body, both in its prelapsarian state and in its postlapsarian state. His accolades heaped on the body are almost as rhetorically elevated as some of his negative statements. "Likewise, in regard to the structure of the human body, one must have the greatest keenness in order to weigh, with Galen's skill, its articulation, symmetry, beauty, and use," Calvin said as he praised the body. The workmanship of God in the body is such that "God's glory shines forth in the outer man." In talking of the resurrection of the body, Calvin called the body "God's temple," a term he used also in regard to the soul. Finally, in looking at one of the most basic bodily functions, the suckling of a child, Calvin in a remark on Psalm 8:2 proclaimed that "infants, while they nurse at their mothers' breasts, have tongues so eloquent to preach [God's] glory that there is no need at all of other orators."[14] Calvin's pain partly accounts for his negative rhetoric. The question is, what accounts for the positive rhetoric?

I will proceed along two related lines. First, I will explore Calvin's thought on Christ's human body and the role it plays in the Christian's salvation. Second, I will look at how, according to Calvin, it is through the human body that the Christian is put in touch with the act of salvation that is mediated through the human body of Christ. Both lines of thought are best explored in the context of Calvin's eucharistic teaching. The role of Christ's body and the Christian's body in the schema of salvation made up a situation that, in the end, contributed to Calvin's affirmation of the human body, an affirmation that led Calvin to assert that the body is something that warrants resurrection.[15]

Calvin's View of Christ's Body and Its Role in Salvation

Margaret Miles, in an article titled "Theology, Anthropology, and the Human Body in Calvin's *Institutes of the Christian Religion*," approaches the question of the body in relation to Calvin's theology, and specifically in

14. *Inst.* 1.5.2 (CO 2:42); *Inst.* 1.15.3 (CO 2:136); *Inst.* 3.25.7 (CO 2:736); *Inst.* 1.5.3 (CO 2:43).

15. The argument is meant to supplement rather than supplant other views; in terms of understanding the body in Calvin's thought, it contributes to Engel's perspectival view.

relation to God's glory. The upholding of the glory of God is seen as the central aspect of Calvin's theology, and so the human body is seen in that light. By approaching the matter in this way, Miles concludes that, at best, Calvin was ambivalent toward the body and that the body as such was, at best, a neutral entity in Calvin's theology.[16]

In response and for further advance, I make two suggestions. First, though the glory of God is certainly an important aspect of Calvin's thought,[17] such praise, as with anything good in human life, according to Calvin, is achieved only through the mediation of Christ. So, it seems to me, one can legitimately use Christ as a jumping-off point for understanding the human body. Even the glory of God itself, Calvin believed, is mediated through the Christ figure. Second, it is difficult properly to analyze Calvin's view on many topics by referring solely to his magisterial *Institutes of the Christian Religion*.[18] With these two things in mind, it would be helpful to look at Calvin's view of how Christ's human body mediates salvation as it is expounded in his commentary on the Gospel of John.

In Calvin's comments on the Fourth Gospel, there is a clear statement about how righteousness comes from God to humanity. He worked out this statement in the context of his eucharistic theology as he examined the sixth chapter of John, which contains the bread-of-life passages.

Calvin argued that Christ's flesh is life-giving to the souls of believers because it is the instrument God has chosen to bestow new life on believers. In commenting on John 6:27, where Jesus speaks of working for the "meat" (KJV) that abides unto eternal life, given by Jesus and sealed by God, Calvin declared that God ordained Christ to the purpose of serving as spiritual food

16. See Miles, "Theology, Anthropology, and the Human Body." For a critique of Miles's views and her use of the *Institutes*, see James Goodloe, "The Body in Calvin's Theology," in *Calvin Studies V*, ed. John H. Leith (Davidson, NC: Davidson College, 1990), 112–13, and esp. 116–17n57.

17. God's glory is tied to God's goodness: God deserves glory because God is the *fons bonorum* (fount of good things). Moreover, already in the 1536 *Institutes*, Calvin associated Christ in his *humanity* (in a body) with that goodness. See *Inst.* '36, 51–52 (CO 1:66).

18. Reliance solely on the 1559 *Institutes* assumes that Calvin's views never changed or that historical circumstances were not important in shaping certain aspects of his thought. I argue for the importance of looking at Calvin in terms of development, in *The Clearest Promises of God: The Development of Calvin's Eucharistic Teaching* (New York: AMS Press, 1995). Calvin's more negative statements about the body may be a result of his experiential situation rather than being intricately related to this theology. The term "prison" as applied to the body became more frequent the later the edition of the *Institutes*. Several of the occurrences of the word "prison" were new with the 1559 edition; few were present in 1536. So, it seems that as Calvin's own body became weaker and more painful, the rhetoric of the body as a prison increased. Moreover, the worst tropical (figurative) offender to modern sensibility, the human as "a five-foot worm," appeared first in the 1559 edition (*Inst.* 1.5.4 [CO 2:44]).

to the believer.[19] Yet in Calvin's thought, that spiritual food is directly tied to Christ's human body. At his exegesis of John 6:51, where Jesus calls himself "the living bread," Calvin explicitly laid out the hierarchy of salvation, as he understood it, and how that salvation is accommodated to human capacity through a series of instruments, the end result of which is to present Christ's body as the living bread that serves as spiritual food to the believer.

Calvin explained it this way: First, righteousness comes from God alone. There is no other source of righteousness than God. However, as the Second Person of the Trinity, Christ also shares in the Godhead's righteousness and thus can also be seen as the one from whom righteousness springs. But to bring that righteousness to human beings, Christ, the Second Person of the Trinity, became incarnate in the person of Jesus Christ. In his office as mediator, Christ brings righteousness to his people. Yet as mediator, Christ is fully human as well as fully divine, which means that he has true flesh, a truly human body. Moreover, it was in that body that salvation was accomplished, for it was in the body that Christ was sacrificed to atone for sin. The righteousness of Christ then is transferred from his divinity, where righteousness intrinsically belongs, to his body. It is there, in the body, that the righteousness of God and its offer to God's people is most fully manifested. Therefore, that flesh "communicates to us a life that it borrows from elsewhere."[20] In this sense, then, Christ's body is considered life-giving in Calvin's eucharistic thought. Righteousness flows to the Christian through a hierarchy of instruments: from God (which includes the Second Person of the Trinity), to the mediator, and from the divine essence of the mediator to his body. Calvin then concluded: "Therefore it follows that in it [the body of Christ] are placed all the parts of life, so that none can rightly complain that he is deprived of life because it is hidden and far off."[21]

If the instrumental nature of Christ's body in the role of salvation does not seem to be emphasized heavily enough by the above explication, Calvin later made it absolutely clear that he did view Christ's body in terms that make it the essential instrument God uses to grant righteousness to believers. He explicated this view in his exegesis of John 6:63, where Jesus proclaims that it is the Spirit that quickens, therefore the flesh profits nothing (cf. KJV). How did Calvin take the passage? He explained it in a way reminiscent of the

19. CNTC 4:154 (CO 47:140).
20. CNTC 4:167 (CO 47:152–53).
21. CNTC 4:167–68 (CO 47:153). Calvin's notion of the humanity of Christ, in its bodily aspect, as being the instrument by which God mediates salvation, seems to echo Augustine's opinion when he says of Jesus, "For how far forth he was a man, so far forth was he mediator" (Augustine, Confessions, 2 vols. [Cambridge, MA: Harvard University Press, 1970], 2:203).

manner in which he dealt with the power of the Eucharist, where the instrument is dead and lifeless without the quickening effect of the Spirit. In regard to the flesh, Calvin stated:

> For where does the flesh get its quickening power, but because it is spiritual? . . . But those who raise their eyes to the power of the Spirit with which the flesh is imbued, will feel from the effect itself and the experience of faith that quickening is no empty word.
>
> We now understand how the flesh is meat indeed and yet profits nothing. It is meat in that, by it life is procured for us, in it God is reconciled to us, and in it we have all the parts of salvation accomplished. It profits nothing if considered in its origin and nature; for the seed of Abraham, which in itself is subject to death, does not give life, but receives its power of feeding us from the Spirit. Therefore we also must bring the spiritual mouth of faith that we may be truly nourished by it.[22]

As in the Eucharist, the instrument is made alive and effective by God through the Spirit, whose work it is to enliven all of God's instruments and creatures. Therefore, according to Calvin, Christ's body is life-giving because it has been ordained as an instrument of God for that purpose.[23] Thus Calvin insisted that the Christian must partake of the substance of Christ's body, for in it "have all the parts of salvation [been] accomplished."[24]

This emphasis of Calvin also explains why in his eucharistic polemics he was so insistent that the body of Christ retain its human nature: it is intrinsically linked to the means of salvation. To strip Christ's body of its human nature is to make nil God's salvation, for it denies the instrument God has chosen to give salvation to believers. This explains Calvin's insistence on Christ's body remaining in heaven: it is the nature of a body so to do, and to change that nature so that it can be everywhere at once actually changes the nature of the body in a way that makes it seem less human and thus more remote (and therefore, for Calvin, nonsalvific). It must retain its full human nature, including specificity of place, if it is to serve as an instrument that seems near at hand for humans rather than at a distance.[25]

---

22. CNTC 4:175 (CO 47:159).

23. The word "flesh" denotes for Calvin more than the body. However, it includes the notion of body, though flesh is not completely defined by that reality. When God uses "flesh" as an instrument, the bodily aspect is certainly included. In the case of unregenerate humans, "flesh" means all that is over against God; however, since there is naught in Christ that is unregenerate, flesh for him means being human, characterized by having a body.

24. CNTC 4:175 (CO 47:159).

25. Thus, at John 6:55–56 one sees Calvin's warnings: "They are false interpreters who lead souls away from Christ's flesh" and "If you want to have anything in common with Christ, you must especially take care not to despise the flesh" (CNTC 4:170–71 [CO 47:155–56]).

Thus when Calvin spoke of partaking of Christ, full body-and-blood Communion, he literally meant participation in a real and true human body. To speak of eating the body of Christ meant for Calvin that the Christian is nourished by and gains union with a real human body. There is, literally, a fleshly body involved in the Christian's spirit feeding on Christ (though the body is literal, the feeding itself, however, must be understood spiritually in the sense of nourishment rather than manducation [chewing]). That is why Calvin insisted on substantial partaking of the body of Christ in the Eucharist, for it is the human body of Christ that is the accommodated instrument of God's salvation. It is the thing by which righteousness comes to believers.

Calvin's View of the Human Body and Its Role in Appropriating Salvation

If Calvin's anthropology were truly so bleak in its view of the human body, one would expect to find the locus for the Christian's appropriation of salvation to reside in the soul, comprised of understanding and will, according to Calvin.[26] Faith, which appropriates God's gift of salvation, is actually sometimes seen as primarily an intellectual phenomenon in Calvin[27] (thus the stereotype of Calvin as the cold logician of faith). Yet just as Christ's body has a central role in mediating salvation, so also the human body of the believer has a central role in appropriating the knowledge of that salvation. What I am saying here is that, according to Calvin, one most fully knows and understands the salvific event of Christ through the body and its senses rather than through the intellectual capacity of the soul alone, apart from the body.

At first hearing, this may sound a bit rash. It is, however, no more rash than Calvin's own statements on the matter, again found especially in his eucharistic theology. There is this statement that first appeared in the 1539 *Institutes*: "To be sure, whatever is clearer, accordingly it is more capable of sustaining faith. In truth the sacraments convey the clearest promises."[28] If this is not clear enough in its implications, then heed what else Calvin had to

26. *Inst.* 1.15.7 (CO 2:142).

27. "In the 1536 *Institutio*, Calvin, like Luther, insisted that above all faith was trust and hope. In 1539 he made more of the intellectual nature of faith" (Jean-Daniel Benoit, "The History of the Development of the *Institutio*: How Calvin Worked," in *John Calvin*, ed. G. E. Duffield [Appleford, UK: Sutton Courtenay, 1966], 104).

28. CO 1:941, "Nempe ut quaequae est manifestior: ita est ad fulciendam fidem magis idonea. Sacramenta vero et promissiones afferunt clarissimas."

say of the sacraments. They attest God's "good will and love toward us more expressly than by word."[29]

The question is why, and the answer is simple: sacraments convey a better understanding of salvation to the Christian than the Word alone because the sacraments appeal to all of the bodily senses: taste, feel, smell, sight, and (with the adding of the Word to the sacramental sign) hearing.[30] The human body plays a crucial instrumental role in Calvin's theology in assuring the Christian that salvation is one's own. Since union with Christ, union with not just his spirit but also his body, constituted the essence of Christian life for Calvin, then it is the Sacrament of the Eucharist that most assures the believer that such a union takes place. It is an assurance most effective because of the bodily aspects involved. To be sure, Calvin wanted the soul to be lifted up to heaven,[31] but the starting point of that ascent is the instrument of bodily sense.

By taking a look at *Institutes* 4.14.6, it is clear why such is the case. Since Christians live in the flesh, things of divinity are shown under the flesh so that they may be known. This is God's accommodation to humanity's "dull capacity." By means of bodily things, then, Christians are taught. The physical signs, things that appeal to bodily senses, are termed "tutors," "pictures," and "mirrors" of things divine. Indeed, though the Word of God is seen as the foundation, when "sacraments are added, [faith] rests more firmly upon them as upon columns."[32]

Moreover, Calvin was certain that such instrumental advance toward God is part of how God works because God always, in every circumstance, is a mediated God. The Christian simply could not bear direct contact with God.[33] Thus God comes to humanity through the mediatorial instrument of Christ.[34] Yet the church does not have Christ directly either, for he bodily resides in heaven. So Christ, too, is mediated through the structures of the church. As

29. *Inst.* 4.14.6 (CO 2:945).

30. For a full demonstration of the extraordinary role the senses play in Calvin's theology, see Randall C. Zachman, *Image and Word in the Theology of John Calvin* (Notre Dame, IN: University of Notre Dame Press, 2007).

31. This is a reference to Calvin's famous use of the Sursum Corda: through the eucharistic action that presents the symbols of bread and wine, the believer's heart (and mind) is lifted up to heaven to commune with Christ's body. But the initial rung of the ladder of ascent is the sign of bread and wine, in the context of Word and worship, as perceived by the senses.

32. *Inst.* 4.14.6 (CO 2:945).

33. See Calvin's comments on Exod. 33:20, where he states that unmediated contact with God would immediately destroy any human being because of God's "incomprehensible brightness" ("incomprehensibilis fulgor," CO 25:111).

34. Ford Lewis Battles termed this God's "supreme act of condescension" (Battles, "God Was Accommodating Himself to Human Capacity," in *Readings in Calvin's Theology*, ed. Donald McKim [Grand Rapids: Baker Academic, 1984], 23).

such, the instruments that the church has at its disposal, ordained by God, are the ways Christians receive Christ, and thus receive God and God's salvation.[35] Therefore, God's presence is conveyed by instruments. And it is the appeal to bodily senses by the eucharistic action of Word joined to sign that serves as the initial instrument by which Christians gain entrance to God's presence.

Conclusion

Since Calvin's theology of God is instrumental, to speak of things as instruments is not to denigrate them: it is to put them in their proper place in relation to God. God remains the efficient cause of all good things, but those good things are carried by instruments of grace. As such, to say that Christ's body is instrumental in conferring salvation on the Christian and that the body and its senses are instrumental in appropriating knowledge and understanding of that salvation is not to denigrate the instruments but to understand their role. These instruments play roles ordained by God for the purpose of saving God's people. Thus theologically, christologically, anthropologically, and eucharistically, one cannot truly speak of Calvin's view of the human body as anything but a wonderful gift and instrument of God, through which God saves God's people. This view is not negative or curiously ambivalent. In no way is the body neutral in the order of salvation; it is essential to it. And only by looking beyond rhetoric to the actual function of body in Calvin's thought can one appreciate its role.

From this functional perspective, then, we should view whatever Calvin had to say of the body. If the negative rhetoric can be explained by pain as well as the history of Western thought on the body, as I think it can be, then the positive seems to be rooted in the way Calvin viewed the function of the body in the order of salvation. And that function is best examined in the context of Calvin's properly theological concerns, such as in his eucharistic theology, rather than in his relation to philosophy.[36]

35. In his comment on Gen. 28:17, Calvin actually calls the sacraments "the gates of heaven" ("sacramenta dici possunt coelorum portae," CO 23:394).

36. The eucharistic context is important for two reasons. The first is apparent from this chapter: in the eucharistic theology the function of the body becomes apparent. Another, and in some ways even more foundational, argument rests on the assumption that to view Calvin's theology properly one must recognize its shape; I ascribe to the notion that the shape of Calvin's theology is eucharistic. This point has been made well by Brian A. Gerrish in *Grace and Gratitude: The Eucharistic Theology of John Calvin* (Minneapolis: Fortress, 1993). The idea, however, is not new. An older statement that still bears reading is John Williamson Nevin, *The Mystical Presence: A Vindication of the Reformed or Calvinistic Doctrine of the Holy Eucharist* (Philadelphia: J. B. Lippincott, 1846; repr., Hamden, CT: Archon Books, 1963).

If seen in such a manner, then the place of the resurrection of believers' bodies seems to be less problematic than if we take a purely philosophical approach to Calvin's work. Simply put, because of this argument for the central role of the body in the scheme of salvation, the body is to be honored; indeed, it warrants a resurrection. Though Calvin distinguishes between the immortality of the soul and the resurrection of the body, both depend on the power of God; indeed, the resurrection of the body points to "God's boundless might."[37]

Moreover, even Calvin's insistence on recognizing the importance of the immortality of the soul as it is played out in *Institutes* 3.25.6 is to be seen not as a denigration of the body but as recognition that there is some part of the Christian that is continually and forever in union with God through Christ Jesus. In other words, what has once been joined to God in right relationship can never be severed. Here Calvin's discussion shows his foremost concern that union with Christ be a *permanent* union, one that is unfailingly protected even at and beyond the point of death. What Calvin seeks to accomplish at 3.25.6 is less a brush-off of the body than an appreciation of the never-ending quality of God's love.[38]

Thus Calvin's treatment of the resurrection of the body in *Institutes* 3.25.7 is not in any way peripheral to his anthropology: it is central. The body, as God's temple, is not simply to fall away; the death of the body is accidental to its nature, not essential to its nature; the body, which bears the death of Christ in it, also profits from his resurrection, so that the Christian may, in the end, be in all things as Christ.[39] And that, really, is the point of all of Calvin's theology, theological anthropology included.

---

37. *Inst.* 3.25.4 (CO 2:733).
38. *Inst.* 3.25.6 (CO 2:735–36). Calvin's concern to protect the Christian's living and lively union with Christ goes back, I believe, to his earliest writing, the *Psychopannychia* (written, 1534; published, 1542). Again, the point is one of assurance: to know that not even death severs the living bond between Christ and his members.
39. *Inst.* 3.25.7 (CO 2:736–37).

5

PREACHING AND PRESENCE

Constructing Calvin's Homiletic Legacy

The Need for a Legacy

How is God to be known, especially if one is a Calvinist? On the face of it, the problems are insurmountable—or at least, *the* problem is so. For if one takes a view mistakenly but still commonly held, that at the heart of Calvin's theology sits an absolutely transcendent God, one is left in a quandary about how the human and divine can be bridged in any way.[1]

This is said, perhaps as a Calvin scholar who knows better, somewhat tongue in cheek. The truth of the matter, however, is that Calvin's God remains unknown to many. Calvin's teaching about God's presence has been presented in such an unbalanced manner that it affects not only popular attitudes toward Calvin but even those who do research on the theology of John Calvin. A few examples should suffice.

1. Indeed, this line of thinking has led David Wright to remark on the "fearful caricature of the Calvinist Deity: an arbitrary, heartless despot, disposing of the destinies of human beings in this life and the next with capricious cruelty—the kind of God tailor-made by and for the tyrant of Geneva, John Calvin himself, for whom dispatching awkward dissidents to the funeral pyre was all in a day's work" (David F. Wright, "Calvin's Accommodating God," in *Calvinus Sincerioris Religionis Vindex* [*Calvin as Protector of the Purer Religion*], ed. Wilhelm H. Neuser and Brian G. Armstrong [Kirksville, MO: Sixteenth Century Journal Publishers, 1997], 3).

Some years ago, Leroy S. Rouner, a professor at Boston University and sometime general editor of the Boston University Studies in Philosophy and Religion series, wrote a piece called "Transcendence and the Will to Believe." Though the piece was somewhat wide ranging—a comparative look at Eastern and Western philosophical and religious ways of belief, with William James serving as the bridge between the two—the Calvinist tradition was repeatedly seen as one of the West's problematic ways of thinking. The problem? Calvin's theology of God's transcendence, which leads to the bugaboo of predestination. As Rouner put it, "Calvin, obsessed with the need for clarity and logical consistency, carefully crafted an increasingly monstrous doctrine which even he found hard to believe." In all this, Rouner used Calvin as a straw man to argue for the need of the experiential in religion. Calvin certainly did hold to a notion of God's transcendence, but he also balanced that with a notion of God's presence. One does not find reference to that balance in Rouner.[2]

A second and more anecdotal story: I once worked with a woman whose father-in-law was a Unitarian minister. She told me of an article he had written—I have never tracked it down—in which he places the blame for modern-day atheism at the feet of Calvin; in particular, Calvin's notion of the transcendence of God is the culprit behind rampant secularity. Calvin removed God so far from humanity, the argument goes, that it was like having no God at all.

A third example details how a one-sided focus on God's transcendence works its way even into Calvin scholarship. A 1999 book by Christopher Elwood, in a chapter on Calvin's eucharistic theology, speaks of the separation of sign from reality in Calvin's rendering of eucharistic meaning. The author explains that such separation is actually due to the transcendent God one finds in Calvin.[3]

2. Leroy S. Rouner, "Transcendence and the Will to Believe," in *Transcendence and the Sacred*, ed. Alan M. Olson and Leroy S. Rouner (Notre Dame, IN: University of Notre Dame Press, 1981), 171.

3. Christopher Elwood, *The Body Broken: The Calvinist Doctrine of the Eucharist and the Symbolization of Power in Sixteenth-Century France* (New York: Oxford University Press, 1999). Elwood's essay on Calvin is chap. 3, "Specifying Power: Sacramental Signification in Calvin's Theology of the Eucharist." He argues that the Eucharist must be viewed within the context of God's absolute power (70, 72–73). If this is *the* context from which the Eucharist must be viewed, then it is not surprising that Elwood thinks, finally, that sign and signified are separated in Calvin's eucharistic thought. The sacramental signs have no inherent power (68), they are "inferior instruments" (70), and they are "in effect degraded" and "reduced to the status of mere instruments" (74). Therefore, we read, Calvin's sacramental view is representational (72). Yet what is lacking is any sense of balance: certainly, the Eucharist is only an instrument (in calling the Eucharist an inferior instrument, Elwood is actually quoting Calvin), but it is an ordained instrument of God's power. The cross itself is instrumental. If one starts from God's

I raise these examples for a reason: to show how one aspect of Calvin's thought—the notion of God's transcendence—is perceived to overwhelm any notion of God's presence with humanity, thus rendering God unknowable. This widely held misreading of Calvin makes the job of a Calvin scholar difficult because it throws up barriers to a more honest rendering of Calvin's theology if one is trying to convey the range and depth and beauty of Calvin's theology to the nonspecialist. Everyone thinks they already know Calvin.

Perhaps here one could speak of Calvin scholars as well. For the very thing that Calvin most insistently called on to show how God is to be known, cognitively and affectively, is the very thing scholarship, traditionally and as a whole, has not been very good at dealing with: the real presence of Christ and union with him as the crux of Christian existence. The reason Calvin is perceived to present a transcendent God *absolutum* is because the thing he balances transcendence with, Christ's presence, may be the least appreciated aspect of his theology, perhaps because it is the thorniest.[4]

Brian Gerrish is correct in his assessment of this situation as he addresses Calvin's views on the Eucharist: real presence is at the heart of Calvin's eucharistic piety, and that is expressly what has not found a home in the mainstream of Reformed thought. Gerrish is also correct, in my opinion, that such a presence as Calvin experienced in the Eucharist is actually the same presence given by the proclaimed Word.[5] Thus, in a roundabout way, I finally come to the thesis of this chapter: by and large, Calvin left no homiletic legacy because what he left has not been received; or if we want to speak in terms of the ancient church doctrine of *paradosis*, what Calvin handed down has been dropped. Thus speaking of Calvin's homiletic legacy involves pointing to the need to construct that legacy and to see what impact it can have for us as we

---

self-revelation, rather than some absolutist stance, then the role of the Eucharist takes on a different character than what Elwood outlines above, a character that has to do with God making Godself known rather than an absolute (and therefore unknowable) God. There is, as Calvin fully knew and taught, an absolutely transcendent aspect of God; but that is God in Godself, not God for us.

4. The greater part of the Reformed tradition has done much to make Christ's presence a spiritual—nonbodily—presence. When pushed to see the evidence in Calvin for some experience of bodily presence, the tendency is and has been to reject such a presence as alien to Calvin's *real* concerns (such as predestination). The clearest example here is Charles Hodge, who will be noted below.

5. It is "a settled principle that the sacraments have the same office as the Word of God: to offer and set forth Christ to us, and in him the treasures of heavenly grace" (*Inst.* 4.14.17 [CO 2:953]). Thus Calvin asserted that in both Word and Sacrament, one first receives Christ, and then his benefits. See also Brian Gerrish, "Calvin's Eucharistic Piety," in *Calvin and Spirituality: Papers Presented at the Tenth Colloquium of the Calvin Studies Society, 1995,* ed. David Foxgrover (Grand Rapids: CRC Product Services for the Calvin Studies Society, 1998), 63–65.

teach about Calvin's theology. Serious attention to Calvin's homiletic work goes a long way toward rebalancing an overblown emphasis on transcendence. Whatever else homiletic theory and homiletic practice shows us in Calvin, it is a God with us.

Calvin and Preaching: What Are We Looking For?

When we speak of Calvin's preaching, we approach one of the two final frontiers, perhaps, in studies of Calvin; the other is exegesis. Calvin the theologian, at least in the sense of quantity, has been the subject of a great tradition of scholarship. Within the last generation, however, many within that tradition find it no longer acceptable to study Calvin as theologian in the traditional manner: by reading solely the great *Institutes of the Christian Religion.* With great vigor, a number of scholars have begun the task of taking on the commentaries and are beginning to relate Calvin's theology and exegesis in fruitful ways.[6]

Calvin's preaching, however, is just now beginning to come into its own as an area of study. A handful of books and articles have begun to form a locus of inquiry from which to examine Calvin and preaching.[7] I want to briefly point to three ways in which we can look at Calvin's homiletic practice and suggest that one of these areas, however interesting historically, is really accidental in some ways to the concern for a legacy; the second is helpful but not foundational; the third holds promise as a key to unlocking something new and exciting for how Calvin is studied and understood.

6. Much headway has been made in working on Calvin's commentaries since T. H. L. Parker's observation that "apart from some well-trodden paths," the study of exegesis in the sixteenth century has "been neglected" (Parker, *Calvin's New Testament Commentaries* [Grand Rapids: Eerdmans, 1971], vii). A brief review of some of this literature, mostly books, can be found in Richard A. Muller, "Directions in Current Calvin Research," in *Calvin Studies IX: Papers Presented to the Ninth Colloquium on Calvin Studies,* ed. John H. Leith and Robert A. Johnson (Davidson, NC: Davidson College, 1998), 83–84. A collection of important articles, many of which touch on Calvin's exegesis, can be found in Richard C. Gamble, ed., *Calvin and Hermeneutics* (New York: Garland, 1992). David Steinmetz made a statement similar to Parker's in "John Calvin and Isaiah 6: A Problem in the History of Exegesis," *Interpretation* 36 (1982): 156–70. Steinmetz then set out to address the problem. His efforts have been celebrated with a volume of essays, complete with a bibliography of Steinmetz's work. See Richard A. Muller and John L. Thompson, eds., *Biblical Interpretation in the Era of the Reformation* (Grand Rapids: Eerdmans, 1997). Other notable recent contributions on Calvin and exegesis include Barbara Pitkin, *What Pure Eyes Could See: Calvin's Doctrine of Faith in Its Exegetical Context* (New York: Oxford University Press, 1999); and Donald K. McKim, ed., *Calvin and the Bible* (New York: Cambridge University Press, 2006).

7. In what follows, these publications will be listed as they are considered.

The Logistics of Preaching

Pioneering work into Calvin's preaching starts, in many ways, with T. H. L. Parker's *Oracles of God*, later revised as *Calvin's Preaching*. This book represents the kind of historical spadework necessary to establish the actual work of Calvin's preaching. Here we find detailed information on when Calvin preached on what, how many times a week Calvin ascended the pulpit, the number of sermons to be reckoned with, and some analysis of the form of Calvin's preaching. The book reveals something to us especially of the day-to-day work of Calvin's preaching.[8]

I will not rehearse here what is said in this book—it is easily enough obtained. What I do say is that, while it serves as a foundation for the study of Calvin's preaching, such studies are not capable, by their very nature, of serving as an entry point for discussing Calvin's homiletic legacy. Such works are intrinsically biographical. They tell us something of Calvin, his situation, the routines of sixteenth-century Genevan church life, and the like. Biography, while shedding light on the circumstances of Calvin, is a writing of a life, not a legacy. We can invoke Calvin's principle of distinction without separation when considering his life and legacy—the legacy flows from the life (thus they cannot be completely separated), yet—they are not the same thing (distinction). No one would say, for example, that Calvin's pattern of preaching should be duplicated in some form, or the length of his sermons are normative, or any such thing. One must look elsewhere for something that constitutes a legacy in preaching.

The Method of Preaching: Pedagogy and Persuasion

Calvin preached through books of the Bible. Parker and others can be consulted on how many sermons were preached on which books.[9] But the point is that, as far as pedagogy was concerned, Calvin believed that the Bible's message was contained in its books, which had authors. For Calvin, in preaching as well and in exegesis, the point in studying books of the Bible

8. T. H. L. Parker, *Calvin's Preaching* (Louisville: Westminster John Knox, 1992); idem, *The Oracles of God: An Introduction to the Preaching of John Calvin* (London: Lutterworth, 1947). Serious work on Calvin's sermons began with Erwin Mülhaupt, *Die Predigt Calvins: Ihre Geschichte, ihre Form, und ihre Religiösen Grundgedanken* (Berlin: de Gruyter, 1931). This led, in part, to work on Calvin's manuscript sermons and their publication (little by little and ongoing) in the *Supplementa Calviniana*. Other helpful works on Calvin and preaching include Richard Stauffer, *Dieu, la création et la Providence dans la prédication de Calvin* (Berne: Peter Lang, 1978); and Wilhelmus H. Th. Moehn, *"God Calls Us to His Service": The Relation between God and His Audience in Calvin's Sermons on Acts* (Geneva: Librairie Droz, 2001).

9. See Parker, *Calvin's Preaching*, appendix 1, 153–62.

was to "unfold the mind of the writer."[10] Since he believed in a contextual reading of Scripture—that verses fit within larger fragments held together by an authorial mind in an overall view of the subject[11]—Calvin thought it best to go through each book of the Bible a few verses at a time, *lectio continua*, explicating with clarity and brevity the meaning of the author. Once explicated, the meaning was universalized in the sense that fit with Calvin's belief that the message of the Bible had as much to do with the present as the past. This process is called, perhaps somewhat mistakenly, application.[12]

In sketching this procedure for preaching, we speak of the craft of homiletics, which clearly has two distinct parts: determining the message of Scripture, a matter of pedagogy (how one is taught and how one best learns), and then an appropriate presentation of the meaning of that message, or persuasion. Let us look briefly at each of the two parts.

By all accounts, Calvin used the full range of available critical tools at his disposal to wrestle with the meaning of Scripture. In his sermons and his commentaries, one can discover references to ancient history, geography, philology; one also finds that Calvin used the tradition of interpretation available to him. Though the hand of the scholar is displayed more lightly in sermons than in commentaries, it is there nonetheless. Calvin certainly saw it as the preacher's job to equip himself for the task of interpretation as fully as possible, with all the tools available, not disdaining to use even pagan authors if therein one could find help in shedding light on a problem of scriptural

10. Since preaching is an oral interpretation of Scripture, I assume that Calvin's statement here applies as much to preaching as to the written commentary. The quote comes from Calvin's dedicatory letter to Simon Grynaeus in his first biblical commentary, an exposition of Romans (CNTC 8:1 [CO 10:403]). Many articles written during the last twenty years on Calvin's exegesis start with this statement.

11. See Calvin's remarks in his commentary on Isa. 14:12: "But when passages of Scripture are seized on thoughtlessly and the context is ignored, it should not surprise us that mistakes arise everywhere" ("Sed quum temere arripiuntur scripturae loci, nec attenditur contextus, nos errores passim oboriri mirum non est," CO 36:277). See also Parker, *Calvin's Preaching*, 81–82, 90, 93, 132–33, 137–38.

12. Parker, *Calvin's Preaching*, part 4, "From Exegesis to Application." "Application" seems to me too "external" a word; it implies the past being taken and put into contact with the present. Although Scripture speaks of the past activity of God, it is not about the past. As Richard Muller says about Calvin's understanding, "Scripture, as God's Word, is a present revelation" (Muller, "The Foundation of Calvin's Theology: Scripture as Revealing God's Word," *Duke Divinity School Review* 44 [1979]: 15). Maybe the word "transformation" would better convey Calvin's notion of how the message of God's Word works. Dawn DeVries states it nicely when she says of the gospel story, "The hearer does not so much intellectually appropriate the story as *participate* in it" (DeVries, *Jesus Christ in the Preaching of Calvin and Schleiermacher* [Louisville: Westminster John Knox, 1996], 32).

interpretation.[13] Once one has so educated oneself, then it in a sense became a matter of teaching the congregation what is necessary in order to realize the meaning of a passage of Scripture in its fullness. Preaching has, thus, a didactic function: the congregation leaves worship knowing more about God's Word than before.

This knowledge, however, is more than cognitive; it is also affective. And this is where the notion of persuasion comes in. To simply convey bare Gospel history, for example, is not sufficient for preaching. To be sure, one should know the Gospel history, but such knowledge by itself is not enough; the message, after penetrating the mind, must make its way to the heart.[14] And the approach appropriate to such affective appeals is that of persuasion.

A number of works deal with the notion of persuasion in Calvin. William Bouwsma, for example, speaks of Calvin's desire that his theology persuade within the context of the general Renaissance environment, which placed a pragmatic value on thought, leading to a pragmatism of action. For Bouwsma, this means an antisystematic Calvin because the rhetorical by nature militates against a strict systematic approach.[15] Also jumping off from the Renaissance interest in rhetoric, Olivier Millet has written as well on the drive within Calvin's theology to work persuasively, meaning rhetorically.[16]

13. As Calvin says in the *Institutes*, "If we regard the Spirit of God as the sole fountain of truth, we shall neither reject the truth itself, nor despise it wherever it shall be found" (*Inst.* 2.2.15 [CO 2:198]).

14. "Faith rests not on ignorance, but on knowledge" (*Inst.* 3.2.2 [CO 2:399]). "Indeed, most people when they hear this term [faith], understand nothing deeper than a common assent to the gospel history" (*Inst.* 3.2.1 [CO 2:397–98]). "And it will not be enough for the mind to be illuminated by the Spirit of God unless the heart is also strengthened and supported by his power" (*Inst.* 3.2.33 [CO 2:425]). Knowledge of God, to be true, must take "root in the heart" (*Inst.* 1.5.9 [CO 2:47]).

15. On the general place of rhetoric in Calvin's theology, see William J. Bouwsma, "Calvinism as *Theologia Rhetorica*," in *Calvinism as Theologia Rhetorica*, ed. Wilhelm Wuellner (Berkeley: Center for Hermeneutical Studies in Hellenistic and Modern Culture, 1987), 1–21, esp. 1, where Bouwsma states: "The rhetorical tradition, given new life by Renaissance humanism, supplied *the* dynamic element in Calvin's thought" (emphasis added). On Calvin as "antisystem," see William J. Bouwsma, "Calvin and the Renaissance Crisis of Knowing," *Calvin Theological Journal* 17 (November 1982): 190–211, esp. 194, 199, 208–9. For a more appreciative view of "system" in Calvin, understood as a coherent whole held together by governing principles, see Gerrish, "Calvin's Eucharistic Piety," 54–56.

16. "La rhétorique . . . est en effet la doctrine à visée pratique don relève entièrement cet exercice de la parole dans *la mésure où* il se veut efficace, c'est-à-dire persuasif" (Olivier Millet, "*Docere/Movere*: Les catégories rhétoriques et leurs sources humanistes dans la doctrine calvinienne de la foi," in Neuser and Armstrong, *Calvinus Sincerioris Religionis Vindex*, 35). Speaking of faith as persuasion, Millet powerfully explains the implications for preaching: "La foi définie comme persuasion restaure la prédication chrétienne, parole prononcée comme instrument du

What interests me most, however, is to examine what in language Calvin thought constituted persuasive speech, and on this matter he was quite clear: it is the language of metaphor that moves hearts. Calvin knew that metaphors are inherently inexact but said he was willing to sacrifice some exactness of definition to find the persuasive metaphor that impresses on the heart the meaning of Scripture.[17] This seems to me to be an extremely important principle in Calvin's preaching; though he did, actually and for pedagogical reasons, want to make the things of Scripture clear, he also wanted to make those things clearly present to the heart of believers. The fact that he believed metaphor worked best to accomplish this end is something we will return to; for now it is just to be recognized.

Still, are pedagogy and persuasion, considered in and of themselves and as Calvin expressed them, things that we want to consider as constituting Calvin's homiletic legacy? Though I think they lend themselves a bit more toward the making of a legacy than logistics, in and of themselves, I do not think they make up the heart of a legacy, though certain aspects of them can be helpful as we reflect on preaching.[18]

---

salut, elle invite aussi implicitement les prédicateurs chrétiens à assumer dans toutes ses dimensions les ressources du langage humain" (ibid., 51). David F. Wright calls into question some of the trends in using rhetoric as a way of talking about Calvin the theologian. While critically appreciative of Millet's work, Wright is less impressed by others who have recently worked on Calvin as "rhetorical theologian." Wright argues that Calvin is more concerned with biblical truth than with rhetoric (Wright, "Was John Calvin a 'Rhetorical Theologian'?" in Leith and Johnson, *Calvin Studies IX*, 69).

17. "Although a figurative expression is not so distinct, it gives a more elegant and significant expression than if the thing were said simply, and without figure. Hence figures are called the eyes of speech, not that they explain the matter more easily than simply ordinary language, but because they attract attention by their elegance and arouse the mind by their lustre, and by their lively similitude better penetrate the soul" (John Calvin, *True Partaking of the Flesh and Blood of Christ*, in *Selected Works of John Calvin: Tracts and Letters*, ed. Henry Beveridge and Jules Bonnet, vol. 2, *Tracts*, part 2, ed. and trans. Henry Beveridge [Edinburgh: Calvin Translation Society, 1849; repr., Grand Rapids: Baker Books, 1983], 567 [CO 9:514]). The last part of the translation has been slightly altered to better represent what Calvin actually wrote. In commenting on Matt. 13:10, Calvin indicated that not only is the figurative word "more efficacious in affecting the mind but it is more perspicuous. It is important, therefore, both to consider how a thing is said and what is said" (CNTC 2:63 [CO 45:357]). See also Jane Dempsey Douglass, "Calvin's Use of Metaphorical Language: God as Enemy and God as Mother," *Princeton Seminary Bulletin* 8 (1987): 19–32, esp. 19–20.

18. "Indeed it will be an unattractive way of teaching, if the masters do not work out carefully what are the needs of the times, what suits the people concerned, for in this regard nothing is more unbalanced than absolute balance (*perpetua aequalitas*)" (Calvin, commenting on Matt. 3:7, in CNTC 1:120 [CO 45:116]). Here Calvin is commenting on John the Baptist's preaching repentance to the Pharisees, but the point has general application. It speaks to whether one should speak/preach, rhetorically or otherwise, in the same manner as Calvin. Obviously not. But it is not only audience and rhetorical methods (persuasive speech) that change. What

The Purpose of Preaching

There is a sentence from one of Calvin's sermons that should give every preacher pause while ascending the pulpit. It is his strongest statement on the purpose of preaching, or if you like, its role in the great drama of salvation. "If the gospel be not preached," Calvin proclaimed, "Jesus Christ is, as it were, buried."[19] Is this exaggeration on Calvin's part? I think not. He was presenting to his congregation what he considered to be the usual means of God's redemptive activity.[20] According to Calvin, preaching is the instrument God uses to span time and space and to bring Christian, Christ, and cross together. Preaching is the bridge between the work of the cross and the grace

I have called pedagogy changes as well. Pedagogy, broadly understood, is about the means of teaching—oneself as well as others. Calvin approached the text, pedagogically, with the resources of humanistic learning, especially a concern for language and context. Some see this approach as the start down the path of modern historical criticism. Luke Timothy Johnson, for example, lays the "sins" of modern historical criticism at the feet of the early Protestant Reformers (primarily Luther, who represents "the Reformation"), especially in their insistence on the literal meaning as the primary meaning of Scripture and in what he considers to be their flawed approach to the text—historical. On this, see Luke Timothy Johnson, *The Real Jesus: The Misguided Quest for the Historical Jesus and the Truth of the Traditional Gospels* (San Francisco: HarperSanFranscico, 1996), 67–69. Johnson talks about how the *real* Jesus is the Jesus who lives in the community of the faithful. Yet this is exactly Calvin's point—but he tied that real presence in community to the instrument of Scripture by power of the Holy Spirit. Still, Johnson's point is well taken if one understands him to mean that the *method* of interpretation (modern historical criticism) cannot be what reveals the living Jesus by its nature. This is why, as helpful as Calvin is as one example of how to approach Scripture pedagogically—precritical or precursor to modern, depending on one's interpretation—one can certainly distinguish that approach from what I take to be the purpose of preaching. Simply put, prevailing paradigms of interpretation change over time.

19. John Calvin, *The Mystery of Godliness and Other Selected Sermons* (Grand Rapids: Eerdmans, 1950), 25, on 2 Tim. 1:8–9 (CO 54:41; there is a bit more punch to the French: "Or si l'Evangile ne se presche, voilà Iesus Christ qui est comme enseveli"); see also his sermon on 1 Tim. 2:5–6: "We may therefore perceive that the death and passion of our Lord Jesus Christ would be unprofitable to us, unless it were witnessed by the gospel" (*Mystery of Godliness*, 208 [CO 53:176]); and sermon on 2 Tim. 1:9–10: "If the gospel were taken away, of what advantage would it be to us that the Son of God had suffered death, and risen again the third day for our justification? . . . Jesus Christ shows Himself openly to those who have the eyes of faith to look upon Him, when the gospel is preached" (*Mystery of Godliness*, 48 [CO 54:61]; the original does not contain the words "for our justification").

20. See Calvin's comments on Rom. 10:14: "The Word, accordingly, is required for a true knowledge of God. But it is the preached Word alone which Paul has described, for this is the normal mode which the Lord has appointed for imparting His Word." See also his comment on Rom. 10:17: "This is a noteworthy passage on the efficacy of preaching, for Paul declares [testatur] that faith is produced by preaching. He has just stated that by itself preaching is profitless, but when the Lord is pleased to work, it is the instrument of His power" (CNTC 8:231, 233 [CO 49:205, 206]). Later, at Rom. 10:21, Calvin wrote, "In procuring our salvation by the ministers of His Word, God stretches forth His hands to us exactly as a father stretches forth his arms" (CNTC 8:236 [CO 49:210]).

of God experienced in the present. This is one of the many attributes that preaching and sacraments share with one another: grace is offered in the here and the now, through the instruments God has chosen to present and to make present the new life in Christ.[21]

We shall consider at greater length (below) what it meant to Calvin to have new life in Christ. Let it be sufficient here to say that new life is received only *in* Christ, with an emphasis on the "in." The Christian experience is defined by the fact that it is an experience of Christ, and Calvin believed that such an experience has to do with the present rather than with the past. It is with the living Christ that the Christian has to do, and it is the living Christ to which the Christian must be joined to gain the benefits of Christ.

But to speak of communion with Christ, one must ask in what way one has access to Christ. The answer is that one has access to Christ through the means appointed by God, and the primary means are through preaching. "We receive [Christ]," Calvin said, "clothed with his Gospel."[22] What is more, what Calvin meant here by Christ being clothed in the Gospel is that Christ comes in the Gospel as proclaimed. This is not to place the written Word in an inferior position: it is God's revelation and testimony to the incarnate Word, and all preaching must be measured against it. But it is the spoken Word, proclaimed to the community, that embodies Christ. This may well be because, for Calvin, the written Word that testifies to Christ must come alive in contemporary circumstances.[23] Preaching spans the gap that separates the

21. As Brian Gerrish has said, "The idea of Christ's living presence, effected through the Word of God, is the heart of Calvin's gospel" (B. A. Gerrish, "John Calvin and the Reformed Doctrine of the Lord's Supper," *McCormick Quarterly* 22 [1969]: 92). Though Calvin made this point in numerous places, it is said particularly well in his sermons: "So then, may we so esteem the spiritual grace which is given us in our Lord Jesus Christ, and which is offered in our Lord Jesus Christ, and which is offered us every day by the preaching of the gospel" (John Calvin, *Sermons on the Saving Work of Christ*, selected and trans. Leroy Nixon [Grand Rapids: Eerdmans, 1950; repr., Hertfordshire, UK: Evangelical Press, 1980], 148, on Matt. 27:27–44 [CO 46:913–14]); and preaching on Matt. 28:1–10: "He is willing to have a common life with us, and that what He has may be ours, even that He wishes to dwell in us, not in imagination, but in fact" (ibid., 195 [CO 46:953]).

22. *Inst.* 3.2.6 (CO 2:401).

23. It is by the power of the Holy Spirit that the Word comes alive. On the relation of Spirit, Word, and preaching, Richard Muller says, "God's Spirit is so conjoined to the Word that preaching becomes at once a communication of God's will and an instrument of the Spirit in working salvation. Calvin establishes the closest possible relation between the words of the preacher, the Word of God, and the work of the Spirit without exalting the human instrument beyond his station. Preaching makes the Word of God present to faith because God has so willed" (Richard A. Muller, "The Foundation of Calvin's Theology," 125). I would expand this train of thought, however, to make explicit that the Word presents Christ, and him bodily. More will be made of this in what follows. Because the role of the Spirit is to unite believers with Christ, Willem

"then" nature of the events of the Gospel from the "now" nature of redemption. A Gospel that remains in the past, that speaks of disciples who faithfully responded to Christ without indicating how disciples faithfully respond in the present, is no Gospel at all; it is bare history, according to Calvin, even if it is about divine things, and as bare history it may tickle the fancy but it will not move the heart.[24]

Calvin, as many have pointed out, was a theologian of experience,[25] and thus matters simply of memory did not interest him. In his discussions of the soul, Calvin held on to the traditional notion of reason and will as functions of the soul, leaving out memory.[26] Perhaps it is subsumed in some way under the function of reason. While holding to the importance of knowing the past, Calvin emphasized that by itself recollection is not life.[27]

We have to recognize that, for Calvin, it was not the preachers themselves who gave preaching its importance; it was the Spirit of God. Calvin viewed preaching as instrumental, just as he viewed the Eucharist; the power to operate the instrument lies outside the instrument, and without that power

---

Van 't Spijker is correct when he states, "Unity with Christ keeps the scriptural principle from degenerating into a legalistic scheme used in a formulistic way. Scripture comes alive in fellowship with Christ" (Van 't Spijker, "Calvin's Friendship with Martin Bucer," in Foxgrover, *Calvin Studies Society Papers, 1995, 1997,* 174).

24. See *Inst.* 3.2.1 (CO 2:397–98) and note 3 that accompanies it by McNeill; and CNTC 11:349–50 (CO 52:121), where Calvin comments on Col. 3:10 and speaks of knowledge as transformation, not as "simple and bare." For more on the relation of gospel history to faith, see Thomas J. Davis, "Historical Knowledge and True Wisdom: Objectivity, Faith, and Freedom," *Fides et Historia* 29, no. 3 (Fall 1997): 20–22. Dawn DeVries sums up nicely *why* the gospel must be more than mere history for Christians, according to Calvin, when she explains that the gospel is not just an announcement; it is also the gift of Christ present (DeVries, *Jesus Christ in the Preaching of Calvin and Schleiermacher,* 16).

25. For a few examples, see John T. McNeill, "John Calvin: Doctor Ecclesiae," in *Readings in Calvin's Theology,* ed. Donald K. McKim (Grand Rapids: Baker Academic, 1984), 12; Bouwsma, "Calvin and the Renaissance Crisis of Knowing," 204, 210; and Ford Lewis Battles, "Calculus Fidei," in *Calvinus Ecclesiae Doctor,* ed. Wilhelm H. Neuser (Kampen: Kok, 1978), 87. Indeed, some suggest that Calvin was "existentialist" in his thinking. See Gerald J. Postema, "Calvin's Alleged Rejection of Natural Theology," *Scottish Journal of Theology* 24 (1971): 424; and John New Thomas, "The Place of Natural Theology in the Thought of John Calvin," *Journal of Religious Thought* 15 (1958): 108. Calvin wrote of how "each believer experiences within himself" the truth of Scripture (*Inst.* 1.7.5). Joel Beeke reminds us that, when Calvin spoke of experience, however, it is not bare experience of which he spoke but of "experience grounded in the Word" (Beeke, "Making Sense of Calvin's Paradoxes on Assurance of Faith," in Foxgrover, *Calvin Studies Society Papers, 1995, 1997,* 19).

26. *Inst.* 1.15.7 (CO 2:142).

27. So, on the one hand, one must have a knowledge of the gospel (*Inst.* 3.2.29 [CO 2:421–22]), but on the other hand, the gospel is beneficial only if one is joined to Christ (*Inst.* 3.2.30 [CO 2:422]).

the instrument is lifeless and void.[28] But to say this is not to denigrate preaching for Calvin but simply to understand its working: God uses preaching as an instrument to make Christ known, fully and present. And whereas God may not be bound to use the instrument, Christians are.[29] To speak of instrumentality is simply a way of reckoning with how God works; even Christ's death on a cross is instrumental: in and of itself it has no value. God did not have to use the cross as the means of salvation, but God chose it because it best suited God's purpose to show Godself as a giving Father full of love, according to Calvin's thought.[30] In like manner, God has chosen preaching, and God invigorates the preaching of ministers by the power of God's Spirit so that Christ truly comes in the spoken Word to reside with his people; or to reverse the direction as Calvin so liked to do, preaching lifted the congregation to Christ, to participate in Christ and thus gain all the benefits he offers.

As Calvin saw it, the purpose of preaching, in short, is that it is an instrument, along with others such as the Holy Supper, that unites the Christian with Christ. If we want to talk about constructing a homiletic legacy for Calvin, this is the place to start. When and how often preaching takes place, the question of pedagogy and persuasion in the preaching act—all take a backseat to what was fundamental for Calvin: in preaching, Christ is present. That is the goal, that is the content, that is the raison d'être of preaching. Everything else flows from recognition of this experience.

28. "This is a noteworthy passage [Rom. 10:17] on the efficacy of preaching, for Paul declares that faith is produced by preaching. He has just stated that by itself preaching is profitless, but when the Lord is pleased to work, it is the instrument of His power" (CNTC 8:233 [CO 49:206]). In his comments on the next chapter of Romans (11:14), Calvin wrote, "Let us, however, understand that preaching is an instrument for effecting the salvation of believers. Although it can accomplish nothing without the Spirit of God, yet through the inward working of the Spirit it reveals His action most powerfully" (CNTC 8:248 [CO 49:219]). In relation to the sacraments, see *Inst.* 4.14.12 (CO 2:950).

29. "For, although God's power is not bound to outward means, he has nonetheless bound us to this ordinary manner of teaching" (*Inst.* 4.1.5 [CO 2:750]). In speaking on the same passage, Calvin remarked, "It is a singular privilege that [God] deigns to consecrate to himself the mouths and tongues of men in order that his voice may resound in them" (ibid.). This is a common theme in Calvin's sermons.

30. "[God] was well able to rescue us from the unfathomable depths of death in another fashion [than by Christ's death], but He willed to display the treasures of his infinite goodness when He spared not His only Son" (Calvin, *Sermons on the Saving Work of Christ*, 51 [CO 46:833]), preaching on Matt. 26:36–39. Though Calvin held to a version of the satisfaction theory of the atonement (see esp. *Inst.* 2.17.4–5 [CO 2:388–90]), I do not think he was quite as "Anselmian" as some suggest (see, e.g., DeVries, *Jesus Christ in the Preaching of Calvin and Schleiermacher*, 98) because for Anselm there was something of ontological necessity about Christ's sacrifice, whereas for Calvin it was a chosen instrument, not an ontological necessity, an instrument that Calvin thought best exemplifies God's goodness.

Preaching and Presence: Proclaiming the Heart of the Gospel, Examining the Heart of Calvin

Next I move to what may, on the face of it, seem to be an odd place: Calvin's exegesis of Ephesians 5. This text deals mostly with how Paul directs Christians to conduct themselves in the world, and the latter part of the chapter deals specifically with the relationship between husband and wife (leading into Eph. 6, on the relationship between parents and children).

Much used and abused, this passage in Ephesians speaks of wives being subject to their husbands and husbands loving their wives. But then Paul brings in the imagery of Christ and the church and speaks of the relationship between Christ and church as similar to that between husband and wife. The two are one, Paul proclaimed, speaking of both husband/wife and Christ/church. An extraordinary thing takes place in Calvin's commentary. For Calvin, often depicted as one devoted when possible to a literal and clear and plain reading of Scripture, took this passage as an opportunity to speak of the Lord's Supper. And he knew his opponents would fault him. "In short, Paul [here] describes our union to Christ, a symbol and pledge of which is given to us in the Holy Supper. Some assert that it is a twisting of this passage to refer it to the Lord's Supper, when no mention is made of the Supper, but only of marriage; but they are very mistaken. Although they teach that the death of Christ is commemorated in the Supper, they do not admit a communication such as we assert from the words of Christ. We quote this passage against them."[31]

Why did Calvin take this opportunity to speak of the Supper? It is because, for Calvin, the Supper is the place where union with Christ is most fully pictured; and this passage is about union, as Calvin made clear when he wrote: "This is a remarkable passage on the mystical communication which we have with Christ." Furthermore, Calvin stated emphatically that the union with Christ enjoyed by the Christian is not one simply of a shared humanity: it is not about incarnational likeness or similarity. Rather, staying with the marriage metaphor, Calvin spoke of the prototypical husband and wife, Adam and Eve, and how Eve in her creation was bone of Adam's bone, and how her life was derived from his flesh. In the same manner, Calvin proclaimed, are Christians made into one body with Christ because of communication in his substance. Christians are indeed flesh of Christ's flesh and bone of his bone, Calvin averred. According to Calvin, "This is no exaggeration, but the simple truth."[32]

31. CNTC 11:208–9, commenting on Eph. 5:30 (CO 51:225–26).
32. CNTC 11:208–9 (CO 51:225–26), commenting on Eph. 5:29–31; quotations from comments on Eph. 5:29 and 30, respectively. Calvin used the Eph. 5:30 passage to make the same

The Ephesians passage that relates the mystery of Christ's union with the church to the union of husband and wife ends with a declaration that so mirrors Calvin's own feelings on how the Supper feeds the Christian that it bears repeating in full here, for it is typical of the way Calvin ended discussions of the union of Christ with the Christian:

> [Verse] 32. *The mystery is great.* He [Paul] concludes with wonder at the spiritual union between Christ and the Church. For he exclaims that this is a great mystery. By which he implies that no language can do it justice. It is in vain that men fret themselves to comprehend, by the understanding of the flesh, its manner and character; for here God exerts the infinite power of His Spirit. Those who refuse to admit anything on this subject beyond what their own capacity can reach, are very foolish. When they deny that the flesh and blood of Christ are offered (*exhiberi*) to us in the Lord's Supper, they say: "Define the manner or you will not convince us." But I am overwhelmed by the depth of this mystery.[33]

This passage nicely fits the pattern that Brian Gerrish has pointed out as the shape of Calvin's theology: there is gift (grace), and then there is gratitude[34]—better stated in this case, perhaps, as awe at the mysterious way in which God has joined Godself to sinful humanity.

Why this excursus on the Eucharist? First, it is to remind us briefly of Calvin's view that, in the Supper, it is Christ who is given, and given in the fullness of his humanity, which means bodily. Though the Spirit works the mystery of union, it is no mystery what Calvin plainly said: the union the Christian has with Christ in the Eucharist is not a union of Christ's spirit with the Christian's spirit (or at least not just that); rather, it is the sustenance of the Christian's spirit and body with the very substance of Christ's body.[35] With that kept fully in mind, we should remember a second thing: Calvin believed

---

point in his 1545 Catechism (CO 6:125–26): "Le Seigneur Iesus nous y promet que nous sommes os de ses os, chair de sa chair."

33. CNTC 11:209–10 (CO 51:226–27), commenting on Eph. 5:32.

34. Brian A. Gerrish, *Grace and Gratitude: The Eucharistic Theology of John Calvin* (Minneapolis: Fortress, 1993).

35. See esp. *Inst.* 4.17.8–9 (CO 2:1007–9). In section 9, Calvin did mention that Christ cleaves to Christians "wholly in spirit and body." The emphasis, however—probably because of the conflict over "true presence"—is on Christ's body. Also see Calvin's comments on 1 Cor. 6:15: "We should note that the spiritual union which we have with Christ is not a matter of the soul alone, but of the body also, so that we are flesh of his flesh etc. (Eph. 5:30). The hope of resurrection would be faint, if our union with Him were not complete and total like that" (CNTC 9:130 [CO 49:398]). One of the first of contemporary scholars to take the idea of Christ's body seriously as gift was G. P. Hartvelt, *Verum Corpus: Een Studie over een Centraal Hoofdstuk uit de Avondmaalsleer van Calvijn* (Delft: W. D. Meinema, 1960).

that what is received in the Sacrament is the same thing that is received in the Word, especially the preached Word.[36]

Dawn DeVries has pictured for us the function of Calvin's preaching as a sacramental Word; she makes the point that the function of the preached Word for Calvin is to make Christ present.[37] In my mind, this is entirely consistent with Calvin's thought: preaching is about the present, not the past, just as the Eucharist is about the present, not the past. Or perhaps we might better say that Word and Sacrament are instruments that bridge past and present so that the grace originating with the work of Christ in his earthly life—including ministry, passion, death, and resurrection—continues in the present in the believer's life. But the reason Word and Sacrament work as a bridge is because of Christ himself. Much as the humanity of Christ serves as the mediatorial principle between the righteousness of God and its application to the Christian, so too does the humanity of Christ serve as that which mediates between what happened in the past and how that work becomes present gift and grace.[38]

But over and over Calvin asserted that, to have these benefits of Christ, one must first have Christ himself.[39] A number of works deal with what it means to have Christ himself. Calvin referred to this experience as participation in Christ, communication in Christ, communion with Christ, union with Christ, and mystical union. Dennis Tamburello has shown how important the notion of union with Christ was for Calvin, and how it related to Calvin's broader thought on questions concerning justification and sanctification.[40] Charles Partee, in a fine

36. *Inst.* 4,14,7 (CO 2:945): "It is therefore certain that the Lord offers us mercy and the pledge of his grace [that pledge being Christ] both in his Sacred Word and in his sacraments." That Word here refers to preaching. Note that *Inst.* 4.14.1 (CO 2:941–42) sets out the topic of the chapter as relating sacraments to "the preaching of the gospel." See also *Inst.* 4.14.17, cited in note 5 of the present chapter.

37. DeVries, *Jesus Christ in the Preaching of Calvin and Schleiermacher*, ix, 16–18, 27.

38. On Christ's humanity (body) as the mediatorial principle for righteousness, see CNTC 4:167 (CO 47:152–53), commenting on John 6:51. Or, as Calvin approvingly quoted Augustine: "As God, [Christ] is the destination to which we move; as man, the path by which we go" (*Inst.* 3.2.1 [CO 2:398]). See also his comments on 1 Tim. 3:16: "We cannot know Jesus Christ to be a mediator between God and man, unless we behold him as man" (Calvin, *Mystery of Godliness*, 17 [CO 53:323]). On Christ's past work made present in the Christ who is present, see DeVries, *Jesus Christ in the Preaching of Calvin and Schleiermacher*, 31, 95.

39. For example, see *Inst* 4.17.11 (CO 2:1010); for a fuller explication (and references), see Thomas J. Davis, *The Clearest Promises of God: The Development of Calvin's Eucharistic Teaching* (New York: AMS Press, 1995), esp. 48–50, 80–84, 100–103, 151, 158, 171–72, 215–16. These passages indicate how Calvin moves, chronologically, from equating Christ with his benefits to distinguishing the two, insisting that reception of Christ comes before receiving his benefits.

40. Dennis Tamburello, *Union with Christ: John Calvin and the Mysticism of St. Bernard* (Louisville: Westminster John Knox, 1994).

article, revisits the question of a central dogma in Calvin's theology and points
to union with Christ as being a central dogma, if not *the* central dogma.[41]

I add my own agreement to these voices, though with a caveat. In particular, Tamburello, in his notion of union, focuses on the spiritual nature of the
union. He does not imply that Calvin thought there was a mixing of spiritual
substances; he is quite right to point out that Calvin believed nothing of the
sort. But Tamburello does focus on the union of wills as a way to think about
the Christian's union with Christ, and while that is involved, he so emphasizes
that aspect of union that it tends to spiritualize Calvin's idea of union with
Christ—again, spiritualize in the sense of union having to do with a communion of the Christian's spirit with Christ's spirit.[42] Yet what Calvin made
explicit was that the communion Christians have with Christ is with Christ's
body, and that it is Christ's body that first feeds the Christian's soul yet also
feeds the Christian's body. It is the body of Christ that nourishes the soul unto
eternal life, yet it is also the body that nourishes the Christian's flesh so that
resurrection is assured.[43]

---

41. Charles Partee, "Calvin's Central Dogma Again," *Sixteenth Century Journal* 18, no.
2 (Summer 1987): 191–99. See also idem, "Calvin's Polemic: Foundational Convictions in the
Service of God's Truth," in Neuser and Armstrong, *Calvinus Sincerioris Religionis Vindex*,
97–122, esp. 114–16.

42. Tamburello, *Union with Christ*, 40, 100–101, 105; but cf. 93.

43. "Such is the presence of the body that the nature of the Sacrament requires: one we say
manifests itself here with a power and effectiveness so great that it not only brings undoubted
assurance of eternal life to our hearts but also assures us of the immortality of our flesh. Indeed,
it is now quickened by his immortal flesh, and in a sense partakes of his immortality" (*Inst.*
4.17.32 [CO 2:1033]). Though in Calvin the above passage is rare in its explicitness relating
Christ's resurrected flesh to the Christian's, one sees the logic of it at work less explicitly in a
number of places. To "eat" Christ's body is to be united to him so that his life flows into the
Christian; it is to be in union with him. "We must hold fast to that fellowship which the apostle
proclaims: that we arise because Christ arose. For nothing is less likely than that our flesh, in
which we bear about the death of Christ himself, should be deprived of Christ's resurrection"
(*Inst.* 3.25.7 [CO 2:738]). There is here, it seems, a connection between being united to Christ
and resurrection of the flesh. Also in the same place, in speaking of the resurrection of the flesh,
Calvin quoted Paul: "So that the life of Jesus Christ may be manifested in our mortal flesh" (CO
2:736). When Calvin spoke of the life of Christ being manifested, he usually was speaking of
his life in the body. The place Calvin cited is 2 Cor. 4:11, where he commented, "The best cure
for adversity is to know that just as Christ's death was the gate of new life, so we at the end
of all our miseries shall come to a blessed resurrection, for Christ has joined us to Himself on
condition that if we submit ourselves to die with Him in this world [undergo suffering on behalf
of the gospel], we shall share His life." Again, Christ's action in his body (to which Christians
are joined and from which they are nourished) is related to resurrection of the flesh (CNTC
10:60 [CO 50:55]). Calvin also said that Christ's resurrection is the "substance" (hypostasis) of
Christian resurrection (CNTC 9:318 [CO 49:542]), commenting on 1 Cor. 15:12. Thus Christian
resurrection comes about by participation in the body of Christ, which, for Calvin, every time
he spoke explicitly of such, meant a joining to Christ bodily.

One nucleus of Calvin's thought, therefore, is the body of Christ as the food of the Christian. The body is the place of salvation. Without it, everything else goes. And it is here that David Wright's insight is helpful, I think, for grasping the importance of this concept in understanding Calvin, although I do not claim that Wright himself applies it to this particular assertion. He makes a more general point. Speaking to the International Calvin Congress, Wright said that we miss something important in Calvin if we assume that accommodation—which has received much attention since Ford Lewis Battles's essay on the subject—was only an exegetical tool for Calvin.[44] In other words, the assumption sometimes made is that, in reading Scripture, Calvin used the notion of accommodation to explain a particularly troublesome passage from the Bible—if the passage seemed to attribute something unworthy to God, for example.[45] More to the point, however, accommodation played a much bigger role in Calvin's thought: it was not just about explaining Scripture; it was the heart of Scripture. More than that, for Calvin it constituted the heart of the Gospel, because the Gospel is Christ, and Christ in his humanity is God's accommodation par excellence.[46]

Accommodation, therefore, was not simply a tool; it was not even primarily about the form of scriptural interpretation and theology; it was, for Calvin, about the content of salvation. God reveals Godself to fallen humanity, God redeems fallen humanity, God sustains redeemed humanity through God's action and presence in the body of Christ. The body of Christ is the sine qua non of Christian life. The Christian experience is nothing more and nothing less than participation in that body. And that, for John Calvin, is how God is to be known. Scripture, Sacrament, and preaching point to that body and present it; the Holy Spirit joins the Christian to it. Calvin was never able to fully comprehend, much less explain to others, the details of the mode of union. He was content simply

44. Wright, "Calvin's Accommodating God," 3–33, esp. 15–16, where Wright argues that accommodation affects not only the form but also the substance of revelation: God accommodates himself, his Word, and his will.

45. Calvin did, however, use this as one way of employing the notion of accommodation, especially when he spoke of how God communicated in terms accommodated to the "rudeness" of the ancient Hebrews. See *Inst.* 1.14.3 (CO 2:119).

46. See David F. Wright, "Calvin's Pentateuchal Criticism: Equity, Hardness of Heart, and Divine Accommodation in the Mosaic Commentary," *Calvin Theological Journal* 21 (1986): 33–50, esp. 44: "This . . . commentary contains some instances of divine accommodation as impressive as any found in Calvin's other writings and pointing forward to the *supreme accommodation of God* to the measure of mankind in the incarnation" (emphasis added). Battles made much the same point on the "supreme act" of accommodation of God in Christ, in Ford Lewis Battles, "God Was Accommodating Himself to Human Capacity," *Interpretation* 31 (1977): 38, as he looks at Calvin's commentary on 1 Pet. 1:20: "In Christ God so to speak makes himself little."

to have experienced it, and having experienced it, to bow down in praise and wonder. And if we miss that in Calvin, we miss everything.[47]

What Now? Constructing a Legacy: Possible Directions

Once we recognize the importance of union with Christ and acknowledge that, for Calvin, such a union is a participation in the true body of Christ, what are we to do with it? One response would be simply to ignore it. One thinks back to the Nevin-Hodge debate of the nineteenth century, and one is reminded that much of the Reformed tradition stands with Charles Hodge. John Nevin might have been one of the first to bring out Calvin's notion of mystical union, but just because it was something Calvin believed does not mean that the idea has to be dealt with. Many might agree with Hodge that, after all, the notion is a bit odd and is alien to Calvin's thought.[48] Here one is somewhat reminded of the debates over the role of the body in Luther's teaching of the Lord's Supper. It has been variously called alien, leftover Catholicism, and a renegade element best swept away by the more-Protestant principle of justification by faith alone.[49] Yet as one reads essays such as that by Kyle Pasewark, one realizes that there are riches unrealized if one simply ignores the role of the presence of the body in Luther.[50] It might seem to some the more rational thing to do; it tidies things up a bit. But too much real insight is lost if wrinkles are simply ironed out of theology.

What are we, then, to gain by taking seriously what Calvin himself took most seriously: the presence of Christ, especially in preaching? In the spirit of an exploratory first word, I will make several suggestions.

The Reclamation of Christ's Humanity in Preaching

Here I put forward a suggestion: given Calvin's own use of figures of speech—he knew well and spoke at length on metaphor, metonymy, and

47. See the letter to Peter Martyr Vermigli, CO 15:722–24; see also CNTC 11:209 (CO 51:227).

48. John Williamson Nevin, *The Mystical Presence: A Vindication of the Reformed or Calvinistic Doctrine of the Holy Eucharist* (Philadelphia: J. B. Lippincott, 1846; repr., Hamden, CT: Archon Books, 1963); Charles Hodge, "Doctrine of the Reformed Church on the Lord's Supper," *Princeton Review* 20 (April 1848): 227, 275–78.

49. Paul Althaus, *The Theology of Martin Luther*, trans. Robert C. Schultz (Philadelphia: Fortress, 1966), 321–22; Adolf von Harnack, *History of Dogma*, trans. Neil Buchanan from the 3rd German ed., in 7 vols. bound as 4 (Gloucester, MA: Peter Smith, 1976), 2:267.

50. Kyle A. Pasewark, "The Body in Ecstasy: Love, Difference, and the Social Organism in Luther's Theory of the Lord's Supper," *Journal of Religion* 77, no. 4 (October 1997): 511–40.

synecdoche—I think it not unwarranted to look for the ways figures of speech may help us out, or at least expand the horizon of possibilities, when speaking of the present Christ in Calvin.[51] In one of his sermons, Calvin himself spoke about how truth is more forcefully conveyed when figures of speech are used.[52]

Perhaps it would be helpful to think of Calvin's talk of Christ's body as a synecdochal expression for Christ's human life. Synecdoche is a figure of speech wherein a part is used to express the whole. To say "I have a roof over my head" means "I have a house to live in." "Roof" is used to stand for the notion of house. In like manner, Calvin's insistence that we are saved by our participation in Christ's body and that we are fed by Christ's body can be read as drawing life from Christ's humanity. This is not to dispel the notion that when Calvin spoke of Christ's body he did not mean only Christ's body: he meant at least that. Did he mean more? I think so. Being human demands having a human body; we see Calvin as insistent on this in his eucharistic teaching, and one can read at length about this in his commentary on the ascension in Acts.[53] But the reason Calvin demanded that Christ's body remain in heaven, even in the eucharistic celebration—hence the requirement of the Christian being lifted up to heaven in mind and spirit to be joined with Christ there—was because he thought the body, with its limitations, to be requisite for true humanity. And for Calvin, Christ must retain full humanity even after resurrection because the humanity of Christ is the mediatorial principle in Calvin's theology. In the humanity of Christ, the Christian sees incarnated the will of God. It is the humanity of Christ to which the Christian has access.[54] Thus, while certainly not denigrating the divine nature of Christ, it is the human nature of Christ and the deeds of the human Christ that serve as the revelation of God's

---

51. I take my cue from Calvin himself, as he preached about reading Scripture: "For it is important to know how Scripture uses words. Surely we need not stop simply at words, but we cannot understand the teaching [la doctrine] of God unless we know what procedure, style, and language he uses" (Calvin, *Sermons on the Saving Work of Christ*, 13 [CO 47:465]), commenting on John 1:1–5.

52. See note 17 above.

53. CNTC 6:21–26 (CO 48:1–3), commenting on Acts 1:1–2. See below, chap. 7, "'He Is Outwith the World . . . That He May Fill All Things': Calvin's Exegesis of the Ascension and Its Relation to the Eucharist."

54. "We must have recourse to this link [Jesus Christ in the flesh; the French "ceste union" is stronger, I think, than the word "link" implies] of God's majesty, and the state of man's nature together" (Calvin, *Mystery of Godliness*, 15 [CO 53:522], on 1 Tim. 3:16). As T. H. L. Parker has said, "When we think of the Word of God, we are not to imagine an unknown being; we are to think of Jesus of Nazareth" (Parker, "Calvin's Concept of Revelation," part 2, "The Revelation of God the Redeemer," *Scottish Journal of Theology* 2 [1949]: 339; see also note 38 above).

plan of salvation. And it is in the acts of the body—hunger, thirst, pain, suffering, death, resurrection—that Christ is most clearly God's revelation. Any preaching that does not present the drama of Jesus's life, death, and resurrection from the perspective of his human life will not convey the heart of the Gospel.[55]

The Reclamation of Christ's Presence in Preaching

Returning to an earlier quote from Calvin, we read: "If the gospel be not preached, Jesus Christ is, as it were, buried."[56] How did Calvin mean this proclamation? Certainly, he did not mean it in an objective sense; the gospel history has a reality apart from belief or unbelief, knowledge or ignorance, of individuals, groups, nations, and races. But the point for Calvin was that what he called "bare history" could not of itself be salvific. It is the joining-to-the-present Christ that is salvific. And Christ is present, Calvin declared, clothed in the gospel—especially the gospel as preached. Language, the words the preacher utters, is the tool by which God makes present the Word, Christ incarnate.[57]

One of the most innovative homileticians of our own time has built his career on examining the very question under consideration here: the presence of Christ via the Word. David Buttrick, in a remarkable series of books, has done much to educate ministers about the power of words to form consciousness. What is more, Buttrick has detailed how words make reality present to consciousness. In his *Preaching Jesus Christ*, among other works, Buttrick shows how the reality of Christ is tied to our proclamation of him, and how much of that proclamation is tied to concrete metaphors.[58] Much of what he has done can be related to Calvin's sentiment: without preaching, Christ remains buried. Again, this is not to be taken in an absolute sense, but it is indicative of the importance of preaching as an ordained tool for making Christ present with his church.

55. As Calvin wrote, "Let those who want to discharge the ministry of the Gospel aright learn not only to speak and declaim but also to penetrate into consciences, so that men may see Christ crucified and that His blood may flow" (CNTC 11:47 [CO 50:202–3]), commenting on Gal. 3:1–5.

56. See note 19 above.

57. Preaching on John 1:1–5, Calvin proclaimed, "When the gospel is proclaimed to us, it is a manifestation of Jesus Christ" (Calvin, *Sermons on the Saving Work of Christ*, 14 [CO 47:466]); preaching on 2 Tim. 1:9–10, Calvin said, "Jesus Christ shows Himself openly to those who have the eyes of faith to look upon Him, when the gospel is preached" (Calvin, *Mystery of Godliness*, 48 [CO 54:61]).

58. David Buttrick, *Preaching Jesus Christ* (Philadelphia: Fortress, 1988).

The Reclamation of a Present Faith

Another point at which there is some convergence between Calvin and Buttrick: Christian faith is about the present life. Calvin did speak of the future life; indeed, some have said that the whole of Calvin's theology is a meditation on the future life.[59] Ford Lewis Battles's insight is helpful here; Calvin did have a concern for the future life, but his concern was not solely about the future life, and to read Calvin in that manner would be to undo the balance he struck between future and present, between hope and faith.[60]

Another of Buttrick's books speaks of *The New and the Now*. In talking of preaching, he details how one's sermons cannot simply be a dwelling in the past: that would confine God's activity to the past. Hence, for all the helpfulness of the historical-critical method in biblical exegesis, preaching cannot finally be simply a recapitulation of the findings of the historical-critical method because that imprisons the message of the gospel in the unreachable past.[61] Antiquarianism can be interesting, but it is not the basis for a changed life. To speak of a present faith is not simply to believe that something once happened; neither is it simply to believe that something will happen sometime. A present faith sees a living Christ working among his elect now, under all the contraries of historical ambiguity, secure enough in the foundations of Christ's historical works and hopeful enough of that work's glorious and universal completion—enough to act now as part of the new creation.[62]

What is more, Christian preaching cannot be about a future that does not impinge on the present. Eschatology is less about the future per se than it is

59. Martin Schulze, *Meditatio futurae vitae: Ihre Begriff und ihre Stellung im System Calvins* (Leipzig: Dieterich, 1901).

60. "Hope of the future life should feed our present life and give it meaning and purpose" (Battles, "Calculus Fidei," 105).

61. David Buttrick, *Preaching the New and the Now* (Louisville: Westminster John Knox, 1998); see also his article that relates some of the problems of preaching to the problems of the historical-critical method: "Interpretation and Preaching," *Interpretation* 35, no. 1 (January 1981): 46–58, esp. 49. The point is not that the historical-critical method cannot be helpful or should not be used; rather, it is that a simple recapitulation of its findings does not make for preaching, because preaching is about *now*. Buttrick also deals with the problem of treating the text like an "object," aping some of the assumptions more appropriate to scientific inquiry.

62. On the past's relationship to the present, DeVries says, "The sermon does not merely point back to saving events that happened in the life of the Jesus of history, but rather *itself conveys*, or is the medium of, the presence of Christ in the church" (DeVries, *Jesus Christ in the Preaching of Calvin and Schleiermacher*, 95). On the future's relation to the present, Paul Traugott Fuhrmann is perceptive: "Calvin's works have a *tension toward the future*" (Fuhrmann, "Calvin, the Expositor of Scripture," *Interpretation* 6 [1952]: 203). Buttrick seems to be a good Calvinist in saying, "We preach from future promise to present tense," and, "Our hope is grounded in a sense of God's future purposes that, in a way, are coming to us every day" (Buttrick, *Preaching the New and the Now*, 135, 140).

about how God's future works itself into present experience and expression. I think this corresponds well to Calvin's understanding: in the Christ who is present, Christ's past action is wed to his future kingdom, and the Christian finds oneself in a community living out God's purpose with Christ as one's head.

The Reclamation of a Community of Faith

The last sentence points to another way in which a legacy constructed from Calvin's thought on preaching would be helpful: Calvin preached to a community. What is more, he preached to a community with the understanding that, through the instrument of preaching, Christ himself would be present and, as present, would serve as the head of a body. Christ is not so much the savior of individuals as he is the savior of the church, to which individuals are joined by the Holy Spirit as members of one body. Christian faith for Calvin was personal and experiential, but it was not individualistic.[63]

Here it would be helpful to remind ourselves about Calvin's understanding of hermeneutics as he went about the task of exegesis and homiletics. Calvin believed that figures of speech had their foundation in something real and, if you like, literal. Though he appreciated metaphor and used it, at the root of all metaphor is a literal reality that serves as the guarantee for the truthfulness of figures of speech.[64]

Thus it is the body of Christ literally—the integrity of the "continuing flesh of Jesus," as Charles Partee puts it[65]—that is at the heart of all Calvin's talk of the church as the body of Christ. The church as the body of Christ is tied to the real body of Christ; the union of Christ with Christians in body serves as the foundation for the union of Christians with one another in that holy fellowship of the church. At the base of Calvin's talk of the body as a metaphor for the church is a literal body, and that matched for him the reality of Christian faith; it also is consistent with his exegetical method. One sees this relationship ordered in Calvin's exegesis of 1 Corinthians 11, the passage where Paul exhorts the Corinthians to discern the body of Christ in the Eucharist (11:27–32). Luther thought this discernment had to do only with Christ's true body; Zwingli said this discernment had to do with the church as the body of Christ. Calvin said it is about both: First, it is about the true

---

63. See note 67 below.

64. See Robert H. Ayers, "Language, Logic, and Reason in Calvin's *Institutes*," *Religious Studies* 16 (1980): 289, where he talks of Calvin's "need for grounding metaphors in something of literal significance."

65. Partee, "Calvin's Polemic," 98.

body of Christ, and this is primary. But the discernment of the social body of Christ, the church, flows from this first discernment. The church as body rests on Christ's own body present.[66]

This means that Christian experience by nature is always experience within the context of the church as the body of believers.[67] This is a message that needs to be grasped, appreciated, and communicated. There is a well-known study of Calvin's spirituality that ends with Calvin as an individualist.[68] He was not. The body of Christ serves as the foundation for the body of the church. And in a culture that currently sees spirituality as individualistic and antichurch if not altogether antireligion,[69] a reclamation of Calvin's corporate vision of the church is sorely needed.[70]

66. See below, chap. 9, "Discerning the Body: The Eucharist and the Christian Social Body in Sixteenth-Century Protestant Exegesis." One might say that just as the eucharistic bread, when presented, must remain bread to truly signify Christ's body, so Christ's body, when used to signify the church, must remain true body according to Calvin's principle of similitude between sign and thing signified. See esp. *Inst.* 4.17.15 (CO 2:1015): "Let it therefore remain certain that in the Supper the flesh of Christ is not truly and fittingly promised to us to be truly food unless the true substance of the outward symbol corresponds to it."

67. Indeed, Calvin seemed to equate reception into the church with engrafting into Christ (*Inst.* 4.15.1 [CO 2:962]). What is more, preaching belongs to the church, because God "deposited this treasure in the church" (*Inst.* 4.1.1 [CO 2:745]). Also, see Calvin's comments on Eph. 4:16 on the corporate nature of Christian faith (CNTC 11:185 [CO 51:203]). As has been observed, "Calvin asserts that God deals not so much with individuals, as with people in community" (G. S. M. Walker, "Calvin and the Church," in McKim, *Readings in Calvin's Theology*, 220). Tamburello also puts it well: "Christ's promises are made to individuals, but only insofar as they are members of the community" (Tamburello, *Union with Christ*, 97). Thus there is a good balance between the personal and the communal. The experience of God is personal, but it has as its context the community of the redeemed. This is not individualism.

68. Lucien Joseph Richard, *The Spirituality of John Calvin* (Atlanta: John Knox, 1974), esp. 17, 180–83.

69. See Robert Wuthnow, *After Heaven: Spirituality in America Since the 1950s* (Berkeley: University of California Press, 1998), 2: "Most Americans say their spirituality is private—that it must develop without the guidance of religious institutions." See also 74, 76–77.

70. See again note 67 above and Calvin's comments on Eph. 4:16, which are stunning in the way they present the interconnectedness of body. As one would expect, Calvin's vision and concern came out in sermons as well. For example: "Let us be so united to [Christ], that it may be not only for each one of us that such a thing may be said, but for all in general. Let us have mutual concord and brotherhood together, since He has sustained and borne the condemnation which was pronounced by God His Father upon us all. So let us aim at that, and let each one come here not only for himself (as I have said), but let him try to draw his companions to it, and let us so urge one another on to walk steadfastly, noticing always that our life is a road which must be followed to the end, and that we must not grow weary in the middle of the journey, but let us profit so much day by day and let us take trouble to approach those who are out of the road; let this be all our joy, our life, our glory and contentment, and let us so help one another until God has fully gathered us to Himself" (Calvin, *Sermons on the Saving Work of Christ*, 65 [CO 46:846]), commenting on Matt. 26:36–39. On the notion of individual spirituality outside the church: "We shall not have access to God by prayer, unless we be joined together; for he

The Reclamation of Love Acting from Faith

Finally, a word about Christian action in the world. Some perceive Calvin to be so otherworldly that surely, we think, they have never read his work, or so misread his work because of such strong preconceptions about who Calvin was. An anecdote, with name politely withheld:

I was at a major presentation by someone who is head of a well-known, prestigious school. In talking about religion for the public good, she told a story about serving on a dissertation committee that oversaw a student's work on Calvin's actions on behalf of the poor. She expressed amazement. "Who would have thought Calvin would care anything about this-worldly concerns like food," she exclaimed. Yet many of us know quite well, thanks to the work of a number of scholars, that Calvin was interested in the way the church was to care for the poor.[71] But think of that assumption! This scholar had such an image of Calvin as so otherworldly that she had a hard time reconciling her preconceptions (misconceptions) about Calvin with the textual evidence in the dissertation.

To reclaim Calvin's notion of the presence of Christ bodily in preaching is to reclaim a Christ whose presence as human demands that we pay attention to humanity. Flowing from faith in Christ and him crucified, Calvin saw a love that cared for neighbors not only in spirit but also in body. A faith that proclaims Christ present bodily cannot be accused of being anti-body, and a faith that announces Christ's presence announces God's presence as well, as dwelling with God's people.[72]

Conclusion

It has been argued that "the uneasy relations between presence and absence . . . are the dialectical conditions of Western metaphor."[73] If, at root, language

---

that separates himself from his neighbors shuts his own mouth, so that he cannot pray to God as our Lord Jesus Christ has commanded" (Calvin, *Mystery of Godliness*, 189 [CO 53:190]), commenting on 1 Tim. 2:8.

71. See Jeannine E. Olson, *Calvin and Social Welfare: Deacons and the Bourse Française* (Selinsgrove, PA: Susquehanna University Press; Cranbury, NJ: Associated University Presses, 1989); and Elsie Anne McKee, *John Calvin: On the Diaconate and Liturgical Almsgiving* (Geneva: Librairie Droz, 1984).

72. "Let us remember that the Word of God is preached to us, that God dwelleth among us, and is present with us" (Calvin, *Mystery of Godliness*, 118 [CO 53:309]), commenting on 1 Tim. 3:14–15.

73. Ed Folsom and Carey Nelson, introduction to W. S. Merwin, *Regions of Memory: Uncollected Prose, 1949–82*, ed. Folsom and Nelson (Urbana: University of Illinois Press, 1987), 1. Battles says something similar of Calvin, though in a more positive way: "Our grasp of all

about God must be accommodated to hearers, as Calvin thought, then we are left with that unforgettable phrase from the works of the poet W. S. Merwin: "Language [is] a vehicle of the unsayable."[74] Presence and absence. Christ is in heaven bodily: absence. You are joined to Christ bodily by the Spirit's work: presence. God is transcendent: absence. God is near: look at Christ bodily presence. Christians are engaged in the work of mystery, of declaring the hidden and revealed God.[75] Calvin's work taught that the proclamation of that mystery comes through the humble instrument of preaching. Language is, indeed, the vehicle of the unsayable. No wonder the Holy Spirit must bless the words and work their outcome. And that, as Calvin also taught, is not a cause for resignation but a call to preparation.[76]

Christian truth has this dynamic polarity—between absence and presence, between nothing and infinity" (Battles, "Calculus Fidei," 104).

74. Merwin, *Regions of Memory*, 199. It is interesting to relate this to Alister E. McGrath's statement that "Calvin does not, and does not believe that it is possible to, reduce God or Christian experience to words." He goes on to talk of the way he perceives Calvin as viewing the relationship between (1) the experience of the risen Christ and (2) the words that channel that experience (McGrath, *A Life of John Calvin: A Study in the Shaping of Western Culture* [Oxford: Blackwell, 1990], 132).

75. A fine entry into the notion of the hidden God in Calvin's thought is Brian A. Gerrish, "'To the Unknown God': Luther and Calvin on the Hiddenness of God," in *The Old Protestantism and the New: Essays on the Reformation Heritage* (Chicago: University of Chicago Press, 1982), 131–49.

76. As note 28 above indicates, Calvin thought preaching powerless without the work of the Holy Spirit. From a human perspective, however, one must prepare to be used by the Spirit, especially if one is to preach. As Calvin stated in a sermon on Deut. 5:23–27, "No one will ever be a good minister of the word of God unless that one be first of all a scholar" (CO 26:406). This was said by Calvin in the context of stating (a) that God has set up the ministry of the Word to announce God's teachings unto salvation, and (b) that such an office is obviously different than that performed by the prelates of the Roman church.

6

REFLECTIONS ON A MIRROR

Calvin's Preaching on Preaching (Deuteronomy 5)

In 1555 in midyear (June 7–July 18), John Calvin ascended the pulpit in Geneva to deliver a series of sermons on Deuteronomy 5.[1] He was preaching through the entire book of Deuteronomy, a task that took more than one year.

Deuteronomy 5 tells the story of the Ten Commandments, delivered to the children of Israel through Moses. As the narrative goes, Moses stood between the people and God, thus serving as an intermediary, and then announced God's law. Though God talked to the people from within the fire on the mountain, the people were afraid, so Moses re-presented to them all that God spoke. Moses relayed the Ten Commandments to the people, and the chapter ends with the people voicing their desire that God speak to them through Moses. God approved, and so Moses served as God's mouthpiece.

In his exposition of these verses from Deuteronomy 5, Calvin proceeded in his usual way, trying to lay bare the meaning of the text. He sought to explain how Christians should understand the Ten Commandments, paying special attention to how the commandments should be applied to their lives. Calvin spoke in a quite expansive manner, seeing the commandments as a beginning point rather than being complete and full in and of themselves (thus, just as

1. These sermons can be found in CO 26:235–419.

Jesus did, Calvin dealt with the subject of anger under the commandment that forbids killing).

Even though Calvin saw it as his purpose to lay bare the meaning of the text,[2] thus perhaps leading to some level of constraint in how he interpreted the chapter, he still managed within the framework of the passage to create a space in which some concerns that lay near and dear to his heart could be explored and explicated. So, though the exposition centers on the Ten Commandments and the circumstances of their promulgation, we also find herein ruminations that lead to two important points: (1) how one should think about God, and (2) the role of preaching in the drama of God's self-revelation. Calvin made explicit connections between God's mode of self-revelation and the way preaching is used in that revelation: in these sermons on Deuteronomy 5, we find clear indications of what Calvin thought happened in the act of preaching.

One of the strongest emphases in these sermons centers on the way Calvin believed that God communicates with human beings. All communication from God, all revelation, is accommodated to human capacity. David Wright has written specifically on the role of accommodation in the Deuteronomy sermons, pointing out that herein one is safe in saying that the notion of accommodation is not simply a way for Calvin to interpret hard passages of Scripture; it is instead a notion at the heart of Calvin's understanding of God's modus operandi.[3] This understanding of God's accommodation to human capacity frames Calvin's sermons on Deuteronomy 5.

Indeed, such accommodation is necessary, Calvin declared. God's face cannot be seen without the beholder perishing.[4] Therefore, he asserted, God gives the people tokens and signs of God's presence: God "shows himself to them in a visible way."[5] Thus instead of overwhelming God's children with God's glory, "it pleases him to have regard for us and our rudeness."[6] The appearance of God's glory would keep humans from approaching God altogether.[7] Even though, Calvin said, God has made Godself known from the beginning,

2. As Calvin himself saw it, the task of the exegete should be to "unfold the mind of the writer," something he said in his very first commentary, the one on Romans. See CNTC 8:1 (CO 10:403).

3. David F. Wright, "Calvin's Accommodating God," in *Calvinus Sincerioris Religionis Vindex* [*Calvin as Protector of the Purer Religion*], ed. Wilhelm H. Neuser and Brian G. Armstrong (Kirksville, MO: Sixteenth Century Journal Publishers, 1997), 3–33.

4. "Que les hommes ne peuvent voir la face de Dieu, qu'ils ne perissent" (CO 26:249).

5. "Se monstrant d'une façon visible" (CO 26:249).

6. "Qu'il luy plaist d'avoir regard à nous, et à notre rudesse" (CO 26:248).

7. "Car nous ne sommes pas encores participans de la glorire de Dieu, et ainso nous n'en pouvons approcher" (CO 26:248).

God has always done so by stooping, accommodating, to make God's presence known and bearable.[8] God hides God's glory because it would simply overwhelm human capacity: God's glory must remain hidden.

How then, according to Calvin, does God accomplish this accommodation? One of the most developed metaphors in the Deuteronomy sermons in this regard is that of "nursemaid." Calvin preached that God speaks as a nursemaid rather than according to God's own nature. God babbles, speaks baby talk, as a nursemaid speaks to an infant, according to Calvin. God does so in Scripture, through the apostle Paul, through Moses, indeed through all the prophets. By doing so, God engages in acts of abasement, condescension, yielding Godself to Christians out of respect for their childish capacity.[9]

What is it, according to Calvin, that God seeks to communicate through these acts of condescension? A series of themes emerges as one examines how Calvin preached about God's condescension to human capacity: images, verbs, adjectives that convey, in Calvin's mind, God's disposition to the people. God, Calvin thought, used figures familiar to God's children so that by those figures God could become familiar to them. All seem founded on the notion of God as Father.

That "Father" is a root metaphor in Calvin's sermons is no surprise: it has been examined by Brian Gerrish, for example, who sees it as one of the primary root metaphors in Calvin's theology.[10] It should be expected, then, that Calvin described God as Father in every sermon on Deuteronomy 5. And though this figure of speech is used extensively throughout the sermons, Calvin gave it special prominence as he preached on verse 16, the commandment having to do with honoring one's father and mother. The name "Father," Calvin asserted, belongs particularly to God alone; indeed, human fathers are such because God has imprinted the mark of father on them. In an interesting twist

8. On God lowering Godself to make God's presence known, Calvin wrote, "Selon nostre portee il descende pour nous faire sentir qu'il est present." On accommodation, he wrote, "Mais il s'accommode à nous," this so that humans could bear it ("mais selon que les hommes le pouvoyent porter"). All quotes are from CO 26:248.

9. "Retenons donc que nostre Seigneur n'a point parlé selon sa nature. Car s'il vouloit parler son langage, seroit-il entendu des creatures mortelles? Helas non. Mais comment est-ce qu'il a parlé à nous en l'Escriture Saincte? Il a begayé. S. Paul dit qu'il s'est fait comme une nourrice avec les enfans, quand il a presché l'Evangelo: quand il parle de soy, il n'y a nulle doute qu'il ne monstre la bonté de Dieu, lequel l'a ainsi gouverné par son sainct Esprit. Et ce qui est en S. Paul, nous le trouvons aussie bien et en Moyse, et en tous le Prophetes. Notons biens donc que Dieu s'est fait quasi semblable à unce nourrice, qui ne parlera point à un petit enfant selon qu'elle seroit à un homme: mais qu'elle à sa portee. Ainsi donc Dieu s'est comme demis: d'autant que nous ne comprendrions pas ce qu'il diron, sinon qu'il condescendit à nous" (CO 26:387).

10. See Brian A. Gerrish, *Grace and Gratitude: The Eucharistic Theology of John Calvin* (Minneapolis: Fortress, 1993), 25–31.

on how one should understand the metaphor, Calvin claimed that earthly fathers are such only insofar as God has been pleased to make them partakers of the title: God has set that mark on them.[11] All fatherhood proceeds from God, and the Christian's union with Christ points to the proper understanding of God's parental relationship to God's children.[12] Through the symbol of earthly fatherhood, God draws the Christian by an accommodated means "most proper and convenient to our nature."[13]

For Calvin, the point of the father image was to show that the nature of God is love. In discussing the law, Calvin remarked that the root of obedience is love—a love that is not forced but is, instead, a "singular pleasure" to the Christian; it is a blessing, because of love, to be governed by God's will and to be conformed to it.[14] Yet it is not within the Christian to love God unless the Christian has first been touched by the love of God. As Calvin proclaimed more eloquently, "This love cannot be here in us until we have tasted the goodness of our God. For as long as we conceive God to be against us, that makes us shun him. So, do we want to love him? Do we want to be reformed, dutifully rendering obedience so that we take all our pleasure in serving him? Then we have to know that he is our Father."[15] Thus, according to Calvin, it is only through the comprehension that God, as Father, is a loving God that one is able to turn to God and be received as a child of God.

Throughout the sermons, Calvin qualified even this idea, the idea that God, through the accommodated figure of fatherhood, shows love for God's people. Love, for Calvin, had to do with God's predisposition toward the Christian, indeed, but it also had to do with how God, as a loving Father, conveys knowledge of Godself, of human sin, and of redemption. As a loving Father,

11. "Cest honneur donc est propre à Dieu seul, d'estre nommé pere, et ne peut convenir aux hommes, sinon entant qu'il luy plaist de leur communiquer. Or maintenant puis que ce tiltre de Pere est comme une marque que Dieu imprimee aux hommes" (CO 26:312).

12. "Quand nous oyons que tout parentage procede de Dieu, comme sainct Paul le prononce, et que nous sommes par ceste union de Iesus Christ ramenez là" (CO 26:312).

13. "Plus propres, et convenables à nostre nature" (CO 26:310). Preaching on a different verse, Calvin commented that "Our Lord . . . shows that he wants to win those who belong to him in a friendly way . . . [so] he acts the father" ("Nostre Seigneur . . . monstre qu'il veut gagner les siens par un moyen amiable . . . fait office de pere," CO 26:417).

14. "Ainsi notons que le commencement d'obeissance et comme la source, et la fondement, et la racine, c'est amour de Dieu, que nous ne soyons point forcez de venir à luy, mais que nous y prenions nostre plaisir singulier: cognoissons aussie que c'est nostre vraye beatitude, et que nous ne demandions sinon d'estre gouvernez selon sa volonté, et d'y estre du tout conformez" (CO 26:267).

15. "Ceste amour ici ne peut estre iusques à ce que nous ayons gousté la bonté de nostre Dieu. Car cependant que nous concevons Dieu contraire à nous: il faut que nous le fuyons. Le voulons-nous donc aimer? Voulons-nous estre reformez à son obeissance pour prendre tout nostre plaisir à son service? Il faut que nous ayons cogneu qu'il est nostre Pere" (CO 26:267).

God approaches the Christian with all sweetness, which is the true natural
disposition of God, according to Calvin.[16] It is notable how often this word
"sweetness" and others like it appear in these sermons.[17]

It is the word "douceur," and its variants, that dominates the way Calvin
thought that God reached out to humanity. It can be interpreted as "sweetness,
gentleness, or kindness." Calvin spoke the word as a way of characterizing
God's love. One can explore several instances of the word's use (as well as
related words). The incarnation of Christ, Calvin declared, is an exhibit of
God's "so sweet and friendly fashion." Christians are drawn to God "with all
gentleness." God comes to Christians in a "gentle and familiar fashion." God
wins people by "friendliness." God uses "gentleness" with Christians. Calvin
spoke of how God brought the people out of Egypt and "nourished [them]
in all sweetness and gentleness." Calvin continued, "God draws us gently, as
a father." God allures Christians gently. Many more examples can be found,
but I will add just one more: "Just as a father does not want to press his child
too hard, so it is that God uses a fatherly gentleness in the Gospel."[18] There
is, then, in these and other uses of the words variously translated as "gently"
or "sweetly" the sense that Calvin viewed God as a tender Father, one who
drew near to God's children and sought to attract them in a manner consistent
with the quality of love that God wished to communicate.

In these sermons Calvin constructed an image of a God who is a loving
Father, gentle with God's children. The result is an emphasis on God's initiative in acting to show love and to save. Though Calvin himself did not use this
imagery, I come away from these sermons with a sense that, metaphorically,
God works so hard to overcome the gap between Father and children that God
must wipe the sweat from God's brow. Though hopelessly anthropomorphic,
such an image conveys Calvin's sense that the issue of divine separation from

16. "Voila donc le vray naturel de Dieu, c'est qu'il ne demande sinon d'attirer les hommes
en toute douceur" (CO 26:268).

17. Yet even with this talk of "sweetness," Calvin does think that God chastises God's
children; also, Calvin believed those who hated God would be punished (e.g., see CO 26:268).
Perhaps this is why some push the image of Calvin into the realm of caricature, as David Wright
has observed, cited in note 1 of chap. 5 above. Yet to read these sermons, it is clear that Calvin
preferred to speak of God's gentleness, mildness, and sweetness, and he did so at great length.
Such language certainly seems to run counter to the common image of Calvin as a tyrant
preaching a tyrannical God.

18. "D'une façon tant douce et amiable" (CO 26:242); "avec toute douceur" (CO 26:251);
"d'une façon douce et familiere" (CO 26:253); "amitié" (CO 26:254); "humanité" (gentleness
used here in the sense of humaneness; CO 26:273); "nourri en toute douceur et humanité" (CO
26:276); "Dieu . . . nous attirera doucement comme un pere" (CO 26:281); "doucement" (CO
26:289); "ainsi qu'un pere ne voudra point estroittement presser son enfant: ainsi est-ce que
Dieu en l'Evangile use d'une douceur paternelle" (CO 26:398).

humanity is one that God seeks to remedy. Some think that Calvin developed a doctrine of God's transcendence that essentially created an unbridgeable gap between God and humanity.[19] There is no doubt that Calvin fully appreciated and articulated that God in Godself is utterly transcendent. Yet Calvin balanced his notion of transcendence with the affirmation that God can be found, heard, and understood in ways appropriate to human nature because of God's own work to make Godself available through the means appropriate to creatures of flesh and blood.

Calvin preached that God "is content to let his glory remain hidden from us so that we are not undone by it."[20] How, finally, are the good things of God, and the good that is God, revealed in the fullest way? Calvin proclaimed that God declared Godself in a familiar way, "by the means of our Lord Jesus Christ, who is [God's] lively image."[21] Thus, according to Calvin, "God has declared himself to you by visible and plain signs," signs that people "are able to bear."[22] In Christ, however, there is the ultimate act of accommodated revelation. Calvin preached that "God gave us his heart in the person of our Lord Jesus Christ."[23] Thus, for Calvin, Christ is the act of accommodation that serves finally to validate most clearly all true visible evidences of God. It is Christ who reveals who God truly is for the Christian, and this so that the Christian may know, love, and obey God.

As shown in chapter 5 above, for Calvin the Christ who makes God known is a Christ who is present through preaching as an instrument of the Holy Spirit. Some questioned the need for mediation, for means of grace, or the notion that the divine and invisible could be made present and living through the human and visible. In these sermons, Calvin gave a response to this line of thinking: "And so, let us give this honor to God, that he should have the freedom to show himself to us as it pleases him, and as he knows to be expedient."[24]

Throughout the Deuteronomy 5 sermons, Calvin constructed and presented his understanding of a God who accommodates Godself through visible signs to exhibit God's paternal love, a God who deals gently with Christians while seeking to move them toward love for the God who intentionally

19. See notes 1 and 2 in chap. 5 above.
20. "Il est content que sa gloire nous soit cachee, afin que nous n'en soyons point abysmez" (CO 26:248–49).
21. "Par le moyen de nostre Seigneur Iesus Christ qui est seu image vive" (CO 26:248).
22. "Dieu s'est declairé à vous par signes visibles et notoires" (CO 26:247); "pouvoyent porter" (CO 26:248).
23. "Dieu nous à donné son coeur en la personne de nostre Seigneur Iesus Christ" (CO 26:242).
24. "Et ainsi faisons cest honneur à Dieu, qu'il ait ceste liberté de se manifester à nous, comme il luy plaira, et comme il cognoist estre expedient" (CO 26:405).

stoops down to the human level. Once we understand how Calvin established this way of thinking about God, what can be said about preaching in this context?

The first step in answering this question is to examine a metaphor Calvin frequently used throughout these sermons: the figure of "mirror." As with the word "gentleness," the use of the word "mirror" occurs in the majority of these sermons on Deuteronomy 5. In all cases, Calvin used the word to indicate how one sees and comes to acknowledge divine truth. This notion works in a variety of ways. Because God created humankind in God's image, one can see oneself in the men and women of the world insofar as the mirror of humanity reflects the image of God.[25] Christians themselves should be as "mirrors in order to attract the poor unbelievers and win them for our God."[26] Calvin admonished the rulers: they should rule justly, yes, but they should rule in such a way that God "may be served and honored by all, and that they may be as mirrors in order to show good example."[27] Finally, Calvin preached that "the Law should be a mirror to us so that we may contemplate the poverty that is in us."[28] A little later, Calvin expounded at length on the commandment that prohibits lust and covetousness, and he concluded: "It is most true that the law of God is as a mirror, the purpose of which is to show to us our impurities."[29]

The point here is to show how "mirror" was used by Calvin to convey the idea that God's divine and spiritual truth is conveyed through physical signs, which serve as mirrors of God's will and disposition. This brings us to the most important use of the term "mirror," at least for our purpose in this chapter.

In the first sermon on Deuteronomy 5, Calvin stated that, when talking of Moses, "God appointed him to be as a mirror to all prophets and to all those who have the charge of teaching in the church of God."[30] Thus, according to Calvin, all ministers stood in the line of the prophets, and all should look to Moses as an example. Calvin thought that Moses served as a model for how to understand the duties of the ministerial office.

25. CO 26:304.
26. "Comme miroirs pour attirer les povres incredules, et pour les gagner à nostre Dieu" (CO 26:308).
27. "Soit servi et honoré de tous, et qu'ils soyent comme miroirs pour monstrer bon exemple" (CO 26:317).
28. "La Loy nous doit estre un miroir pour contempler la povreté qui est en nous" (CO 26:373).
29. "Il est vray que toute la Loy de Dieu est comme un miroir pour nous monstrer nos ordures" (CO 26:382).
30. "Dieu l'a constitué comme un miroir à tous Prophetes, et à tous ceux qui ont la charge d'enseigner en l'Eglise de Dieu" (CO 26:237).

When Calvin claimed that Moses shone as a mirror for preachers, what did he mean? I believe he was asserting that God continued, through the line of apostolic ministry, to entrust God's Word to the lips of human beings. In other words, Calvin believed that God's self-revelation came to the church through preaching.

Calvin's penultimate sermon on Deuteronomy 5 was an exposition on the role of the minister—mirroring Moses—in serving as the messenger of God.[31] To this point, Calvin has built up a schema whereby God accommodates Godself to human capacity, doing so by stooping to make Godself known through the material means best suited for creatures of flesh and blood. In this sermon, Calvin was essentially setting up the ministry of the Word as a mirror by which God makes known the Gospel. Calvin declared that humanity benefited because it pleased God to have the Gospel preached by "men like unto us."[32] According to Calvin, since the whole history of God's interaction with God's people has been one of accommodation, it was no great step to understand that God "ordains people who expound his will to us, as if he were speaking."[33]

Calvin actually made a general principle from this situation. "It is worth much more to us that the Word of God be preached to us by the mouths of men than if God himself should thunder from heaven."[34] And though rogues might complain about having people like themselves proclaiming God's Word— something they think unworthy of God—Calvin responded that the manner of God's self-revelation was up to God as God saw fit, and so it was a matter of honoring God to accept the means God had chosen.[35] For indeed, Calvin preached that "God shows here that when he sends us his Word, it is in order to be joined to us and that we may also be united to him."[36]

---

31. This chapter obviously focuses on the role of the minister in a quite limited context: these sermons from Deut. 5 and the Mosaic example of how God uses people to reveal God's presence and will. For a more general introduction to the office of pastor (complete with bibliographic references to the larger literature), in terms of practice especially, see Darlene K. Flaming, "The Apostolic and Pastoral Office: Theory and Practice in Calvin's Geneva," in *Calvin and the Company of Pastors: Calvin Studies Society Papers 2003*, ed. David Foxgrover (Grand Rapids: CRC Product Services for the Calvin Studies Society, 2004), 149–72.

32. "Hommes semblables à nous" (CO 26:397).

33. "Constitue gens qui nous exposent sa volonté, comme s'il parloit" (CO 26:398).

34. "C'est qu'il nous vaut beaucoup mieux que la parolle de Dieu nous soit preschee par la boucher des hommes, que si luy-mesmes tonnoit du ciel" (CO 26:399). Indeed, in a previous sermon, Calvin counseled that, because God has ordered it so that humans are instruments of the Word, Christians should "receive it [the preached Word] as if we saw God's majesty face to face" ("recevons-la tout ainsi que si nous voyons sa maiesté face à face," CO 26:400).

35. See note 24 above.

36. "Dieu monstre ici, que quand il nous envoye sa parolle, c'est d'estre conioint à nous, et que nous soyons aussi unis à luy" (CO 26:410).

Herein we find that at this point Calvin moved to conjoin his notion of God's revelation and the preaching of the Word by tying the two together with the metaphor of the mirror. As God is loving, as God is paternal, as God moves in all gentleness, so too should the minister mirror all that, so that not only the words but also the life of the minister reflect God's goodness as in a mirror. Perhaps it is the notion of that kind of mirroring, at least in theory, that enabled Calvin, in a sermon on John 1:1–5 ("In the beginning was the Word . . ."), to declare, "When the Gospel is proclaimed to us, it is a manifestation of Jesus Christ."[37] Thus God, through Christ, through the proclamation of the Word, stands among God's people, a presence that uplifts the faithful, as a mirror reflecting upward.

37. John Calvin, *Sermons on the Saving Work of Christ*, selected and trans. Leroy Nixon (Grand Rapids: Eerdmans, 1950; repr., Hertfordshire, UK: Evangelical Press, 1980), 14; CO 47:466.

7

"HE IS OUTWITH THE WORLD . . . THAT HE MAY FILL ALL THINGS"

Calvin's Exegesis of the Ascension and Its Relation to the Eucharist

I n introducing a collection of prose writings by the American poet W. S. Merwin, the editors characterized Merwin's work: "[His] metaphors are those of simultaneous proximity and distance, presence and absence, the eerie irresolution of historical knowledge. . . . The uneasy relations between presence and absence, some would argue, are the dialectical conditions of Western metaphor."[1] The "uneasy relation between absence and presence" was also something that preoccupied many of the thinkers of the sixteenth century; indeed, it was one of the areas of most bitter polemic. This should not be surprising: at a gut level, sixteenth-century thinkers knew that the power of controlling language was real power, especially as Reformation thinkers wrestled with the notion of a Word that, in their belief, acts in history.

The story is perhaps familiar: as we examine the terrain of sixteenth-century Protestant theology, we think that the landmarks are easily recognizable: most emphatic on presence—meaning the presence of Christ bodily in the Eucharist—was Luther; most emphatic on bodily absence from the eucharistic

---

1. Ed Folsom and Carey Nelson, introduction to W. S. Merwin, *Regions of Memory: Uncollected Prose, 1949–82*, ed. Folsom and Nelson (Urbana: University of Illinois Press, 1987), 1.

celebration was Zwingli.[2] These are the poles, north and south, of Protestant eucharistic polemic in the sixteenth century, and it is usual to read of eucharistic theology from this period being parceled out into respective hemispheres; this was a way to understand where a person stood on the question of the presence of Christ in the Eucharist.

While skipping over the question as to whether Luther and Zwingli *should* serve as polar opposites on the question of presence, we shall examine a case that at one time or another has been assumed to exemplify the thought of both poles: John Calvin's notion on the presence of the ascended Christ in the eucharistic celebration. This case is important for at least two reasons: it represents an attempt to hold absence and presence in dialectic so that both exist—this is important because both carry benefits that Calvin believed should be preserved. Also, it underscores the importance of reading Calvin's commentaries alongside his *Institutes*,[3] for we will find in the commentaries the clue that makes Calvin's understanding of the dialectic of absence and presence comprehensible.

The first question to ask is this: is Christ truly present and offered to believers in the Eucharist? Calvin affirmed this consistently after 1539 (though not before); as he explained to Cardinal Sadolet, "We loudly proclaim the communion of flesh and blood, which is exhibited to believers in the Supper; and we distinctly show that that flesh is truly meat, and that blood truly drink—that the soul, not contented with an imaginary conception, enjoys them in very truth."[4] If one is to believe Calvin, this is enough of an affirmation, and nothing else needs to be said. As is clear from the historical evidence, however, much more was said, partly because of polemical circumstances in which some demanded that Calvin explain himself, partly because Calvin himself, I think, felt a need to try to put his experience, which he considered to be a basic Christian experience, into words. And the explanation became problematic in some ways because, as Calvin worked out his eucharistic teaching, he was

2. Oftentimes left out of the discussion altogether is Caspar Schwenckfeld, who thought that, at the time of Jesus's ascension, the human body disappeared altogether and was replaced by a divine body. Nothing human, as such, was left of Christ. At least for Zwingli, Christ, though absent, retained a human body.

3. There has been a steady trend in Calvin studies that recognizes the importance of the commentaries in the development and expression of Calvin's thought. One thinks of Elsie Mc-Kee's seminal essay as one of the major turning points in this regard: "Exegesis, Theology, and Development in Calvin's *Institutio*: A Methodological Suggestion," in *Probing the Reformed Tradition: Essays in Honor of Edward A. Dowey, Jr.*, ed. Elsie Anne McKee and Brian Armstrong (Louisville: Westminster John Knox, 1989), 154–72.

4. John Calvin, "Reply to Letter by Cardinal Sadolet to the Senate and People of Geneva," in *John Calvin: Selections from His Writings*, ed. John Dillenberger (New York: Anchor Books; repr., Missoula, MT: Scholars Press, 1975), 99 (CO 5:400).

unwilling to solve the dilemma of presence and absence by letting one pole be dissolved into the other.

The questions that follow "Is Christ truly present?" are two: How and in what manner?

With regard to how, Calvin stated his belief that through the descent of Christ's power by his Spirit working on the eucharistic celebration, through Word and elements, Christ reached down to Christians so that they could be raised in heart and mind to heaven.[5] While this is important to recognize, it is also clear that the whole issue of how depends on the manner of presence, which is tied to the question of the nature and function of Christ's body. Therefore, we will focus on the manner of Christ's presence.

Because of Calvin's attempt to hold the absence and the presence of Christ's body together, especially if one asks about the true participation in Christ's body in the eucharistic act, it is easy to come to divergent conclusions. Both sets of conclusions seem to rest on clear-cut assertions made by Calvin himself, with neither set finally being able sufficiently to account for Calvin's range of thought and use of language when it comes to the way Calvin understood Christ's presence. If one reads the language about Christ's ascended body as having to be in a place, because the definition of body requires locality, then one ends with Kilian McDonnell's assertion: "There is in [Calvin's] eucharistic doctrine . . . an unmistakable local sense. . . . For Calvin, the Ascension experience has to do with body, space, movement from an earthly here to a heavenly there. . . . One cannot interpret Calvin's eucharistic doctrine without this strong spatial element." This seems to carry, for McDonnell, the primarily negative consequence of underscoring, to some extent, Christ's absence; Calvin's sacramental realism is therefore "weak."[6] This emphasizes Calvin's talk of absence as a way to undercut the notion of presence.

5. In a sense, there is a dual action involved in Calvin's notion of the Eucharist as a means of grace: a downward action, a descent of the Holy Spirit on which rides the power and energy of Christ; and also an upward action, by which the eucharistic celebration, through Word and Sign animated by the Spirit's power, serves to lift the Christian's heart and mind to heaven. Randall Zachman sees a tension in Calvin's thought here: descent seems to be a function of the Spirit serving at Christ's direction, and ascent involves the believer's use of symbols to effect an "anagogic ascent" (Zachman, *Image and Word in the Theology of John Calvin* [Notre Dame, IN: University of Notre Dame Press, 2007], 340–42).

6. Kilian McDonnell, *John Calvin, the Church, and the Eucharist* (Princeton, NJ: Princeton University Press, 1967), 263, 367. The first quote is, in part, McDonnell's attempt to discount the view of Wilhelm Niesel, who argues that distance is more metaphysical than spatial in Calvin's eucharistic teaching. McDonnell states that, because of a passage from Calvin that speaks of the Spirit joining things separated in space (*Inst.* 4.17.10), "Niesel's position must therefore be rejected" (263n59). For Niesel's position, see Wilhelm Niesel, *Calvins Lehre vom Abendmahl im Lichte seiner letzten Antwort an Westphal* (Munich: Chr. Kaiser, 1930), 92;

Reading the selfsame Calvin, one can turn to the work of John Williamson Nevin. If one reads Calvin's language about the necessity of truly partaking of the body of Christ for salvation, wherein Calvin emphasizes the instrumental nature of the body as the medium of salvation,[7] then one ends with Nevin's statement that Calvin's talk of communion with Christ in the Eucharist is "a real communion with the Word made flesh; not simply with the divinity of Christ, but with his humanity also. . . . The participation is not simply in his Spirit, but in his flesh also and blood. It is not figurative merely and moral, but [also] real, substantial, and essential."[8] Here is a reading of Calvin that points to bodily presence, and perhaps it does so without giving full play to Calvin's statements on absence.

It may be helpful to examine this conundrum by stating two theses that appear to be contradictory, examining how Calvin asserted the benefits of both absence and presence. Then we may see how they can be understood so as to present a synthesis of absence and presence rather than a dissolution of the one into the other.

Thesis one: Calvin believed that it is absolutely essential for the ascension to be understood as the removal of Christ's body from earth to heaven so that it is corporeally absent from believers. Calvin's understanding of salvation depended on this.

Thesis two: Calvin thought it absolutely essential that believers have access to the body of Christ in heaven so that it is present corporeally to them. Calvin's understanding of salvation depended on this.

In regard to thesis one, perhaps the bluntest statement about the location of Christ's body is found neither in the *Institutes* nor the commentaries but in the *Consensus Tigurinus* (1549), the eucharistic agreement between Geneva and Zurich that Calvin and Bullinger hammered out. Article 25 states: "And that no ambiguity may remain when we say that Christ is to be sought in heaven, the expression implies and is understood by us to intimate distance of place. For though philosophically speaking there is no place above the skies, yet as the body of Christ, bearing the nature and mode of a human body, is finite

---

cited in McDonnell, *John Calvin*, 263n59. This chapter supports Niesel, at least so far as to understand Calvin's references to space as something other than literal space; McDonnell does not duly consider Calvin's commentaries when coming to his conclusions about Niesel's position.

7. On this point in Calvin, see pages 84–87 in this book, which deal especially with material in Calvin's commentary on John that details the role of the body of Christ in the salvation process.

8. John Williamson Nevin, *The Mystical Presence: A Vindication of the Reformed or Calvinistic Doctrine of the Holy Eucharist* (Philadelphia: J. B. Lippincott, 1846; repr., Hamden, CT: Archon Books, 1963), 58.

and is contained in heaven as its place, it is necessarily as distant from us in point of space as heaven is from earth."[9]

Although one should not take the *Consensus* as truly representative of Calvin's position on matters eucharistic, the notion that Calvin placed Christ bodily and locally in heaven is certainly reinforced in the *Institutes*. In his section on the Eucharist, Calvin referred to Christ's ascension and declared: "Also, 'departing' and 'ascending' do not signify giving the appearance of one ascending and departing, but actually doing what the words state. Shall we therefore, someone will say, assign to Christ a definite region of heaven? But I reply with Augustine that this is a very prying and superfluous question: for it is enough for us to believe that he is in heaven."[10]

But the question for this move is, really, why? Why *must* Christ's body be contained in heaven? It is certainly clear that it was not because of Calvin's

9. The articles of the *Consensus Tigurinus* may be found in John Calvin, *Selected Works of John Calvin: Tracts and Letters*, ed. Henry Beveridge and Jules Bonnet, vol. 2., *Tracts*, ed. and trans. Henry Beveridge (Edinburgh: Calvin Translation Society, 1849; repr., Grand Rapids: Baker Books, 1983), 212–20, esp. 220 with art. 25 (CO 7:735–44, quote on 743). In many ways, the *Consensus* on some items represented the limits to which Calvin would agree to compromise rather than serving as a clear expression of his own thought. There are points where the *Consensus* clearly did not represent Calvin's thought. On the *Consensus* and Calvin, see, among others, Timothy George, "John Calvin and the Agreement of Zurich (1549)," in *John Calvin and the Church: A Prism of Reform*, ed. Timothy George (Louisville: Westminster John Knox, 1990), 42–58; Paul Rorem, "Calvin and Bullinger on the Lord's Supper, Part 1," *Lutheran Quarterly* 2 (Spring 1988): 155–84; idem, "Calvin and Bullinger on the Lord's Supper, Part 2," *Lutheran Quarterly* 2 (Summer 1988): 357–89; and Thomas J. Davis, "The *Consensus Tigurinus* and the Task of Interpretation," chap. 2 in *The Clearest Promises of God: The Development of Calvin's Eucharistic Teaching* (New York: AMS Press, 1995), which gives a history of interpretation and bibliographic references related to the *Consensus*. To my knowledge, the most recent work on the *Consensus* is a paper that Wim Janse presented to the 2006 International Congress on Calvin Research at the Johannes à Lasco Library, Emden, Germany, August 22–26, 2006.

10. *Inst.* 4.17.26 (CO 2:1025). See also Calvin's comments on that portion of the creed that declares that Christ "ascended into heaven and is seated at the right hand of the Father," along with Calvin's assessment of the benefits derived from Christ's ascension (*Inst.* 2.16.14–16 [CO 2.381–83]). As the quote above reads, it seems, in this instance, to support McDonnell rather than Niesel, and it certainly at least seems—without considering other materials, especially the passages in Calvin's commentaries that I will examine below—to support McDonnell rather than Nevin when Nevin says of Calvin, "What he means in fact is sufficiently plain. . . . Neither ascent nor descent here are to be taken in any outward or local sense; they serve merely to express metaphorically the relation of the two orders of spheres of existence. . . . The whole *modus* of the sacramental mystery transcends the category of space" (John Williamson Nevin, "Doctrine of the Reformed Church on the Lord's Supper," *Mercersburg Review* 2, no. 5 [September 1850], repr. in John Williamson Nevin, *The Mystical Presence and Other Writings on the Eucharist*, ed. Bard Thompson and George H. Bricker [Philadelphia: United Church Press, 1966], 351–52). Nevin does not take seriously enough Calvin's insistence on the reality of Christ's departure in his attempt to guard the real presence in Calvin's thought (though I think, in the end, Nevin's understanding of Calvin hits closer to home than McDonnell's).

literal reading of the Acts passage on the ascension. No more than Luther did Calvin think, when Scripture spoke of Christ ascending to the right hand of the Father, that that phrase in itself meant a specific location. Calvin was quite clear that the "right hand of God" did not designate place but a dignity and power: indeed, "here it is a question, not of the disposition of his body, but of the majesty of his authority. Thus, 'to sit' means nothing else than to preside at the heavenly judgment seat." Here we have a metaphor about Christ's power and reign. Indeed, to speak of it is to acknowledge that "all things were entrusted to his decision."[11]

To speak of Christ ascending to the Father's right hand did not serve as a rationale for Calvin's insistence on the circumscription of Christ's body to a specific locale in heaven. Rather, it was because Calvin viewed the containment of a body in a place as a quality of body that is essential, not accidental, to the notion of body. And it is a matter of salvation that Christ's body remain fully human, because Calvin understood Christ's body to be the instrument of salvation. In speaking of the benefits of the ascension, Calvin made this clear.[12] In Calvin's theological outlook, therefore, the absence of Christ's body from earth seems to be requisite for salvation to occur.

But then there is thesis two. Believers must partake of the true body of Christ in order for the salvation won therein (Christ's body) to apply to them. Calvin may have spoken of bread and wine as symbols of Christ's body and blood, but he believed them to be symbols of a present reality, not an absent one. The Eucharist truly offers what it signifies, Calvin said over and over: the Lord's Supper is not a matter of bare and empty signs. And the offering, according to Calvin, is not an offering simply to the imagination or the understanding: what is offered is the same body that died on a cross, not a memory of that body. Indeed, one must have Christ bodily, Calvin repeatedly asserted, if one is to have his benefits. Christ offers his true body and blood in the Eucharist, and that offering is received by Christians as their spirits are joined to Christ's body in participation; his body also guarantees the immortality of their own bodies as well as feeding the spirit unto eternal life. It is Christ's body that is the life of the spirit; where Christ's body is not, the spirit perishes.[13]

How, then, does reading Calvin's commentaries alongside his *Institutes* help us understand what he meant to say? Quite simply, it is this: in the commentaries, as far as I can tell, Calvin remarked most clearly on the figurative

11. *Inst.* 2.16.15 (CO 2:383).
12. On this, see above, chap. 4, "Not 'Hidden and Far Off': The Bodily Aspect of Salvation and Its Implications for Understanding the Body in Calvin's Theology."
13. Again, for a fuller explication of this, I refer the reader to chap. 4, "Not 'Hidden and Far Off.'"

nature of speech when talking about the ascension of Christ to heaven. First, let us examine what Calvin wrote specifically on "place" in his commentary on Acts, how he perhaps qualified it, and then turn to his commentary on Ephesians, looking at the verse to which Calvin directed the reader when considering the Acts material on ascension.

Commenting on Acts 1:11, where it says Jesus was taken up, Calvin declared, "For when Christ is said to be taken up to heaven, spatial distance is clearly indicated." This sounds clear enough, except that, immediately following that declaration, Calvin offered this qualification:

> I grant that the word "heaven" is taken in various ways: sometimes for the air, sometimes for the whole system of the spheres, sometimes for the glorious Kingdom of God where the majesty of God has His proper abode, however much He fills the world. Wherefore Paul places Christ above all heavens (Eph. 1:21) because He is above the whole world and holds the highest station in that habitation of blessed immortality. . . . But this is no reason why He *may* not be absent from us, and that by this word "heaven" there *may* not be meant a separation from the world. However much they may protest, it is evident that "heaven" into which Christ was received is set over against the fabric of the world. His being in heaven therefore means that He is outwith [outside of] the world.[14]

So, at first Calvin averred that distance in space is clearly indicated by the ascension passage, but then he qualified the statement by acknowledging that the notion of heaven itself has to do with something more than space: reality. Heaven, in terms of the kingdom of God, is not a place above the spheres but a different order of reality, or as Calvin put it, something "set over against the fabric of the world."

Tensions abound. Right before the passage of Calvin's cited above, he wrote, really seeming to frame the discussion of the ascension, "We must not desire to have Him present with us bodily in the world." The clouds that enveloped Jesus at the time of the ascension teach Christians that they must not seek him here on earth. A little later Calvin asked, "Who can fail to see that those words [of the angels] indicate that He is corporeally absent from the world?" Calvin then declared, "The desire for His corporeal presence is condemned." But then, within the selfsame section, Calvin wrote, "Nevertheless, I willingly confess that Christ is ascended that He may fill all things." The body does remain in a place: it is not everywhere in substance but is everywhere in power. But then Calvin said, "I grant moreover that He is present with us both in the Word and the Sacraments. Nor is it to be doubted that all are truly

14. CNTC 6:34–35 (CO 48:13), emphasis added.

made partakers of His flesh and blood, who by faith receive the symbols of His flesh and blood." And then comes the language of presence that seems to insist on real partaking: "But Christ in extending to us the bread in His Supper invites us to heaven that by faith we may receive life through His flesh and blood." In this case, however, Christ is not being sought bodily "in the world," yet Calvin does seem to indicate that Christ can be sought bodily and as present "in heaven."[15]

If one follows Calvin's comments on the ascension in Acts, it becomes clear that, for him, heaven is the place of God's rule, which is no place at all but fills all places without being contained thereby. Christ in power and majesty and as God also rules in heaven in this omnipresent manner, and Calvin admitted that Christ is present with believers in this manner. But he also asserted that Christ's body cannot be presumed to be present locally because of this doctrine of divine ubiquity; indeed, body as body must be in a place. Hence, one finds the talk of distance of place, especially as a way of guarding against Christ's body being drawn out of the realm of heaven, however understood, to earth.

Yet there seems to be no real resolution in this part of Calvin's commentary on Acts; the tension remains because of the way Calvin spoke of the very notion of distance. In his Acts commentary, he referred to the teaching of Paul on the ascension, so one must read the Acts commentary in relation to the Ephesians commentary, wherein Calvin commented on Paul's notion of Christ being in heaven yet filling all things.

Writing on Ephesians 1:20, a passage that speaks of Christ sitting at the right hand of God, Calvin commented that the designation "right hand of God" "does not mean some particular place but the power which the Father bestowed on Christ." Later, Calvin added that the kingdom and power of Christ are everywhere diffused and that the ascension does not bind Christ to a place. But then he qualified that statement by saying, "His humanity, it is very true, is in heaven and not in earth."[16] This makes it sound as if Calvin believed that Christ's spirit is everywhere while his body is in heaven. Bodies must be in a place because that is their nature; Christ's body as body is an instrument of salvation and thus must remain human and therefore must be contained as in a place. Calvin declared that that place is heaven; but though Calvin did say that, he almost always added, when pressed to explain, that heaven, as such, is not a place.

15. CNTC 6:34–35 (CO 48:12–14).
16. CNTC 11:136–37 (CO 51:158).

Now, let us skip to Calvin's comments on Ephesians 4:10, where Paul wrote of Christ's ascension above all the heavens. Here one finds Calvin's most intriguing comment, which complicates any notion of Christ's body being in a place as such: "When Christ is said to be in heaven, we must not take it that He dwells among the spheres and numbers the stars. Heaven denotes a place higher than all the spheres, which was appointed to the Son of God after His resurrection. Not that it is strictly a place outside the world, but we cannot speak of the Kingdom of God except in our own way."[17] What I take this passage to mean is that talk of place, in relation to heaven or the kingdom of God, was figurative for Calvin. We speak, Calvin seems to be saying, of heaven up above and separated from us by space, not because that is the way it is, but because that is the only language we have to understand how the world is separated from heaven.

This passage and its view of language of heaven's space as in some way figurative, it seems to me, are reinforced if we go back and look at the Acts commentary again. In examining Stephen's vision of Christ in heaven as related in Acts 7:56, Calvin dealt with the type of sight he thought Stephen needed for seeing into the heavens. He stated that Stephen's seeing resulted from his lifting his eyes to heaven and leaving the world behind, and he claimed that such a seeing is possible for all Christians as an inner state, since the power and grace of God is near and dwells within Christians. Then Calvin moved on to the question of "how the heavens were opened." He declared: "As far as I am concerned, I consider that nothing was altered in the nature of the heavens, but a new sharpness of vision was given to Stephen, to penetrate past every obstacle right to the invisible glory of the Kingdom of Heaven. . . . [Stephen] says that the heavens are open to himself, in the sense that nothing impedes him from the sight of the glory of God. From that it follows that the miracle was produced not in the heavens but rather in his eyes."[18]

Combined with what Calvin said (above) about leaving the world behind and lifting one's eyes to heaven, it seems that what Calvin meant here is that the sight of the kingdom has to do with seeing with the eyes of faith. This means seeing an invisible kingdom made manifest because the obstacle of earthly things is removed so that God's glory may be seen; indeed, not only God's glory but also Christ himself "reigning in that flesh in which he had suffered

---

17. CNTC 11:176–77 (CO 51:195). The phrase translated "but we cannot speak of the Kingdom of God except in our own way" is actually a bit stronger in Latin (sed quia de regno Dei loqui, nisi more nostro, non possumus); quia indicates a "factness," if you like, so that the clause could easily be translated, "but we cannot, for a fact, speak of the kingdom of God except in our own way."

18. CNTC 6:218 (CO 48:167–68).

humiliation."[19] Thus, the sight of heaven is not about rending the heavens or about telescopic sight that crosses the distance of space. As Calvin said, it is a change within: it is faith.

How, then, does this finally help with the dilemma of Calvin's insistence that Christians partake of the true body of Christ for salvation while at the same time maintaining that that body is absent in space? How did the notion of a Christian's spirit being lifted to heaven to feast on Christ there make sense to Calvin? For, if one is going to insist that humanity, to remain truly human (whether it is the humanity of Christ or the humanity of Christians), must retain its limitations, it makes no more sense that a human spirit can ascend to heaven than that a human body can be ubiquitous[20] if—and this is the big if—the notion of space on both ends, the space between heaven and earth, is thought of as literal space with a straight line being the shortest distance between point A and point B.

But there is at least reason to entertain the hypothesis that Calvin did not mean space literally; he said, as we read above, that the talk of such space is actually an accommodated way of speaking. As such, this accommodated language is the only language Calvin thought could be profitably used; it is a type of language that reflects human ways of speaking and knowing rather than one that corresponds perfectly to divine reality. Given this, then, let me suggest a way to analyze Calvin's thought on the ascended Christ in heaven, a way that, while not using his words, may mirror his meaning.

Here, then, is my hypothesis regarding Calvin's language on ascension: Separation from Christ is not a function of distance; rather, distance is a metaphor for separation. In other words, separation from Christ is not a function of physical removal, but it is that language of physical removal that best conveys to the human mind the reality of separation. To put it yet another way, the notion of distance was Calvin's way of speaking about the radical divide that separates the heavenly from the earthly, the divine

19. CNTC 6:218 (CO 48:168).

20. Indeed, this very conundrum presents itself in Calvin's comments on the Stephen passage: "Finally, although this power is diffused through heaven and earth yet some people wrongly imagine that Christ is everywhere in His Human nature. For the fact that He is confined to a certain place does not prevent Him putting out His power through the whole world." So Christ, in his body, is in a place, yet that place was often defined by Calvin as not really being about place. He continued, however: "Accordingly if we desire to be aware of His presence by the efficacy of His grace, we must seek Him in heaven; as for example He revealed Himself to Stephen from there." And as noted above, Stephen saw not Christ's divine power but his body (CNTC 6:219 [CO 48:168]). Here again appears the tension of absence and presence, and that bodily. Christ's body is not on earth, but it is available, according to Calvin, to Christians who dwell on earth by a miraculous "lifting to heaven," which is not a lifting except as metaphor—it is a seeing into a divine reality.

from the human. After all, when he wrote on the ascension in the *Institutes*, Calvin clearly spoke of absence as a true and bodily absence but not necessarily (or always) as a spatial absence. Rather, he spoke of apprehension: "Carried up into heaven, therefore, [Christ] withdrew his bodily presence from our sight, not to cease to be present with believers still on their earthly pilgrimage, but to rule heaven and earth with a more immediate power."[21] Calvin continued to speak of physical absence, but again, that notion as an absolute absence must be qualified because Calvin himself so qualified it in his commentaries, and such an absence stood in the way of true communion with Christ.

If this can be shown to be a viable reading of Calvin's thought, it means, I think, that Calvin and Luther were somewhat closer on the point of the mechanics of Christ's presence in the Eucharist than has previously been thought. Though it has been pointed out how, in some ways, their thought might have had points of contact, it has mostly been assumed that Calvin stood closer to Zwingli than to Luther on the issue of the ascended body. My suggestion is that it is possible to see Calvin as crossing hemispheres, and even on this matter being, as he always claimed, much more a disciple of Luther than has been recognized. The language they used is different; Calvin's constant refusal to see the Lutheran teaching about ubiquity as being about something other than local presence certainly got in the way.[22] But what Calvin said he experienced in the eucharistic celebration, the presence of Christ, even when that had to do with the matter of the ascended Christ's body, sounds closer to Luther than to Zwingli. He experienced Christ bodily. He just had to think of a way to talk about that while maintaining that the body had ascended and was gone!

I started this chapter with an observation by a couple of editors on the work of W. S. Merwin. I will end with some words penned by Merwin that are drawn from that book. "Language," Merwin says, "is [a] vehicle of the unsayable."[23] In speaking of the Eucharist, and of Christ's presence in particular, Calvin once stated that he experienced it rather than understood it.[24] That is why he, perhaps, had such trouble putting into words exactly what he meant about the eucharistic presence: yet he never tired of proclaiming its mystery, for he seemed sure of the experience. Indeed, we have read here from Calvin's comments on Ephesians 4:10 having to do with the ascended Christ.

21. *Inst.* 2.16.14 (CO 2:381).
22. "I speak always of His body. Their claim that it is infinite is an absurd dream" (CNTC 6:35 [CO 48:13]).
23. Merwin, *Regions of Memory*, 199.
24. See the letter to Peter Martyr Vermigli, CO 15:722–24.

But it seems right to close this chapter with a long quotation from Calvin's comments on Ephesians 5:32, part of a passage wherein Paul has spoken of the union of husband and wife, but which Calvin exegeted as having to do with the union of Christ to the Christian, with particular reference to the Eucharist. Calvin wrote:

> *This mystery is great.* He [Paul] concludes with wonder at the spiritual union between Christ and the Church. For he exclaims that this is a great mystery. By which he implies that no language can do it justice. It is in vain that men fret themselves to comprehend, by the understanding of the flesh, its manner and character; for here God exerts the infinite power of His Spirit. Those who refuse to admit anything on this subject beyond what their own capacity can reach, are very foolish. When they deny that the flesh and blood of Christ are offered (*exhiberi*) to us in the Lord's Supper, they say: "Define the manner or you will not convince us." But I am overwhelmed by the depth of this mystery, and with Paul am not ashamed to acknowledge in wonder my ignorance. How much more satisfactory is this than to undervalue by my carnal sense what Paul declares to be a deep mystery! Reason itself teaches us this; for whatever is supernatural is clearly beyond the grasp of our minds. Let us therefore labour more to feel Christ living in us, than to discover the nature of that communication.[25]

Perhaps this experience, this feeling, about which Calvin had so much to say, is finally unsayable, but human language is all we have, as Calvin knew.

As cited on the first page of this chapter, the "uneasy relations between presence and absence, some would argue, are the dialectical conditions of Western metaphor." And it is metaphor that finally is the language of religious experience. So perhaps one way to approach Calvin would be to shed, once and for all, the Barthian fear of "experience" when dealing with Calvin and take Calvin at his word. Despite the appearance of absence, despite real absence here on earth, there was an experience that Calvin claimed, which he said had to do with the bodily presence of Christ. Others, such as Luther (and the long Catholic tradition), claimed it as well. Certainly, the analysis of doctrine can be helpful and profitable (I do it myself). But we must realize that such seemingly helpful analyses and the structures derived therefrom (whether the notion of a *complex oppositorum* or a *calculus fidei*, for example, two structures that appear especially well-suited to explain the tensions in Calvin's talk of absence and presence) actually can get in the way of studying Calvin if those structures are imposed in such a way as to mask the man himself. In

25. CNTC 11:209–10 (CO 51:226–27).

confessing wonder and incomprehension, Calvin has unmasked himself to an extent. We should first explore what that could possibly mean before moving to cover over what some might consider lapses of—or unacceptable tensions within—doctrinal logic. After all, Christianity for Calvin was a life, with all its experiences, rather than a doctrine.

8

THE COMMUNICATION
OF EFFICACY

Calvin's 1 Corinthians Commentary and the
Development of the Institutes

A little more than a century ago, Benjamin B. Warfield assessed the importance of John Calvin's *Institutes*: "It is saying too little that, in reading this work, we are brought into contact with a great book: would we justly express its eminence, we must say that it is one of the world's greatest books—absolutely the greatest book of its class, . . . 'the most important work in the history of theological science.'" Warfield then sniffed at Philip Schaff's assessment, who said merely that the *Institutes* threw into shadow earlier Protestant theologies, having hardly been surpassed since. Schaff went on to say, as quoted by Warfield, "As a classical production of theological genius it stands on a level with Origin's *De principiis*, Augustine's *De civitate Dei*, Thomas Aquinas' *Summa theologiae*, and Schleiermacher's *Der christliche Glaube*." Though this might sound good to some people, Warfield thought Schaff's "measured terms" represented a "perverse moderation." Warfield was clear in his assessment: Calvin and his *Institutes* do not stand with those other great works; Calvin stands alone.[1]

1. Benjamin B. Warfield, "The Literary History of Calvin's *Institutes*," *Presbyterian and Reformed Review* 38 (April 1899): 181–82, 195.

Those kind of accolades and that kind of perspective led many generations of scholars to view Calvin's *Institutes* as almost sacred text. This attitude, perhaps, is what evoked such statements as Imbart de la Tour's declaration, "The whole of Calvinism is in the *Institutes*,"[2] or Luchesius Smits's assessment, "Calvin was a man of a single book."[3] One even sees it in the standard English translation of Calvin's *Institutes*, at least in some regards: the editor, John McNeill, in certain sections of the *Institutes*, indicated that what was found compactly stated in 1536 had simply been expanded by 1559. Thus he made it seem as if no real change had taken place between those years on such topics as the Eucharist.[4] Everything presupposed in my own presentation today calls that point of view into question.

And that point of view has been called into question now for some time. In an early work by I. John Hesselink, one sees at least the suggestion that the study of the *Institutes* is incomplete without reference to commentaries, sermons, treatises, and letters, though there still seems to be present (emphasizing that this is an *early* work of Hesselink) the notion that the purpose of studying these other works is to probe things in Calvin that are "not explicit in the *Institutes*."[5]

What had been lacking in so much of the Calvin scholarship through much of its existence as a modern endeavor (in terms of the modern scholarly study of Calvin, the start of this existence can be pushed back to nineteenth-century scholars such as John Williamson Nevin, J. H. A. Ebrard, and Herman Bavinck, among others)[6] had been both the perspective and the evidence that,

2. Imbart de la Tour, quoted in François Wendel, *Calvin: The Origins and Development of His Religious Thought*, trans. Philip Mairet (London: William Collins, 1963), 111.

3. Luchesius Smits, *Saint Augustin dans l'oeuvre de Jean Calvin*, vol. 1, *Étude de critique littéraire* (Assen: van Gorcum, 1956), 1. Something of the same sentiment remains in more recent times: see Alister E. McGrath, *A Life of John Calvin: A Study in the Shaping of Western Culture* (Oxford: Blackwell, 1990), 145–47.

4. *Inst.*, 2:1368n24. The problem here is that the comparison to the 1536 edition concerns a passage that denies Christ's bodily presence in the Eucharist but affirms that one receives the benefits. By 1559, Calvin was quite clear that what one receives is Christ first and then his benefits. On this, see Thomas J. Davis, *The Clearest Promises of God: The Development of Calvin's Eucharistic Teaching* (New York: AMS Press, 1995). Part of the purpose of the book is to show the substantial changes that took place between 1536 and 1559; see esp. the summary statement on p. 212 that details the major changes between 1536 and 1559.

5. I. John Hesselink, "The Development and Purpose of Calvin's *Institutes*," *Reformed Theological Review* 24, no. 3 (October 1965): 66.

6. See John Williamson Nevin, *The Mystical Presence: A Vindication of the Reformed or Calvinistic Doctrine of the Holy Eucharist* (Philadelphia: J. B. Lippincott, 1846; repr., Hamden, CT: Archon Books, 1963); idem, "Doctrine of the Reformed Church on the Lord's Supper," *Mercersburg Review* 2, no. 5 (September 1850): 421–549; Johann Heinrich August Ebrard, *Das Dogma vom heiligen Abendmahl und seine Geschichte*, 2 vols. (Frankfurt: Heinrich Zimmer,

more than simply "supplementing" the *Institutes*, other endeavors by Calvin led to developments in his theology that were then worked into his *Institutes*. In other words, Calvin studies lacked the notion of real growth, process, development, and the sense that Calvin was capable of learning new things over the years, leading to substantial contributions to his thinking that then found their way into the *Institutes*. (Yet as Susan Schreiner has shown through an examination of Calvin's sermons on Job, there were developments in Calvin's thought that did not make it into the *Institutes*, such as his notion of the double justice of God.)[7]

Elsie McKee has been one of the leaders in showing the importance especially of Calvin's exegetical work and its relationship both to the development of Calvin's theology and to the development of Calvin's *Institutes*. Though we could point to a number of places, I highlight her 1988 article, "Calvin's Exegesis of Romans 12:8—Social, Accidental, or Theological?"[8] The problem therein explored is that of the twofold diaconate, a concept that posited two categories of deacons: the one raising and managing the funds for distribution to the poor and sick, and the other actually engaged in service to the poor and sick. From whence did this concept arise? One position is that Calvin simply mimicked the structure of social services already in place in Geneva; this would be the "social" of the title, the idea that Calvin simply copied social structures already in place and then made up a theory to match it.[9] A couple of accidental theories—in the sense that the dual diaconate is simply accidental to Calvin's theology rather than springing from it as an integral part of his own thinking—suggest either that Calvin's diaconal arrangements stemmed from the overall plural office theory as a by-product or that Bucer's influence was determinative.[10]

While appreciating the logic of both positions, social and accidental, McKee in her article speaks of how Calvin's exegesis of Romans 12:8 led him to the dual diaconate position. She shows that Calvin's use of Romans 12:8 in the *Institutes* as a proof text of his position on the dual diaconate came after his commentary on Romans (1540); hence, such use of Romans 12:8 was incorporated into the 1543 edition of the *Institutes*, not 1539, as some who argued for nontheological causes suggested (which would place the change before the

1845–46), vol. 2, chap. 5, §§ 36–38; and chap. 6, § 39; and Herman Bavinck, "Calvijn's leer over het Avondmaal," *Vrije Kerk* 13 (1887): 459–86.

7. Susan Schreiner, "Exegesis and Double Justice in Calvin's Sermons on Job," *Church History* 58, no. 3 (September 1989): 322–38.

8. Elsie Anne McKee, "Calvin's Exegesis of Romans 12:8—Social, Accidental, or Theological?" *Calvin Theological Journal* 23, no. 1 (April 1988): 6–18.

9. Ibid., 7.

10. Ibid., 9–10.

Romans commentary). Indeed, this being the case, she is able to suggest, "It seems possible . . . that one cause of development in Calvin's theology was the reformer's struggle with problematic biblical texts—exegetical difficulties that he had to resolve if he was to produce a unified interpretation of Scripture."[11] McKee concludes her fine essay with the admonition to heed the "importance of Scripture in determining the shape of doctrine" in Calvin's *Institutes*.[12] Her work contributes to the important mind-set today among many that one must actually deal with commentaries, especially when working through a scholarly analysis of the *Institutes*.

Taking my cue from McKee, then, I decided to examine the role of the 1 Corinthians commentary in the development of Calvin's treatment of the Eucharist in the *Institutes*. I knew that, in regard to the 1559 *Institutes*, the 1546 Commentary on 1 Corinthians, along with many other works of Calvin, signaled certain developments of his thought that made the 1559 explanation of the Eucharist quite different from the 1536 explanation, found in the first edition of the *Institutes*. Having worked on the 1 Corinthians commentary, I also knew of material there on the power of the Eucharist, on efficacy, that was important in the 1559 *Institutes*. I recognized that one context in which Calvin discussed efficacy was in relating the sacraments of the Old Testament to those of the New. Therefore, I decided to pursue a case study to show that the 1 Corinthians commentary was essential in promoting the language of "efficaciousness" as applied to the sacraments of both Testaments, the discussion of which is found in later editions of the *Institutes*.

My plan of action seemed reasonable. How disappointing, then, that I actually had to go and read Calvin, thereupon discovering that, apparently, I was wrong.

There is material especially pertaining to chapters 10 and 11 of the 1 Corinthians commentary—especially the notion of the power of the Sacrament to give what it promises—that shows up in later editions of the *Institutes*.[13] There are several interesting developments on the type of knowledge the sacrament brings to believers, given in the context of faith.

However, in terms of what I initially wanted to look at in this presentation—the communication of efficacy (that is, the power of the sacrament to give something, whether it is the body of Christ or knowledge)—there is a source behind the commentary on 1 Corinthians in relation to much of the eucharistic

11. Ibid., 12.
12. Ibid., 18.
13. Davis, *Clearest Promises of God*, esp. 155–63.

thought of Calvin. It may seem ironic, given the emphasis of today's session, that that source is the 1543 *Institutes*.

The passage of Scripture under examination here is 1 Corinthians 10:3–4, where Paul draws on the exodus from Egypt and the signs presented to the children of Israel by God: "[They] did all eat the same spiritual meat; and did all drink the same spiritual drink: for they drank of a spiritual rock that followed them: and the rock was Christ." In dealing with this passage, Calvin emphasized that the signs of God are efficacious: they have power to accomplish what they signify, doing so by God's ordinance. In dealing with verse 3, Calvin stated, "When Paul says that the *fathers ate the same spiritual meat*, he first of all gives a hint of what the power and efficacy of the sacrament is; and secondly he shows that the old sacraments of the law had the same power as ours have today." Calvin went on to deny that a sign given by God can be bare or empty. In relating the sacraments of the New Testament to the Old, Calvin disagreed with those who said that the fathers of the Old Testament had the "sign without the reality," but he did insist that "the efficacy of the signs is at once richer and more abundant for us since the incarnation of Christ." Yet the signs of the Old Testament were not "mere figures";[14] they were themselves efficacious, though not in quite the same way as the signs of the New.

In verse 4, Calvin again emphasized the efficaciousness of sacraments under the New and Old covenants. He explained how, under the figure of the rock, Christ was presented to the Hebrew children. Calvin insisted that "it was necessary for them to receive the flesh and blood of Christ, so that they might share in the blessing of redemption." Calvin then explained how such a feat was accomplished: through the power of the Holy Spirit. The work of the Spirit was so powerful, Calvin declared, that "the flesh of Christ, even if it was not yet created, might be efficacious in them."[15]

In this commentary, Calvin seemed to be making a distinction between the sacraments' inherent force and the accomplishments of that force, perhaps between potential and actualized power. In commenting on these verses, Calvin wrote of both the power and the efficacy of the sacraments.[16] For the former, he used the Latin word "vis," which means power, but in the sense of essential force, energy, or virtue. For the latter, efficaciousness and its variants, he used the Latin word "efficax" (and its variants), which means efficacious, yes, but we should realize the full sense of that word: it also means power, power to accomplish (after all, the root verb form means "to accomplish"). Thus when

---

14. CNTC 9:203–4 (CO 49:453–54).
15. CNTC 9:205 (CO 49:455).
16. CNTC 9:203, 205 (CO 49:453, 455).

Calvin wrote of the power and efficacy of the sacrament in this section, he meant the essential force of Christ's body, yes, but he also meant that force realized in action so that it accomplishes its goals.

Such an understanding enabled Calvin to say that the sacraments of the Old Testament "have the same power as ours have today."[17] The reality is given with the sign. It is clear that, though the sacraments of the Old Testament exhibit Christ, and though the power of the sacraments are the same between the two Testaments (for the essential power of Christ must remain the same, since it is part of his being), yet for Christians "the efficacy of the signs is at once richer and more abundant for us since the incarnation of Christ." The accomplishment of power is greater; it is a matter, as Calvin described it, of degrees. Though the substance of the Eucharist always retains its full power, for the substance is Christ, the signs can vary in their efficaciousness.[18]

This way of treating 1 Corinthians 10:3–4, and its theological import, appeared before the 1 Corinthians commentary: it appears in the 1543 *Institutes*. In material new to 1543, one reads of the same concerns as in the 1 Corinthians commentary. There is a tendency to distinguish between the sacraments of the old and new covenants in terms of efficacy, but not in terms of power, and in terms of degrees of accomplishment, not in terms of the reality of the thing itself offered in the sacraments. This distinction is then also applied to the difference between the elect and the nonelect in the church.

If one looks at the chapter on the sacraments in the 1543 *Institutes*, the language that distinguishes the matter or substance of the Sacrament from the Sacrament itself is presented in terms of efficacy. The Sacrament is one thing; the power of it is another. The Sacrament is the sign; the power is Christ himself. The profit of the Sacrament is the partaking of Christ himself. But though the partaking of Christ promises salvation, there are questions of "proportion" in relation to the effectiveness of the sign. The degree of effectiveness reflects the degree to which one possesses Christ, the substance or power of the Sacrament.[19]

At the end of his treatment of the sacraments in general in the 1543 *Institutes*, Calvin inserted new material that references 1 Corinthians 10:4. It is a

17. CNTC 9:203 (CO 49:453–54).

18. CNTC 9:203 (CO 49:454). Calvin said much the same thing in his commentary on verse 4, where, though efficaciousness comes in degrees of accomplishment, such a state does not diminish the inherent power of body and blood of Christ to save. "The Holy Spirit . . . was active in such a way that the flesh of Christ, even if it was not yet created, might be efficacious in them [fathers of the Old Testament]. [Paul] means, however, that they ate in their own way, which was different from ours, and, as I have said already, that Christ is now conveyed to us more fully" (CNTC 9:205 [CO 49:455]).

19. CO 1:948–49.

passage that again distinguishes between the thing of the Sacrament (Christ, its power) and its efficacy. It explores the differences and continuities between the two Testaments. Yet Calvin again affirmed that Christ is offered under the signs of both the Old Testament and the New. The people of the old covenant drank the same spiritual drink as those of the new: Christ himself. But again, in terms of efficacy, the signs of the New Testament are "clearer and brighter," according to Calvin. The degree of efficacy changes with the different signs and with those receiving the signs, but the matter—Christ, the Sacrament's power—is the same. Not all receive in the same proportion. The Sacrament is efficacious, but in varying degrees.[20] Again, much of this thought was later folded into the 1 Corinthians commentary.

Where did this new material in the 1543 *Institutes* come from? Though there are intimations of the above language in the *Short Treatise on the Holy Supper*, that work does not contain the full-blown explanations that the 1543 *Institutes* do, and the use of the word "efficax" (and its variants) to distinguish the level of accomplishment of grace from the power and source of that grace—Christ—is perhaps there in outline form, but not in detail.

Simply put, but I hope not too simply, this trend in Calvin's thinking appears to come from Augustine of Hippo. If one looks at the 1543 *Institutes*, at the sections with which we have dealt here—the ones from the sacraments chapter—one finds an explosion of references to Augustine and citations from Augustine. If one looks at these sections in the context of what has come before and what will come later, it is apparent that Calvin had engaged in an intensive reading of Augustine. If one looks at the references and citations to Augustine in the 1559 *Institutes* with an eye for when things first appeared, it turns out that the large majority of all these references originated with the 1543 *Institutes*. What is more, if one looks at the quantity of material added, there are new sections devoted just to Augustine's view of the Sacrament. Though overall the citations are to a wide variety of Augustine's works, of particular importance for our purposes here are two books, because they were quoted at such length by Calvin in 1543. These works are Augustine's *Homilies on the Gospel of John* and the *Commentary on the Psalms*.

In the 1543 sections on the sacraments mentioned above, places where Calvin carefully tried to distinguish between the matter of the sacrament and the sacramental sign, always in the context of the relationship of the signs of the old covenant to the new (in one section entirely new in 1543 and another where half the material was new), all but one of the quotes from Augustine

20. CO 1:956–58.

came from the John work and the Psalms commentary: specifically, comments on John 6 and on Psalm 78.[21]

And—at last—within the context of John 6 and Psalm 78, Augustine spent time on the sacraments, and in both cases he especially referenced and applied 1 Corinthians 10:3–4. Calvin used and expanded this material from Augustine as he continued to think through sacramental matters in his 1543 *Institutes*.

So what are we left with here? If read one way, my examination of Calvin's 1 Corinthians commentary and the communication of efficacy, if viewed in terms of the influence of that 1546 commentary on later editions of the *Institutes*, does not support McKee's insistence that the commentaries inform the *Institutes* (though she really does not claim that this is true in every instance and with every strand of thought). In a different sense, however, it certainly does support her thesis, because, as I read it, her suggestion does not have to do simply with individual lines in commentaries forming new theological emphases that then work their way into the *Institutes* (though this does, as she has shown, happen at times). The basis of her thesis has to do with how Calvin wrestled with Scripture in the context of his unified view of Scripture. For Calvin, all the parts did have to hold together. It is just that, in this particular case, the way Calvin's doctrine was shaped by Scripture came, at least in large part, I think, not through writing a commentary but by reading commentaries. And for 1543, perhaps Calvin's growing debt to Augustine was recognized by Calvin himself. In that edition, he added a quote from Augustine to end his initial note to the reader, and there it remains still.[22]

---

21. CO 1:948–50, 956–58.

22. "Ego ex eorum numero me esse profiteor, qui scribunt proficiendo, et scribendo proficiunt" ("I profess that I am one of those who writes while growing [advancing, making progress] and grows while writing," CO 1:255).

9

DISCERNING THE BODY

*The Eucharist and the Christian Social Body
in Sixteenth-Century Protestant Exegesis*

Thomas H. L. Parker once observed that "the sixteenth century was, above all things, the age of the Bible. How strange, then, that this area of its history has, apart from some well-trodden paths, been neglected."[1] Since Parker's statement, studies on the Reformers' exegesis, hermeneutics, and general use of Scripture have appeared; yet it remains true that there is much to be learned from the examination of exegetical themes in the Reformers and from comparing how those themes, as articulated, nuance one's understanding of their religious thinking and theology.[2] This may be especially true of

1. Thomas H. L. Parker, *Calvin's New Testament Commentaries* (Grand Rapids: Eerdmans, 1971), vii. See also Richard A. Muller's assessment that, despite great strides that have been made, there is still a continuing need for work to be done on Calvin's exegesis (Muller, "Directions in Current Calvin Research," in *Calvin Studies IX*, ed. John Leith and Robert A. Johnson [Davidson, NC: Davidson College, 1998], 83–84).

2. David Steinmetz's work has been especially noteworthy in terms of looking at the exegesis of Luther and Calvin: *Luther in Context* (Bloomington: Indiana University Press, 1986); and *Calvin in Context* (New York: Oxford University Press, 1995). In honor of Steinmetz's work in this area, a collection of essays has been published: Richard A. Muller and John L. Thompson, eds., *Biblical Interpretation in the Era of the Reformation* (Grand Rapids: Eerdmans, 1996). Also extremely helpful is Susan Schreiner, *Where Shall Wisdom Be Found? Calvin's Exegesis of Job from Medieval and Modern Perspectives* (Chicago: University of Chicago Press, 1994); and

studics that place the Reformers within a comparative context, where one can see how exegetical strategies may have reinforced theological agenda.

Though they would not have recognized it, there was at work within the exegesis of the Protestant theologians a hermeneutical circle; this is taken for granted today. Yet to state the obvious—that in Luther, Zwingli, Calvin, and others there is a hermeneutical circle at work—is not simply to dismiss the exegetical work of these writers, as though the presence of hermeneutical assumptions obliterates the possibility that the text of Scripture could have any power over them to direct its interpretation. The Reformers saw themselves as servants of the Word of God, and it was precisely in their roles as interpreters of that Word that they asked others to judge them and their doctrine.

The point of this chapter is to do just that: perhaps not to judge, but at least to examine how their use and interpretation of Scripture was related to the doctrines they promulgated[3] and how their theologies and exegeses affected one another. More than that, in some cases one can glimpse the ways the Reformers' religious experience may have affected how they were willing to handle a text. Though they looked to "the Word," that Word was not divorced from—indeed, it was foundational to—their religious worldviews. This may seem to smack of "subjectivism," a charge from which many Protestant scholars have traditionally tried to shield early Protestants such as Luther and Calvin (and thus also misread their understanding of Scripture). Yet we need to see how things important to their religious self-understanding could help to shape their reading of Scripture.

For a case study, I will examine how Luther, Zwingli, and Calvin dealt with chapters 10–12 in 1 Corinthians, especially as they considered the notion of "body." In these chapters, Paul speaks of the church as the body of Christ. It is a section of a larger part of Paul's letter that deals with social conflict in the Corinthian church, and Paul mediated that conflict by reference to the Lord's Supper. First Corinthians 10 emphasizes that participation in the Eucharist forms Christians into one body. It ends with an emphasis on how consideration for others should result from a proper understanding of the Supper. In chapter 11, the handing down of the tradition of the Lord's Supper, in textual terms, takes place within the context of social division—the well-to-do are not being considerate of the less well-to-do—the very thing Paul addressed previously. After reciting the tradition of institution, Paul offers a warning: do not eat without discerning the body. It ends with a call for compassion for others.

Barbara Pitkin, *What Pure Eyes Could See: Calvin's Doctrine of Faith in Its Exegetical Context* (New York: Oxford University Press, 1999).

3. My views on this are briefly sketched out in the last two pages of chap. 1 above; what I say there about Luther in particular applies, I think, more generally to all those under consideration here.

Finally, chapter 12 emphasizes that all members of the congregation have something good to bring to the group, and then there is the extended analogy of the Corinthian congregation as the body of Christ. Running into chapter 13, this section again calls believers to extend compassion for others.

The pattern in this section of 1 Corinthians, then, can be seen this way: There is a conflict over how to act, there is reference to the Supper, and there is a call to concern oneself with the care of others. In chapters 10 and 12, Paul specifically refers to the congregation as "the body." Therefore, in the midst of social conflict, when Paul refers to the congregation as the "body"—which carries ethical connotations[4]—it seems reasonable to think that Paul's call in chapter 11 to discern the body is a call to ethical regard for all members of the congregation based on the action of Christ's own sacrifice. At least, this is a reasonable point to include in any consideration of Paul's phrase about "discerning the body."

Certainly, there was an established tradition of viewing the Christian social body as an important aspect of eucharistic theology. With the assumption that Christ's body was truly present in the Eucharist, some medieval commentators were able to focus on the social body of Christians, which they regarded as formed by participation in the Eucharist. Indeed, the inclusion into the social body was seen as one of the Eucharist's primary benefits. Bernard of Clairvaux was so convinced of the efficacy of this social body that he believed weak members could commune in the faith of stronger members.[5] In a period in which the true body of Christ was assumed to be given in the elements, the emphasis on the social body of Christ—the spiritual body of Christ called the church—was not threatening. Indeed, as with Bernard, it was considered a prime benefit of eucharistic celebration.

This strand of thought carried over into the sixteenth century, and before the Protestant conflicts over the presence of Christ's true body in the Eucharist came about, it was a common pastoral/devotional emphasis. One sees it specifically in that most-read of early sixteenth-century writers, Erasmus. As John Payne reminds readers in his book on Erasmus and the sacraments, in Erasmus's treatment of the Eucharist the "emphasis as always is upon the personal and ethical dimension [read social body here] of sacramental participation."[6] Yes,

---

4. Kyle A. Pasewark has published a quite helpful article for thinking through how, in one of the Reformers, the discussion of the body undergirds social and ethical theory: "The Body in Ecstasy: Love, Difference, and the Social Organism in Luther's Theory of the Lord's Supper," *Journal of Religion* 77, no. 4 (October 1997): 511–40.

5. Later famously cited by Luther in "Sermon on the Proper Preparation of the Heart for the Sacramental Reception of the Eucharist" (WA 1:333).

6. John B. Payne, *Erasmus: His Theology of the Sacraments* (Atlanta: John Knox, 1970), 133; see also 131. Payne reads Erasmus as leaning toward the idea that in the 1 Cor. 11 context one is not dealing with the natural body of Christ, but Payne indicates that Erasmus wavered on this

there is union with Christ, but Erasmus emphasized the union of one Christian with another; the Sacrament is individual, but it is also social. Indeed, in his comments in his *Novum Testamentum* on Paul's passage on "discerning the body," Erasmus remarked, "[Paul] injects the mention of the Lord's Supper so that by the memory of that most sacred feast they might be recalled to that seriousness and brotherly fellowship which the Lord exhibited by the distribution of his own body among his disciples."[7] Thus a clear statement and understanding of Paul's emphasis on the body of Christ, which is to be discerned as the social/spiritual body of the church, is certainly au courant as the Protestant discussion got under way.

As the term "body" became problematic among early Protestants, the holding together of the true/natural and spiritual/social body in eucharistic understanding was either affirmed or modified in discussions of the 1 Corinthians material. To see how this happened, we will start with Luther.[8]

Luther

The early Luther shared the opinion of both Bernard and Erasmus. He understood the Eucharist to be primarily social in character; in fact, he thought that the social aspect could, in some sense, direct—indeed empower—its personal use. Luther affirmed Bernard's idea that the joining together of the

---

(132). For further discussion of the point, that Erasmus leaned toward the social/spiritual body interpretation of 1 Cor. 11, see Erika Rummell, *Erasmus' "Annotations on the New Testament": From Philologist to Theologian* (Toronto: University of Toronto Press, 1986).

7. Cited in Payne, *Erasmus*, 131 (the original is in Erasmus, *Erasmus' Annotations on the New Testament: Acts, Romans, I and II Corinthians. Facsimile of the Final Latin Text*, ed. Anne Reeve and M. A. Screech [Leiden: Brill, 1990], 493).

8. Here I will examine Luther's use of the Corinthian material as he related it to the Eucharist. There were four uses Luther made of 1 Cor. 12:12–27: (A) as a proof text for the need for the strong to care for the weak (and/or the honorable for the dishonorable, and how they are to serve and love one another through sharing of gifts) in both the Christian social body and even in the larger society or the "social orders"; (B) as a proof text to exhort the lower classes to keep their places and not aspire to a higher class (or some similar political use); (C) as part of a eucharistic discussion in which the notion of the social/spiritual body of Christ was paramount; and (D) as part of a eucharistic discussion in which the natural body of Christ was paramount, in which "discerning the body" was considered an entirely separate issue from the social/spiritual body discussion of 1 Cor. 12:12–27. This chapter examines only the last two uses. For examples of how Luther used 1 Cor. 12:27 in case A, see, e.g., LW 25:509 (WA 56:514–15); LW 27:59, 359, 393 (WA 40.2:74, 582–83, 606); LW 31:302–3 (WA 2:149); LW 30:124 (WA 12:379); LW 43:120 (WA 23:341); LW 21:98 (WA 32:381), applied here to the relation between husband and wife; LW 13:112 (40.3:544). Examples of case B are much fewer: "To the Christian Nobility," in LW 44:129–30 (WA 6:408–9), uses 1 Cor. 12 to argue against the difference in status between secular and religious. In two cases, Luther used the body analogy to reinforce the immutability of the hierarchical earthly order: LW 46:166 (WA 30.2:112) and LW 12:294–95 (WA 40.2:602).

social body of Christ is such a strong element of eucharistic participation that it can provide the faith needed to partake worthily of the meal.[9] Indeed, much of the thrust of the sermon in which Luther approvingly cited Bernard, the 1518 "Sermon on the Proper Preparation of the Heart for the Sacramental Reception of the Eucharist," was on the role of the church as Christ's spiritual/social body.

A more extended eucharistic analysis by the early Luther is found in his 1519 sermon "The Blessed Sacrament of the Holy and True Body of Christ, and the Brotherhoods." Once again, though Luther recognized the difference between the natural and the spiritual/social body of Christ, the emphasis of the work, quite Erasmian, was on the spiritual/social body. This is Luther's most extended treatment of the 1 Corinthian 10–12 context of the Eucharist. In a lengthy segment on the "significance" of the sacrament,[10] Luther wrote about how the Eucharist "signifies the complete union and the undivided fellowship of the saints." Communion's significance or meaning is the "fellowship of all the saints." To go to the Sacrament, according to Luther, meant "to take part in this fellowship." Reflecting on 1 Corinthians 10:17, Luther stated: "To receive this sacrament in bread and wine, then, is nothing else than to receive a sure sign of this fellowship and incorporation with Christ and all his saints. It is as if a citizen were given a sign, a document, or some other token to assure him that he is a citizen of the city, a member of that particular community. St. Paul says this very thing in I Corinthians 10[:17], 'We are all one bread and one body, for we all partake of one bread and one cup.'"[11] (This explanation does sound quite Zwinglian.)

Luther almost immediately followed this reflection with an explanation of the 1 Corinthians 12 material. The sharing of good and evil, of profit and cost, of having all things in common—such sharing is the significance of the Sacrament. This was, according to Luther, Paul's intention in writing about the body analogy in 1 Corinthians 12: to give the Sacrament a "spiritual explanation." "This comparison," Luther declared, "must be noted if one wishes to understand [the] sacrament." Indeed, Christ's sacrifice of his body on the cross epitomized the significance of the social/spiritual body of Christians,

9. See Luther, "Sermon on the Proper Preparation of the Heart for the Sacramental Reception of the Eucharist" (WA 1:333). Bernard ends the exhortation that Luther affirms with the words, "Go, my brother, and celebrate in my faith."

10. Luther here explained that the Eucharist had three parts: the Sacrament, or external sign (the bread and wine); the significance; and faith. This framework for Luther's eucharistic theology was short lived. For an extended analysis of it, along with further developments, see Kyle Pasewark, *A Theology of Power: Being beyond Domination* (Minneapolis: Fortress, 1993), 58–59, 62.

11. LW 35:50–51 (WA 2:742–43).

and the eucharistic context was set by this understanding for Luther. Luther interpreted the Words of Institution through Paul's body analogy. After reviewing the Words of Institution from chapter 11, Luther commented:

> It is as if he [Christ] were saying, "I am the Head, I will be the first to give myself for you. I will make your suffering and misfortune my own and I will bear it for you, so that you in your turn may do the same for me and for one another, allowing all things to be common property, in me, and with me. And I leave you this sacrament as a sure token of all this, in order that you may not forget me, but daily call to mind and admonish one another by means of what I did and am still doing for you, in order that you may be strengthened, and also bear one another in the same way."[12]

The relation of the eucharistic celebration as described in 1 Corinthians 11 to the social body of the church was clarified by Luther when he explicitly tied the language of discernment to the Christian social body. After making the distinction between natural and spiritual/social body, he claimed that the natural body was present in the Eucharist for the very purpose of signifying that, by participation, Christians were "drawn and changed into the spiritual body." Writing directly on 1 Corinthians 11:29 (on discerning the body), Luther explained the process of discernment, not in relation to the natural body of Christ, but in terms of chapter 12, the spiritual/social body of Christ. Luther ended with this admonition: "Therefore take heed. It is more needful that you discern the spiritual than the natural body of Christ; and faith in the spiritual body is more necessary than faith in the natural body. For the natural body without the spiritual profits us nothing in this sacrament; a change must occur [in the communicant] and be exercised through love."[13] Taking Paul's warning

---

12. LW 35:52, 55 (WA 2:743, 745–46). In the first quote, the German is a bit stronger than "must be noted": "muss man woll mercken." In the second (extended) quote are a couple things to observe in the original: there is no original word used for "property," and it is a bit misleading for it to be there in translation because Luther was dealing with human affections, it seems to me. The joining he described was of souls, not possessions.

13. LW 35:59, 62 (WA 2:749, 751). See also these passages where Luther emphasized the social/spiritual over the natural body: "It is Christ's will, then, that we partake of [the Eucharist] frequently, in order that we may remember him and exercise ourselves in this fellowship according to his example" (LW 35:56 [WA 2:747]); on loss of the Sacrament's power, he says: "All this comes from the fact that they pay more attention in this sacrament to Christ's natural body than to the fellowship, the spiritual body" (LW 35:63 [WA 2:752]). At that time Luther did endorse a symbolic view of the Eucharist that tied the closeness of the spiritual/social body directly to the natural signs of bread and wine as food: "For there is no more intimate, deep, and indivisible union than the union of the food with him who is fed" (LW 35:59 [WA 2:748]). Luther went on to argue how this type of union was superior to other types—nails, glue—and thus served better as a sign. Later Luther vehemently denied the "natural" symbolism of the

to discern the body and giving it a rousing application to the discussion of the social/spiritual body was Luther's strongest statement on this matter.

By 1520, Luther began to emphasize more the individual rather than the social aspect of the Eucharist. At least, he made the social consequence of the Eucharist dependent on the personal (faithful) appropriation of Christ's natural body; hence, he reversed the order. In 1518–19, the social aspect directs the individual; in 1520, the individual directs the social. The works associated with love in the social/spiritual body do not disappear, but they become dependent on faith in the presence of the natural body of Christ, and that faith is now incumbent on individuals and cannot be lodged in the social body. The Sacrament thus became, for Luther, a pledge for individual members.[14]

This development in Luther's thought—the Eucharist as particularly well suited to the individual as an assurance of God's promise of forgiveness, for the presence of the natural body by this time guaranteed the truth of God's promise[15]—took place just as the sacramentarian controversy began to unfold. So, just as Luther was moving to a use of the natural body in the Eucharist as a way to undergird the social body, other theologians began to ask whether the natural body was present at all in or through the elements. This conflict caused Luther to completely overturn his earlier treatment of the Corinthian material. The best example of Luther's new exegetical thrust is found in the 1523 treatise *The Adoration of the Sacrament*.

Luther's use of the Corinthian material occurred in *Adoration* within the context of the debate over the word "is": could the word be taken in its natural sense, or did it have to mean "signify"? This had become important because of the shift in Luther's eucharistic thinking. By 1523, the Eucharist served, for Luther, as a testament that functioned to declare the promise of the forgiveness of sins. For a testament to be effective, its word had to be sure, its promises believable. For Luther, the presence of Christ's natural body guaranteed that

---

Eucharist, arguing that it was the Word, not any natural analogy between sign and thing signified, that tied the bread and wine to the flesh and blood of Christ. By that time, the *primary* meaning of the Eucharist had changed for Luther from one that focused on the social body to one that understood the natural body as the linchpin of eucharistic meaning because it served as a warrant that the Word of God is true. This was discussed in chap. 2 above.

14. For the shift toward individuality in the Eucharist, see Luther's 1523 Maundy Thursday sermon observation in Lenker 11:230 (WA 12:484). Outside the eucharistic context, Luther held on a little longer to the notion that the faith of the church as the social/spiritual body described by Paul in 1 Cor. 12 could benefit the individual and aid one's faith. "The faith of the church comes to the aid of my fearfulness," Luther stated in *Fourteen Consolations*, in LW 42:161–62 (WA 6:131).

15. For one take on this development, see chap. 1 above.

the promises contained in the Eucharist were trustworthy. The word "is" had to be read literally to safeguard the reliability of the testament.

Because of the way the debate had been framed, Luther had to deny that the Words of Institution—and the process of discerning the body—were directly tied to the language of social body that came both before and after Paul's presentation of the Last Supper. To speak of understanding discernment of the body as "participation in" or "incorporation into" the social/spiritual body, or to say that the bread and wine were signs that the "spiritual incorporation is taking place"—such talk was to engage in "clever sophistry,"[16] Luther claimed, even though four years earlier he himself had advocated the same notions that he now condemned in this writing.

Luther's strategy actually involved taking the two possible understandings of Christ's body—natural and spiritual/social—and separating them out in the Corinthian context: chapter 11 refers to the natural body, chapters 10 and 12 refer to the social/spiritual body, and the chapters must remain exegetically distinct. Though Luther admitted that one *might* interpret the chapter 11 material as dealing with the social/spiritual body, that was not good enough. "You have to prove," he wrote, "that it must be interpreted in this way and no other."[17] Luther took this statement to heart, in a way. He discussed the social import of the Eucharist, yet he was clear that the Corinthian material, in dealing with that import, added nothing to the debate over real presence and that Paul's call to discern the body in chapter 11 could not be related to the social body material of chapters 10 and 12.

Zwingli

If the 1 Corinthian trilogy of chapters (10–12) was seen as a problematic source for Luther after 1523, it in many ways became paradigmatic for Zwingli. And although John 6:63, "the flesh profits nothing," and the ascension passage in Acts are important and often commented on by scholars who study Zwingli as a source for his views, it is the Corinthian material that drove his understanding of the Eucharist and enabled him to expand his notion of Christ's presence in the Eucharist.[18]

16. Martin Luther, *The Adoration of the Sacrament*, in LW 36:282 (WA 11:437).

17. LW 36:284 (WA 11:439). Luther was adamant that the passage should not be taken in such a manner. He even made a point of stating that Paul was talking about the body of Christ as a social body in 1 Cor. 12:27, but that Paul was not talking about the body in the same way in 1 Cor. 11. See LW 36:283 (WA 11:437).

18. Historically, scholars have certainly focused on the John and Acts passages. When treating the 1 Corinthians material, however, Zwingli often made statements about the positive role of the

From the beginning, Zwingli's assumption about Christ's body—natural and social—strongly emphasized the natural body. What is more, it was in the eucharistic context that he meditated on that body. So, the difference between Luther and Zwingli was not that Luther ended up emphasizing the natural body and Zwingli the social/spiritual body; rather, it was that the significance of the natural body and its type of presence and power differed for the two. And this difference in viewing the natural body then influenced how the Corinthian social body was to be viewed.

In *Commentary on True and False Religion* (1525), Zwingli wrote about how one should read the words "this is my body" in conjunction with "the flesh profits nothing."[19] This could lead one to the conclusion that the natural body of Christ was not important in the celebration of the Eucharist, according to Zwingli. However, this was not the case. Christ's flesh did profit something—but not in the eating of it; rather, profit was in the recollection of its action. So 1 Corinthians served Zwingli well here because (a) the emphasis is on the commemoration of Christ's death, an act in the natural body that, by faith, is salvific and (b) there is not the direct link between the actual celebration/eating of the Eucharist with the promise of the forgiveness of sins as found in Matthew. It is by faith in "a," Christ's death, that the social/spiritual body of Christ existed—those who "proclaim the Lord's death bear witness by this very fact that they are members of one body"; in regard to "b" above, 1 Corinthians was Zwingli's rationale for viewing the Lord's Supper as a commemoration of Christ's death, not "a remitting of sins."[20]

For Luther (after 1520), the presence of the natural body in the Eucharist was tied to the forgiveness of sins because the body served as guarantee of God's trustworthiness. And since belief that the body was present and eaten was a sign of faith in God's Word, the promise of the forgiveness of sins was effected, according to Luther's mind. For Zwingli, the function of the natural body was its sacrifice for sin, and its presence in the Eucharist added nothing to the certainty of the event of sacrifice. The important point for Zwingli was the

---

body in the Eucharist. In this context, as we shall see, there was more than memorialism. Ulrich Gäbler talks about the "supportive role" the elements of the Eucharist play in the contemplation of faith (Gäbler, *Huldrych Zwingli: His Life and Work*, trans. Ruth C. L. Gritsch [Philadelphia: Fortress, 1986], 137). W. P. Stephens also writes of the supportive role of the Eucharist in faith, especially as it appealed to the senses, which was an important element in Calvin's eucharistic teaching (Stephens, *The Theology of Huldrych Zwingli* [Oxford: Clarendon, 1986], 251–52).

19. Ulrich Zwingli, *Commentary on True and False Religion*, ed. Samuel Macauley Jackson and Clarence Nevin Heller (Durham, NC: Labyrinth, 1981), 228 (SW 3:798). On the page before, Zwingli quoted John 15:5 ("I am the vine"), talking about how Christ is *like* a vine and identifying the language as representational.

20. Zwingli, *Commentary on True and False Religion*, 228 (SW 3:799).

role the event of sacrifice played in the life of faith. Concerning discernment, Zwingli in the 1526 On the Lord's Supper stated: "What Paul has in mind here [1 Cor. 11:29] is that we must all go to the Supper worthily, that is, with a true faith, for those who do not go with a true faith are guilty of the body and blood of Christ, not the body which we eat, but the real [natural] body which Christ gave in death."[21]

Faith in the activity of the natural body, thus, was essential for Zwingli. This activity was recalled in the celebration of the Lord's Supper. And it was not the eating itself that was tied to the remission of sin but the meditation on Christ's work, a bodily work. Brian Gerrish has referred to Zwingli's view as a type of "symbolic memorialism."[22] This certainly is better than thinking of Zwingli's view as a bare memorialism. Still, there may be more to what Zwingli presented than indicated by "symbolic memorialism." For Zwingli, Christ was present to the eye of faith in the Eucharist. But while the natural body was not present, its effects were exhibited. For example, in An Account of the Faith, Zwingli declared: "I believe that in the Holy Eucharist, i.e., the supper of thanksgiving, the true body of Christ is present by the contemplation of faith. This means that they who thank the Lord for the benefits bestowed on us in His Son acknowledge that he assumed true flesh, in it truly suffered, truly washed away our sins by His blood; and thus everything done by Christ becomes as it were present to them by the contemplation of faith."[23] This certainly qualifies how one is to understand Zwingli's interpretation of "the flesh profits nothing."

I think one can argue that, for Zwingli, there is a functional though not substantial presence of Christ's natural body in the Eucharist: one can refer, looking for a word, to a "psychospiritual" presence of Christ's natural body, or perhaps even to a phenomenological presence of his natural body to the consciousness of believers. There is more, I think, to this type of memorialism than Gerrish suggests; and it is certainly more complicated than Zwingli's position is normally made out to be, and perhaps more paradoxical. Perhaps one finds here a drawing out of the tensions of thought in the Erasmian model, a model Zwingli may have had in mind, given his admiration for the humanist.

21. Ulrich Zwingli, On the Lord's Supper, in Zwingli and Bullinger: Selected Translations with Introduction and Notes, ed. G. W. Bromiley (Philadelphia: Westminster, 1953), 231 (SW 4:851).

22. Brian A. Gerrish, The Old Protestantism and the New: Essays on the Reformation Heritage (Chicago: University of Chicago Press, 1982), 128.

23. Ulrich Zwingli, An Account of the Faith of Zwingli, in The Latin Works of Huldreich Zwingli, vol. 2, On Providence and Other Essays, ed. William John Hinke for Samuel McCauley Jackson (Philadelphia: Heidelberg, 1922), 49 (SW 6.2:806).

In his 1526 work, Zwingli then connected the discernment of the natural body's sacrifice to the discernment of the spiritual/social body—but the latter depended on the former for Zwingli. Faith in Christ's sacrifice, according to Zwingli, created the bond that united Christians in one body, and by discerning Christ's bodily work, one was then led to the ethical imperative to discern the social/spiritual body. "Therefore, if we are members of his body," Zwingli averred, "it is most necessary that we should live together as Christians, as Paul says."[24]

Zwingli again made this relation clear in his 1531 *Exposition of the Christian Faith* by speaking of the analogy between symbols and things signified (a move Luther employed in 1519 and later vehemently condemned). First, Zwingli stated that the Eucharist applied to Christ, wherein one discerned that "the Son of God [is] made his own." Second, it applied to the social/spiritual body, as it came into existence as "a true temple and body of the indwelling Holy Spirit." Moreover, a page later, Zwingli wrote about how the sacraments "increase and support faith," especially the Eucharist and especially because the elements reinforced the notion of sustenance.[25] Rather than a bare and simple memorialism, it appears that, in Zwingli, Paul's admonition to "discern the body" took Zwingli along the path of theological development, one cut short, perhaps, by his untimely death at the Battle of Kappel.

John Calvin

To round out our trio of theologians, we now turn to John Calvin. As with Luther and Zwingli, there was development in his thought especially on the notion of Christ's natural body and its role in the Eucharist (to some basic extent, all agreed that the social/spiritual body of Christ was the church). In his first treatment of the Eucharist, as found in his 1536 *Institutes*, Calvin equated receiving the fruits of the Eucharist with having received Christ himself: "In this manner, the body and blood are shown to us in the sacrament [*as if* present in the body]; but in the previous manner [ubiquity, substantial partaking] not at all. By way of teaching, we say he

---

24. Zwingli, *On the Lord's Supper*, 235 (SW 4:858).

25. Zwingli, *An Exposition of Christian Faith*, in Hinke, *Latin Works*, 2:257–59 (*Huldrici Zuinglii Opera*, ed. Melchior Schuler and Johannes Schulthess [Zurich: F. Schulthess, 1841], 57–58). Later, in Bullinger's and Calvin's work on the *Consensus Tigurinus*, Lutherans accused Calvin of dishonesty because they assumed that a document from Zurich would not contain a view of the Eucharist wherein the ritual served to increase faith, because they assumed that Bullinger, heir to Zwingli, would never have really agreed to such a statement. Yet here it is, plainly laid out in Zwingli's work itself.

is in truth and effective working shown forth, but not in nature. By this we obviously mean that the very substance of his body or the true and natural body of Christ is not given there; but all those benefits which Christ has supplied us with in his body."[26]

Many hallmarks of Calvin's mature eucharistic teaching are missing in this passage: true partaking of Christ's body, the role of the Spirit in uniting the Christian's spirit with the true body, the nourishment one receives from union with Christ, and so forth.[27] As Calvin reworked the editions of his *Institutes*, wrote treatises, preached, and produced biblical commentaries, he developed a thorough doctrine of the Eucharist that included all those elements missing in 1536.

By 1546, the time of the publication of his 1 Corinthians commentary, Calvin had clearly moved away from his position in 1536. Indeed, Calvin insisted that the body and the blood of Christ were "really" and "truly" given in the Supper. Real bread represented a real body. Therefore, as Calvin stated, "our souls are fed by the substance of His body, so that we are truly made one with him."[28] So, whereas Calvin believed that the body and blood of Christ were not present in the elements of bread and wine, bread and wine still served as vehicles by which Christians, by the power of the Holy Spirit, partook of the true body of Christ.[29]

Calvin was the only one of the three Protestants under examination who actually wrote a formal commentary on 1 Corinthians 10–12.[30] In his section on this material, Calvin argued against some of the explanations and understandings of Luther—asserting, for example, how "This is my body" could be understood as a figure of speech (as metonymy)—and against some of Zwingli's assertions, condemning, for example, Zwingli's efforts to translate

26. *Inst.* '36, 107 (CO 1:123).

27. For a complete analysis of the ways in which Calvin's 1536 work did not match his mature theology, see Thomas J. Davis, "Calvin's Eucharistic Teaching in the 1536 *Institutes*," chap. 3 in *The Clearest Promises of God: The Development of Calvin's Eucharistic Teaching* (New York: AMS Press, 1995).

28. CNTC 9:246 (CO 49:487).

29. There are both older and newer works that detail Calvin's belief that the Christian does actually commune with the true body and blood of Christ through the vehicle of the Eucharist. This is suggested in John Williamson Nevin, *The Mystical Presence: A Vindication of the Reformed or Calvinistic Doctrine of the Holy Eucharist* (Philadelphia: J. B. Lippincott, 1846; repr., Hamden, CT: Archon Books, 1963); G. P. Hartvelt, *Verum corpus: Een studie over een centraal hoofdstuk uit de avondmaalsleer van Calvijn* (Delft: W. D. Meinema, 1960); several writings of Brian Gerrish, but especially in *Grace and Gratitude: The Eucharistic Theology of John Calvin* (Minneapolis: Fortress, 1993); and Davis, *Clearest Promises of God*.

30. Just like Luther, Calvin used Paul's extended analogy of the body in 1 Cor. 12:12–27 in both a eucharistic context and outside that context. We concentrate here on the eucharistic.

the words "communion in" or "participation in" found in 1 Corinthians 10 as "community" in Christ.[31]

However, Calvin assumed as much as Luther and Zwingli (and Erasmus) that the term "body" referred to both natural and spiritual/social body. How, then, did Calvin relate the notion of discerning the body of Christ in 1 Corinthians 11 to the obviously social contexts of chapters 10 and 12? Calvin commented specifically on discerning the body in chapter 11: "In the Supper God does not cheat the wicked by a mere representation of the body of His Son, but really does hold it out to them." Calvin emphasized that "the body of Christ is *offered* to them." And though Calvin, in his eucharistic theology, thought that the Christian's heart must be lifted to heaven to receive the offer, it was an offer of the natural body of Christ.[32]

Once the fact that the natural body to be discerned was in place, however, Calvin went on, in his commentary on chapter 12, to explicitly link the notion of discernment to the spiritual/social body as well. In a discussion on sharing gifts and upbuilding the social/spiritual body of Christ—in other words, in a discussion of the ethical imperatives demanded by social/spiritual body existence—Calvin made this tie back to chapter 11: "For Christ invests us with this honour, that he wishes to be discerned and recognized, not only in his own Person, but also in his members."[33] Thus Calvin had to deal with the discernment of the natural body because of the theological environment—and because of his religious experience, since he said of the union with the true body of Christ in the Eucharist that he claimed to experience, "I am overwhelmed by the depth of this mystery."[34] Yet he did connect the notion of discernment back to the Pauline emphasis, that the celebration of the Eucharist and the discernment of Christ's body were related to the workings of the spiritual/social body.

What we see in Calvin, therefore, is an attempt to remain true to a particular set of texts—the Corinthian material—while also remaining true to his broader reading of Scripture, by which he came to believe that Christ in body and blood was truly offered through the signs of bread and wine, and true to his experience of union with Christ. While distinguishing between the natural and the social/spiritual body of Christ, Calvin obviously believed the two should be held together (Calvin's famous "distinction without separation").

31. CNTC 9, see passim his comments on chaps. 10, 11, and 12 and in CO 49.
32. CNTC 9:252, 254 (CO 49:492, 493). It seems to me that the original is somewhat more emphatic than the translation for the first quote: "sed re ipsa exhibet."
33. CNTC 9:264 (CO 49:501).
34. CNTC 11:210 (CO 51:227).

A Comparison of Eucharistic Function

Indeed, all three Reformers knew that the idea of the body of Christ could be applied to both the notion of the natural body and the concept of the social/ spiritual body. The context of Scripture controlled which understanding of body was to be used for the Reformers. But in the case of 1 Corinthians 11, with its account of the Last Supper in such an obviously eucharistic context, the question of "discerning the body" became a matter not simply of contextual exegesis but of eucharistic theology as well. The question became, how does one decide what body is to be discerned when there is a eucharistic tradition (1 Cor. 11) embedded within the context of a social/spiritual body discussion (1 Cor. 10 and 12)?

For Luther, once his eucharistic theology had developed beyond the emphases of his early thinking about the sacrament (certainly the case by 1523), and after he had begun to engage in polemics with other Protestants about the proper understanding of Christ's presence in the Eucharist, the notion of order became quite important. Luther came to believe that discernment of the social/spiritual body was of little significance unless one *first* discerned the natural and true body of Christ; in other words, physical eating (of the true body in, with, and under the bread and wine) had to precede spiritual eating[35] (the eating that led to participation in and care for the social/spiritual body and its activities). In Luther's mind, God works through material vehicles to achieve spiritual results. It is true that Luther held to a theology of the Word. But it is nowhere clearer than in his eucharistic theology that Luther thought the Word always to be embodied: the Word itself had an embodied character.[36] The recognition of that Word—and its truth—controlled everything else for Luther, especially the understanding and working of the social/spiritual body (the church as the body of Christ).[37]

35. See LW 146, which is from *Against the Heavenly Prophets in the Matter of Images and Sacraments* (WA 18:136). See also Pasewark, *Theology of Power*, 92–96; and Brian A. Gerrish, "Discerning the Body: Sign and Reality in Luther's Controversy with the Swiss," *Journal of Religion* 68, no. 3 (July 1988): 379.

36. See chap. 2 in this book. God, according to Luther, is omnipresent; God is everywhere. God is also transcendent. But, as David Steinmetz has said, "The transcendence of God is not equivalent to his absence. On the contrary, transcendence means that, while God is present in every creature that surrounds me, his presence is inaccessible to me apart from his Word" (Steinmetz, *Luther in Context*, 24). And in the case of the Eucharist, according to Luther, the Word points to the real body of Christ in the eucharistic elements, and thus Christ's presence is accessible thereby: the incarnate Word made available by the spoken Word.

37. Some have argued that Luther lost a sense of the church as the body of Christ because of the way he concentrated on the natural body in his eucharistic theology. See the classic statement on this in Paul Althaus, *The Theology of Martin Luther*, trans. Robert C. Schultz

For Zwingli, it was the notion of an inward eating, faith, that controlled whatever meaning the outward celebration of the Eucharist would have. He allowed that there could and should be a connection between the two for Christians (though not intrinsically so). In his 1531 *Exposition of the Faith*, one sees the emphasis on order: the inward eating provides for proper understanding and appropriation of the outer, and the inward must precede the outer. "To eat the body of Christ spiritually is equivalent to trusting with heart and soul upon the mercy and goodness of God through Christ. . . . You eat the body of Christ spiritually . . . every time your soul puts the anxious question: 'How are you to be saved?' . . . When you comfort yourself in Christ . . . then you spiritually eat his body."[38] To eat spiritually is to have faith.

After declaring the commemorative function of the Eucharist, Zwingli goes on to say: "But to whom does the [Lord's Supper] bear witness? To believers and unbelievers alike. For whether they receive it or not, it testifies to all that which is of the power of the sacrament, the fact that Christ suffered. But only to the faithful and pious does it testify that he suffered for us. For it is only those who have been taught inwardly by the Spirit to know the mystery of the divine goodness who can know and believe that Christ suffered for us. It is they alone who receive Christ."[39]

So, even though by this time there was some notion in Zwingli that there can be a confluence of outward and inward, that the inward eating of faith could coincide with the outward receipt of the Sacrament, it was not necessarily so; and even if there was some talk of how the Sacrament strengthens faith,[40] the presence of an inward faith and spiritual eating was still primary in the order of meaning. The recognition of the social/spiritual body of Christ (the true church), in its testifying role (constituted through the work of the Spirit), came first, according to the above quote. Once so constituted, then it was possible to recognize the receipt of Christ's natural body, but it was receipt only in the sense of remembering that, in the body, "Christ suffered for us." It was the recognition of a deed, really, rather than a perception of presence.

In some important ways Calvin agreed with Zwingli on certain aspects of his eucharistic emphases (such as the confinement of Christ's human body in heaven after the ascension, a point to which we will return). Yet in terms

---

(Philadelphia: Fortress, 1966), 321–22. He did not. Again, see chap. 2 above, as well as the work cited therein by Dennis Alan Laskey, "In Faith and Fervent Love: The Concept of *Communio* in Luther's Understanding of the Lord's Supper" (PhD diss., Lutheran School of Theology at Chicago, 1983).

38. Ulrich Zwingli, *An Exposition of the Faith*, in Bromiley, *Zwingli and Bullinger*, 258–59.

39. Ibid., 260–61.

40. Ibid., 263. See also Gerrish, "Discerning the Body," 386.

of how one discerns the body, Calvin lined up more closely with Luther. By 1541, Calvin had come to the conclusion that, in the Eucharist, one received first Christ and then his benefits (including the benefit of belonging to his spiritual/social body). In the *Short Treatise on the Holy Supper*, Calvin insisted, "This name and title of body and blood is given to them [bread and wine] because they are as it were instruments by which the Lord distributes them [Christ's body and blood] to us." The signs, he argued, "cannot be at all separated from their reality and substance." And what is that substance? "The substance of the sacraments is the Lord Jesus." Christ must be received in order to gain his benefits.[41] But why? The question of order is actually dependent on the answer to another question: what is the role of Christ's natural body in salvation?

This question may bring the most weight to bear as we look at the Reformers' exegesis of the discernment passage. There may have been some disagreements over the exact interpretation of the body of Christ as a trope for the social/spiritual body of the church. Yet it was their understanding of the natural body of Christ and its role in salvation (and thus in the Eucharist) that fundamentally directed their exegesis of the discernment passage.

And this is problematic. As Brian Gerrish has pointed out, "What, after all, *is* the reality of the real presence? Luther and Zwingli both spoke as though everyone knew what was meant by the glorified body of Christ, the main question being where to find it—in the bread or seated at the right hand of the Father."[42]

The "where" question of Christ's body after the resurrection seems to be easily answered in the Reformers: For Luther, it was in heaven, yes, but because of its sharing in the divine nature, Christ's body was also ubiquitous, therefore meaning that it was in the bread of the Sacrament, just as the Word said. For Zwingli, Christ's body was in heaven, separated from believers, and believers neither had access to it nor need of it. For Calvin, it was in heaven, separated from believers on earth, yet there was a bridge (the Holy Spirit) by which believers could be joined to that life-giving body. But indeed, determining the *reality* of that body was a different matter.

While not addressing this question in terms of metaphysics, it is possible to talk around the question in terms of function. Whether there was a satisfactory answer to the "is-ness" of the resurrected and glorified body in the thought of the Reformers,[43] at least in terms of being able to fully define and explain it,

41. *Short Treatise*, 514, 515, 513 (CO 5:439, 439, 437).
42. Gerrish, "Discerning the Body," 395.
43. Indeed, at least in the case of Luther, Margaret Miles has said, "Luther neglected to draw the careful articulations of earlier thinkers of the exact metaphysical status of the human

one can look at the role of the body of Christ in salvation. Thus one can come to understand, perhaps, the Reformers' exegetical and theological concerns when dealing with passages like 1 Corinthians on discerning the body.

Luther's theology greatly relied on the notion of the incarnation as the embodiment of the Word of God, and this idea was largely tied to his eucharistic thought. As Adolf von Harnack long ago noted, "The Eucharist must be conceived of as the parallel to and guarantee for the Incarnation." Furthermore, Paul Althaus, along with others, has emphasized that Christ's "humanity is the place to which God summons us," and then Althaus points out that in Luther's thought God and salvation are mediated specifically through the humanity of Christ. Thus if God chose to reveal Godself through the humanity of Christ, then that is the only place where God may be found.[44] Thus Luther believed that Christ was mediated through the human body and continued to be so mediated. Ubiquity was possible by the communication of properties (the Chalcedonian solution to the problem of two natures within one person), wherein Christ's humanity shares the divine ability to be ubiquitous. Thus when Luther spoke of Christ's presence in the Eucharist, referring to his natural body, he meant that resurrected body, once and always the mediatorial principal of salvation, able to share in the divine nature to be present to believers everywhere at all times. That body, for Luther, was the sign of the surety of God's promises of forgiveness. That was the body that, for Luther, had to be discerned, first and foremost.

Zwingli's theology was not incarnationally centered in the same way as Luther's. Indeed, his interest in Christ focused primarily on the crucifixion as a satisfaction for sin, and Christ's natural body, insofar as it was important, served as the locus of divine action. Indeed, it has been suggested that Zwingli downplayed the association that might have been made between the Eucharist and the resurrected Christ. Instead, by "concentrating upon the narrative of the death of Christ, Zwingli feels enabled to make ethical points which might lose their force in the light of the resurrection." Indeed, one scholar has gone so far

---

body and its integration with the human personality because of his strong interest in a simplified anthropology that reinforced his interpretation of the justification event" (Miles, "'The Rope Breaks When It Is Tightest': Luther on the Body, Consciousness, and the Word," *Harvard Theological Review* 77, nos. 3–4 [July/October 1984]: 244).

44. Adolf von Harnack, *History of Dogma*, trans. Neil Buchanan from the 3rd German ed., in 7 vols. (Gloucester, MA: Peter Smith, 1976), 7:263; Althaus, *Theology of Martin Luther*, 22, 183, and chap. 4 on the notion of the hidden God who reveals Godself in the Word (as Jesus Christ); Heinrich Bornkamm, *Luther's World of Thought*, trans. Martin H. Bertram (St. Louis: Concordia, 1958), 88, 98; Gerrish, *Old Protestantism and the New*, chap. 8; and Steinmetz, *Luther in Context*, chap. 3.

as to suggest that, in Zwingli, the symbols of bread and wine "have become symbols of a symbol—that is, of Christ's death as a sacrificial deed."[45]

If one refers back to Zwingli's *Exposition of Faith* quoted previously, one reads, "But to whom does the [Lord's Supper] bear witness? To believers and unbelievers alike. For whether they receive it or not, it testifies to all that which is of the power of the sacrament, the fact that Christ suffered." It only had an effect, again as cited previously, when one is able to add to Christ's suffering the words "for us." In terms of Christ's natural body, then, the suggestion is that the function was to serve as the place where God accomplished salvation, a once-and-for-all event. The natural body, as such, then had served its purpose, and its role was fulfilled. In terms of the salvation process, then, the natural body's role belonged to the past, according to Zwingli, not to the present and not under the elements of bread and wine.

Finally, what of Calvin? In this regard, his theology stood closer to Luther, though there were points of contact with Zwingli. For Calvin, the natural body of Christ was the means by which God mediated righteousness to the believer. If one looks in his commentary on John, one finds the following analysis: Righteousness resides in God alone. Christ, as part of the Trinity, shares in that righteousness. Christ, as fully human and divine and because of the principle of the communication of properties, shares that righteousness in his whole person, human and divine. And then Christ, as incarnate Word of God, through his humanity, shares the righteousness of God with humanity.[46] In this regard, the function of the human body was to convey salvation, and that on a continuing basis; hence, in Calvin's way of thinking, there was the need for the Christian to be in union with that body in the present. The commentary on John also emphasized that the Christian had to partake of the substance of Christ, for in it "have all the parts of salvation [been] accomplished."[47]

But though the Christian had to truly partake of the body and blood of Christ and do so in the present rather than remember a past act, Calvin insisted that, as a human body, Christ's natural body must remain in heaven (as Zwingli so insisted). Hence Calvin developed the notion that the Christian must be raised to heaven, for Christ's body is there. But for Calvin this was no barrier. As he wrote in his 1 Corinthians commentary, "The Lord will carry out what you understand the words to mean; that His body, which you do not see at all, is spiritual food for you."[48] According to Calvin, this was ac-

45. Alister E. McGrath, "The Eucharist: Reassessing Zwingli," *Theology* 93 (January/February 1990): 16; Gerrish, "Discerning the Body," 385.
46. CNTC 4:167–68 (CO 47:153).
47. CNTC 4:175 (CO 47:159).
48. CNTC 9:247 (CO 49:488).

complished by the work of the Holy Spirit, who descended in the act of the Eucharist to raise believers up.

Calvin tied his concerns about the presence of the true body (at least its function) to the Zwinglian concern listed above. It was the natural body of Christ that served as the mediatorial principle (that was its function, according to Calvin, who like Luther did not really go into detail about the reality of the glorified body in heaven), the body with which the Christian had to be in union. Yet Calvin at least in part echoed Zwingli's emphasis when he stated, for the first time in his 1542 *Institutes*, "We do not eat Christ duly and beneficially except as crucified, when in a living sense we grasp the efficacy of his death."[49] Thus though not confined to the past, the event of crucifixion weighs heavily in Calvin's understanding of the role of the natural body, and certainly in the more-open way that Zwingli thought of it than in the more-hidden way that Luther viewed the natural body on the cross.

Conclusion

With all that said, it is obvious that there were significant differences among Luther, Zwingli, and Calvin on the question of discerning the body, as there were along so many other fronts. What is more, points of interpretation were affected by the development in their thought—for Zwingli's position developed from 1525 to 1531 as much as Luther's from 1519 to 1523, as did Calvin's from 1536 to the 1560s. Yet it is important to observe that the text of Scripture itself did compel all three, on a highly contentious issue, to at least nod in directions of some commonality. What is more, by paying attention to how they dealt with particular problems of exegesis in their fullness, we can at least, at some points, see movements of thought that belie the sometimes too-naked reading of their theological treatises. Luther, at least the early Luther, was concerned with the social/spiritual body (and continued to be concerned even in his later works, though in a modified form buried in a structure of eucharistic meaning that valued social/spiritual body only within a hierarchical theology of body).[50] Zwingli, particularly as his thought developed, came more and more

49. CO 1:993.

50. Again, Luther's emphasis on the communal aspect of the Supper did not disappear but was subsumed under a hierarchy of meaning dictating that the natural body of Christ had to take precedence over the social/spiritual in order for the social/spiritual to exist. Yet even the natural body was itself tied to the power of the Word of God. Kyle Pasewark argues that it was within the context of the social/spiritual body that remembrance occurred, according to Luther; however, remembrance was not a private act but an act of the church, indeed, an act of proclamation, or preaching (Pasewark, "Body in Ecstasy," 533). Thus what started with the

to consider the role of the natural body in the Eucharist, at least in how the Sacrament symbolized the role of that body in the great drama of salvation. And the talk of discerning the body pushed him to wrestle with the notion of what body was there in the celebration to be discerned (his development of the notion that the congregation may be signified as the body of Christ in the eucharistic act).

Calvin mediated between the two, arguing that discernment had to do with both of the recognized expressions of Christ's body, natural and social. And if one reads Calvin's own religious experience aright, it is an altogether fitting exegetical strategy whereby he tried to stay true both to what he found in Scripture and to what he found within his own heart. Thus as we have seen, though he read into the discernment verse of 1 Corinthians 11 a necessity to recognize the true and natural (whatever that really means) body of Christ (as a response to his maturing theology and his religious experience of union with Christ), he did tie the social/spiritual body back into the exegesis by the next chapter of 1 Corinthians.

Yes, there were hermeneutical circles at work in the exegesis of the sixteenth-century Protestants. Yet there is—despite that fact or because of it—much to be learned by tracing the contours of such circles, seeing where they overlap. Without carrying the metaphor too far, perhaps we can learn as well to see the concentric circles lying within the eucharistic ones, whereby we may plunge more deeply into the center of these theologians' thoughts in order to see the theological heart from whence their eucharistic circles emanate.

Word in the Eucharist ends with the Word. This makes for an interesting point of contact with Zwingli, if Carl M. Leth is right, when he says of Zwingli and the Supper, "The celebration of the Supper in the context of [the] preaching service suggests the Supper as a form of proclamation of the Word. At the least, Zwingli understands the role of the Word—as instrument of God's action—to be powerfully transformative" (Leth, "Signs and Providence: A Study of Zwingli's Sacramental Theology" [PhD diss., Duke University, 1992], 76). This insight also relates Zwingli to Calvin insofar as one allows for the notion that Word and Sacrament together make up a "word-sign," a verbal/visible combination that works together as an instrument of God's power. This pulls Zwingli a little closer to Calvin's "symbolic instrumentalism" (Gerrish's phrase, *Old Protestantism and the New*, 128).

10

HARDENED HEARTS, HARDENED WORDS

Calvin, Beza, and the Trajectory of Signification

Surprise! The Same Old Calvin Stereotype

For several years now, I have been interested in how stereotypes about John Calvin became so stubbornly entrenched in the American consciousness.[1] On occasion, I have had people try to correct me about this stereotyping, commenting that much progress has been made in Calvin research and that the cold, rational Calvin of predestinarian syllogism and system has been replaced by a kinder, gentler Calvin, or at least by the Calvin that serves as the fountainhead of all good American things.[2] Yet despite the—admittedly

---

1. See Thomas J. Davis, "Images of Intolerance: John Calvin in Nineteenth-Century History Textbooks," *Church History* 65, no. 2 (June 1996): 234–48; idem, "Rhetorical War and Reflex: Calvinism in Nineteenth-Century Popular Fiction and Twentieth-Century Criticism," *Calvin Theological Journal* 33, no. 2 (November 1998): 443–56.

2. For a kinder and gentler Calvin, I might refer to Randall Zachman's "Theologian in the Service of Piety: A New Portrait of John Calvin," *Christian Century*, April 23–30, 1997, 413–18, but the responses by readers of the *Century* were quick and negative (*Christian Century*, May 7, 1997, 437). For a font of all good things American, one might point to William Jackman, *History of the American Nation* (Chicago: Hamming, 1913), 2:394, who states, "He that will not honor the memory and respect the influence of Calvin, knows but little of the origin of American liberty." One would have to say that the portrayal of Calvin in general history courses,

halting—advance of Calvin scholarship in the twentieth and early twenty-first centuries,[3] there still remains embedded a strong cultural aversion to Calvin that seems to have taken on a life of its own. However much we Calvin scholars might wish that our work would eventually make its way into the broader streams of Reformation scholarship, which then enters the great river of the historical enterprise, I am afraid that, instead, we run off into quiet pools, at least during those times when we are not paddling upstream against the current. The occasional historical slap on the back for Calvin and the dedication of a few hundred Calvin scholars seems to me to have done little to nuance the overwhelmingly negative image of Calvin.

By way of quick example of how close at hand the stereotypical image is, one can look at the entry on "Science" in the generally quite helpful *Oxford Encyclopedia of the Reformation*. There, toward the end of the informative essay, one finds this introduction of a historical character: "Next to Bruno, the other natural philosopher burned for his ideas in the sixteenth century was Michael Servetus (1509/11–1553), condemned to the flames by Calvin for his antitrinitarian views." Then, while insisting that Servetus was not executed for his scientific views, the author concludes, "Yet both [Bruno and Servetus] exemplify the complex interweaving of science and religion in the first century following the Reformation."[4] The bulk of the author's argument here is that Protestantism was no more open to science than was Catholicism, and the implication seems to be that there is some connection between the burned heretic and his being a scientist.

One could spend some time taking apart the statement made about Calvin executing Servetus: it would include a number of items that involve examining the trial itself, the role of Calvin, the authority of the city government, the especially erroneous notion that Calvin was quick to throw Servetus to the flames (Calvin actually argued for a more humane method of execution and, as often happened, lost the argument with the council). But let the statement

---

however, was much more influenced by John Fiske, generally recognized as the greatest popularizer of history America has known (see *Dictionary of American Biography* [New York: Scribner, 1946–58], s.v. "Fiske, John"), who stated that Calvin was, "among all the great benefactors of mankind, . . . the least attractive. . . . [Calvin was] the constitutional lawyer of the Reformation, with vision as clear, with head as cool, with soul as dry as any old solicitor in rusty black that ever dwelt in chambers. . . . His sternness was that of the judge who dooms a criminal to the gallows" (Fiske, *The Beginnings of New England, or, the Puritan Theocracy in Its Relation to Civil Liberty* [Boston: Houghton, Mifflin, 1889], 57–59).

3. Here see the assessment in Heiko Oberman, *The Two Reformations: The Journey from the Last Days to the New World*, ed. Donald Weinstein (New Haven: Yale University Press, 2003), 99–101.

4. Paula Findlen, "Science," in *The Oxford Encyclopedia of the Reformation*, ed. Hans Hillerbrand et al., 4 vols. (New York: Oxford University Press, 1996), 3:27.

stand for what it is: a blunt correlation of Calvin with religious executions. That would be no great jump. After all, as Heiko Oberman reminds us, "Calvin's condemnation of Servetus and of Sebastian Castellio receives more attention than all the other thousands of sixteenth-century martyrdoms combined."[5]

One could reasonably argue that part of the reason Calvin is seen, historically, as quick to consign heretics to the flame is because his theology—which people commonly assume centers around predestination in its most dreadful possible expression—supposedly has God quick to consign most of humanity to the flames. God hardens hearts, and then, with hard words, Calvin supports this God of decrees who condemns sinners to damnation. There develops a type of one-to-one correspondence among predestination, religious persecution grounded in the very God of the doctrine, and Calvin. Predestination becomes the overriding symbol of Calvin, who then becomes the overriding symbol of religious persecution.

I argue that doctrine and person work together as literal signs of all that was bad about the Reformation, literal in the sense of a linear connection, straight from sign to reality; indeed, sign and reality collapse into one another, and one thus has the problem of dealing with, in any large cultural sense, "John Calvin," not as historical person but as literal sign. "Martin Luther" works in much the same manner, in that he came to signify (and still does) freedom.[6] And if the fountainhead and theological master of the Reformed tradition (at least, according to many) is so historically straitjacketed, one can be sure that Theodore Beza and others who follow, when dealt with at all, will be treated even worse. Or in the case of those trying to free Calvin from his negative stereotypes, the course of action is to push those negative images to those who follow Calvin and blame *them* for the perceived defects of the Calvinist theological system.[7]

What has happened to Calvin and Beza in terms of historical image is symptomatic of larger trends within Western culture, I argue. And these trends

5. Oberman, *Two Reformations*, 98.
6. On this, see esp. A. G. Dickens and John M. Tonkin, *The Reformation in Historical Thought* (Cambridge, MA: Harvard University Press, 1985), 119–49.
7. See, e.g., Ernst Bizer, *Frühorthodoxie und Rationalismus* (Zurich: EVZ-Verlag, 1963); and Hans Emil Weber, *Reformation, Orthodoxie und Rationalismus*, 2 vols. (Gütersloh: C. Bertelsmann, 1937–51). Brian G. Armstrong, *Calvinism and the Amyraut Heresy: Protestant Scholasticism and Humanism in Seventeenth-Century France* (Madison: University of Wisconsin Press, 1969), sums up this school of thought and its negative judgments: "One may lay much of the blame for scholasticism at [Beza's] feet" (38). James B. Torrance also places the blame on Beza for orthodoxy's departure from Calvin in regard to the double decree being read as the heart of orthodoxy (Torrance, "The Concept of Federal Theology—Was Calvin a Federal Theologian?" in *Calvinus Sacrae Scripturae Professor / Calvin as Confessor of Holy Scripture*, ed. Wilhelm H. Neuser [Grand Rapids: Eerdmans, 1994], 19).

also help to explain the differences between Calvin and Beza (and the later Reformed tradition) as well. In *The Unaccommodated Calvin*, Richard Muller has warned against the hazards of picking up general intellectual trends in the sixteenth century and applying them to Calvin as a way to "understand" him (through the category of humanism, for example, claiming it as a lens for reading Calvin without the textual and contextual evidence to show that Calvin was actually moved by humanist principles in particular ways),[8] and this is good counsel. Yet one must also recognize that there is a social nature to human existence and that, when there can be shown to be basic shifts in the culture, those shifts do affect people, whether or not they are aware of it.

What I argue is that a basic change in the orientation of signification occurred, a change that perhaps can be seen as early as the thirteenth century, but which did not begin the process of gaining cultural hegemony until the fifteenth and sixteenth centuries, a change that in later centuries was reinforced. Signification made a shift toward the literal, where direct lines were drawn between sign and thing signified, and both were drawn into closest relationship until one observes almost a collapse of distance between sign and thing signified. Among other things, this meant that a sign, if it was to have a chance of seeming culturally authoritative, must mean only one thing. To show where this shift first began to exhibit substantial consequences, one must for now move away from Calvin and Beza and enter the world of Renaissance art.

A Picture Is Worth a Thousand Words

The shift I propose—a move toward literal signification as authoritative for what should be considered "real"—gained cultural dominance and gathered momentum and validation with the works of the Renaissance artists.[9] The artistic context of this shift can be examined under four categories: First, one can illustrate the collapse of sign and thing signified in the work of Albrecht Dürer and others. Second, one can find the theory that underlies much of Renaissance art in Leon Battista Alberti's *On Painting*. Third, one can examine the meaning of this significatory shift in Leonardo da Vinci. And fourth, one can see the implications of this shift especially in the area of science.

8. Richard A. Muller, *The Unaccommodated Calvin: Studies in the Foundation of a Theological Tradition* (Oxford: Oxford University Press, 2000), 9–10.

9. The emphasis here is on gathering momentum and validated literal signification. It is not to say that literal signification was not at work before this time; it certainly was. But it was one way of understanding signs alongside others (and often considered to be an inferior way), and it was not elevated to the position of being "truest." This changes when—even before science—artistic techniques show results that could not have been achieved without an emphasis on the literal.

Albrecht Dürer, Renaissance Art, and the Trajectory of Apocalyptic Art: Visual Signifying as a Linear Exercise

Albrecht Dürer was the great artist of the Northern Renaissance.[10] During the course of his life (1471–1528), he achieved great fame and was often considered to be the greatest artist outside Italy. He is counted as the greatest printmaker of his time, and his woodcuts graced many Bibles. Dürer ended up writing books on measurement (1525) and human proportion (published soon after his death in 1528).

When much of his development was still ahead of him, what brought him early fame, his woodcuts on the Apocalypse (1498), at least in part show the influence of his visit to Italy earlier in the decade, which turned his interest to form, measurement, and proportion.[11] What I want to focus on is the literal nature of the work (though that is not the whole of the work) brought about by Dürer's attempt to render the sign so that it artistically and in a linear manner captured the reality. I will do so by speaking a little about one of these pictures; then I will compare it to some predecessors and to some that came afterward to show a trajectory of literalness. (This literalness is meant in the sense that a sign can mean only one thing, and in the absence of a reason to make that one thing symbolic or metaphorical or allegorical, it is the literal meaning that is represented in the most literal and graphically true manner.)

For purposes of simplicity, I will focus on the first woodcut from Revelation itself, a woodcut that represented material from Revelation 1:12–16 (see

10. For standard works on Dürer, see Erwin Panofsky, *The Life and Art of Albrecht Dürer*, 4th ed. (Princeton, NJ: Princeton University Press, 1955); Marcel Brion, *Dürer: L'homme et son oeuvre* (Paris: Somogy, 1960); and Christopher White, *Dürer: The Artist and His Drawings* (London: Phaidon, 1971). For a recent work that focuses on the specifically religious context of Dürer's work, see David Hotchkiss Price, *Albrecht Dürer's Renaissance: Humanism, Reformation, and the Art of Faith* (Ann Arbor: University of Michigan Press, 2003). In terms of Dürer's importance, Fedja Anzelewski has said, "All artistic inspiration of this period [in Germany] . . . turned to the genius of Dürer as its point of departure and reached its culmination in this artist's work. . . . He is the only German artist to embody all the aspirations of his time and who, beyond the boundaries of his own country, served as an example to his contemporaries and to future generations" (Anzelewski, *Dürer and His Time: An Exhibition from the Collection of the Print Room, State Museum, Berlin Stiftung Preussischer Kulturbesitz* [Washington, DC: Smithsonian Press, 1967], 29).

11. On this, see Panofsky, *Albrecht Dürer*, 55–57, who thinks the Apocalypse woodcuts "work" because they balance the naturalistic technique with the supernatural intent. Michael Levy, however, sees it a bit differently: "The visions of St. John are expressed with a determined literalness that does not always succeed as art but is part of Dürer's serious intention" (Levy, *Dürer* [New York: Norton, 1964], 46). Also, Francis Russell emphasizes the importance of Dürer's work in Italy as laying the groundwork for his Apocalypse art, especially as it related to perspective (while not quite mastering human proportion), in *The World of Dürer, 1471–1528* (New York: Time, 1967), 67.

Figure 1

fig. 1). The picture was meant to capture the following: "I saw seven golden lampstands, and in the midst of the lampstands one like a son of man, clothed with a long robe and with a golden girdle round his breast; his head and his hair were white as white wool, white as snow; his eyes were like a flame of fire, his feet were like burnished bronze, refined as in a furnace, and his voice was like the sound of many waters; in his right hand he held seven stars, from his mouth issued a sharp two-edged sword, and his face was like the sun shining in full strength."[12]

Certain things can be said about the work that marks it as Renaissance:[13] there is a sense of perspective; both Christ and John are drawn in proportion and are proportional one to the other; there is a sense of detail in the drawing

12. For all the woodcuts discussed in this chapter, see Kenneth A. Strand, *Woodcuts to the Apocalypse in Dürer's Time: Albrecht Dürer's Woodcuts Plus Five Other Sets from the 15th and 16th Centuries* (Ann Arbor, MI: Ann Arbor Publishers, 1968). "Christ among the Candlesticks" is woodcut no. 2, on p. 13, which is fig. 1 here.

13. See Panofsky, *Albrecht Dürer*, 55, in relation to the Apocalypse woodcuts; and 273 for the artist's relationship to Renaissance art generally. See, however, 273–74 for the ways in which Dürer did not follow Renaissance art theory—especially having to do with a literalness of representation that rejected the Renaissance tendency to idealize the human form.

Figure 2 Figure 3

of the hands and the feet. But more than those traditional Renaissance art markers, it is the literal rendering of the seemingly figurative language (after all, similes are used as well as metaphors) of the text that is of interest. When looking at the woodcut, one sees that Christ has sunbeams coming from his head, flames shooting from the sides of his eyes, and a sword proceeding from his mouth. One can easily see how the image literally reflects the words of Revelation 1, and one can imagine that the picture reinforced a literal, rather than symbolic, reading of the text.

For example, the notion of the two-edged sword could mean a variety of things. Based on what follows chapter 1, what is figured by the image of the two-edged sword seems to be the fact that Christ speaks words of both comfort and condemnation. The question is, how does one artistically render such an image, whose meaning clearly goes beyond the literal? Or does one? Or instead, does the literal text trump the possibility of an overflow of meaning?

Dürer opted for the literal, as is clear. The realism of Dürer's woodcut can be seen especially if one compares them to earlier woodcuts on the same theme. For example, if one looks to the work that appeared in two earlier German Bibles (Cologne Bible, fig. 2, and Grüningen Bible, fig. 3), illustrated around the time of Dürer's birth by unknown artists, one sees the final remnants of a style more interested in type than realism.[14] There are the obvious differences: size is used symbolically, so that Christ is much bigger than John. There is not much interest in detail in terms of capturing the finer points of

14. See Strand, *Woodcuts*, woodcuts 16 and 17, on p. 28, duplicated here as figs. 2 and 3.

human physiology: neither feet nor hands look particularly realistic (indeed, Christ's hand is missing a finger in fig. 3). The John figure in one picture has a halo behind his head to indicate his saintliness, but it is achieved by having his head turn at an impossible angle to look at Christ (fig. 3). The other John figure faces Christ, but since John needs the obligatory halo, it is placed in front of his face; so as one looks at the woodcut, one sees the back of John's head as he faces a halo, which apparently cuts everything from John's view; the artist arranged the drawing with part of Christ's gown disappearing behind the full halo (see fig. 2).

Moreover, there is no interest in trying to convey the realism of the description of Christ: where Dürer goes for sunbeams and flaming eyes, these artists are content to use the traditional halo, the plate behind the head. There is a sword, but it is drawn in such a way that it does not start until Christ's beard has ended. In both cases, the sword looks eerily like a modern-day tie with a square knot and a tapered extension. Indeed, in one picture, the stars are held by the left hand rather than by the right, as the text says. And so, though these woodcuts illustrate the words of Revelation 1, it is clear that a thoroughgoing literalism was not considered necessary (if the artists even had the ability to portray such literal realism). And the sword is separated from Christ's mouth; it is close enough to illustrate that Christ's word is a two-edged sword but far enough away so as not to confuse sign with what is being signified by it. And this is the point: when comparing the two pictures, one can literally see that Dürer has collapsed the distance between sign and thing signified.

If we look at the illustrations from Luther's Bibles, it is clear that there we have the heirs of Dürer's outlook,[15] which was the developing outlook of an age, both by artists and by thinkers, and speakers and writers. The 1522 New Testament, the so-called September Bible, was illustrated probably by Lucas Cranach (see fig. 4); editions came out in 1523 and 1524 illustrated by Hans Burgkmaier (see fig. 5); and the first edition of Luther's complete Bible—1534—may have been illustrated by Cranach, but other artists have been suggested. At this point the illustrations all conform more to the Renaissance style, with matters of proportion, size, and detail forefronted. But what sets them apart from Dürer at this point—or at least shows the continued trajectory toward the literal—are their attempts to convey what on the surface appears to be a figurative text in a literal fashion, pressing to the point where it seems impossible to hold figurative and literal together.

15. Ibid., woodcuts 33 and 57, on pp. 38 and 62, respectively, duplicated here as figs. 4 and 5. Details on publication history taken from ibid., 37.

This involves how to maintain a human face to Jesus while remaining true to the words that speak of a sword from his mouth, face shining as the sun, and eyes like a flame of fire. In all cases, the sword is now firmly planted within Jesus's mouth; the attempt to show his face shining as a sun and his eyes flaming with fire results in a stretching of the human form that obliterates it (fig. 5). In figure 4, the artist has placed the flames further from the eyes and moved the sun effect to the edge of Jesus's face, rather than having the beams coming straight from his face; but the

Figure 4

Figure 5

effect is to make the head of Jesus look as if it has been decapitated.

Those illustrations that move toward the most literal of representation, with Christ among the candlesticks of Revelation 1, end up seeming to obliterate the very realism that the artist was trying to capture. The risen Christ has become a monstrosity of sorts. Yet this literalism, this visual signifying as a linear exercise, surely supports and is of the same spirit as the translator's, Martin Luther's,

for whom verbal signifying as a linear exercise (the literal interpretation of
the Scripture) provided the certainty he sought as he held out the Bible as
the fundamental ground and authority of religious truth.[16] In both visual
and verbal sign, the literal sense is the authoritative one, executed through
linearity.

Leon Battista Alberti's On Painting: *Technique and the Control of Meaning*

Leon Battista Alberti was the man referred to by Jacob Burckhardt as
the first universal genius of the Renaissance period[17] (we will later return to
Burckhardt's assessment of Calvin). Born in 1404, Alberti is associated with
the great artistic movement of fifteenth-century Florence, doing his work as
Brunelleschi, Donatello, and Ghiberti led the way of the artistic revolution.
Alberti entered Florence in 1434 as part of a papal delegation and witnessed a
period of remarkable productivity as Florentine culture was, in a sense, sculpted
by the genius of the new art to present a new face to the world.[18]

Alberti was a man of wide learning, and he combined knowledge of painting,
sculpture, architecture, language and letters, mathematics (especially geometry),
natural science, and philosophy to produce *On Painting* in 1435 (Alberti translated his own work from Latin, *De pictura*, into Italian, *Della pittura*).[19] Through

16. Still a basic resource on Luther's work as an exegete is Jaroslav Pelikan's *Luther the Expositor* (St. Louis: Concordia, 1959). See also Scott Hendrix, "Luther against the Background
of the History of Biblical Interpretation," *Interpretation* 37, no. 3 (July 1983): 229–39. There
Hendrix speaks to the levels of interpretation—historical, prophetic, christological—in Luther.
In my understanding, all of these are literal since they are all used to explicate the one legitimate
meaning of a scriptural passage. This is the sense in which, even when a passage is taken as
allegorical by Luther, allegorical interpretation is the one legitimate interpretation: there is a
straight line, as it were (linear), from verbal sign to meaning.

17. Jacob Burckhardt, *The Civilization of the Renaissance in Italy* (1860; repr. London:
Phaidon, 1960), 85–87. Burckhardt's idealized presentation of Alberti was quite influential
though overblown. A book that seeks to present a better historical picture of Alberti—without
the strictures imposed by Burckhardt's interpretation—is Anthony Grafton's *Leon Battista
Alberti: Master Builder of the Italian Renaissance* (New York: Hill & Wang, 2000).

18. For an account of Alberti's arrival in Florence of the 1430s and a description of the city's
artistic environment, see Samuel Y. Edgerton, *The Renaissance Rediscovery of Linear Perspective*
(New York: Basic Books, 1975), 32–37; for a shorter description, but one that also includes a brief
introduction to the Alberti family history, see John R. Spencer, introduction to Leon Battista
Alberti, *On Painting*, trans. John R. Spencer, rev. ed. (New Haven: Yale University Press, 1966),
15–17; see also this work's dedicatory letter to Brunelleschi, in which Alberti himself praised
the works of the Florentine artists (39–40).

19. The above translation by Spencer is based on extant Italian and Latin manuscripts by
which means Spencer tried to create a hypothetical text that he thought most closely mirrored
Alberti's intentions. Another translation, from the Latin text and presenting the Latin alongside the English (Latin verso, English recto), is Leon Battista Alberti's *"On Painting" and "On*

this treatise he tried to provide the theoretical foundation for what he saw happening around him. In this, he was wildly successful. *On Painting* became, in many ways, the handbook for painting in the high Renaissance period, not just because of the technique it espoused but also because of Alberti's approach to the status of painting and the way he elevated the artist from mere craftsman to a person engaged in creating knowledge.[20]

Alberti's work details how, in the production of a painting, the artist can benefit from the use of mathematics, especially geometry and proportion. There are three stages in the process, according to *On Painting*: circumscription, composition, and reception of light. Circumscription has to do with how space is bounded. Composition relates to how the parts of a painting fit together, the relative position of things circumscribed that work together to present the painting's point of view. Finally, there is the reception of light, or the coloring, shades of light and dark (so famously explored later by Leonardo da Vinci).[21]

At the foundation of this process of visual representation is circumscription, and here Alberti introduced the reader to the notions of proportion and ratio. All visible things, he observed, are known only as they relate to other visible things. From this come ideas of big, small, far, near, and so forth. And as should not be surprising, though perhaps not meant in the philosophical sense that would become common, Alberti wrote of how man is the measure of all things. But in this case, he is speaking of the human as a measuring stick. The human should be circumscribed in the appropriate ratios (in thirds) so that one has a well-balanced representation of the human. Then, things to be represented can be circumscribed in proportion to the human figure. And these things, quite literally, are only sensible—in both senses of the word (the sensate and the reasonable)—insofar as they truly reflect the proper proportions in relation to the human figure.[22]

Sculpture": The Latin Texts of "De pictura" and "De statua," trans. with introduction and notes by Cecil Grayson (London: Phaidon, 1972). This is the edition from which I will cite (by title, On Painting). The citation from Spencer's translation for the dedicatory letter to Brunelleschi (see note 18 above) can be found in Grayson's translation of On Painting, 32–33. There is another available English translation: Leon Battista Alberti, "On Painting" and "On Sculpture," trans. Cecil Grayson, introduction and notes by Martin Kemp (New York: Penguin, 1991).

20. As Joan Gadol says in her work on Alberti and his outlook, art "yields knowledge rather than utility" because of its relationship to science and mathematics (Gadol, "Leon Battista Alberti: The Renaissance of Geometric Space in Art and Science" [PhD diss., Columbia University, 1965], 282).

21. A discussion of circumscription, composition, and coloring is the subject, mostly, of the second book (of three) in On Painting, paragraphs 33–50 (the actual text of Grayson's translation of On Painting is best cited by paragraph number, which corresponds to both the Latin text and the English translation).

22. Ibid., 18–19.

To delve a little further into the book, Alberti relied heavily on the rectangle and the triangle as geometric forms by which reality could be most faithfully represented. By proper circumscription through reliance on parallelism, angle, and confluence, sensible reality could be captured on the canvas and preserved as a true representation of the thing under consideration.[23]

Following our purposes, we observe that for Alberti a representation was true less because it looked like what it sought to represent, or that it reflected back so-called reality so that one saw the natural correspondence of the thing represented (though if well done the representation would do both), but it was true especially because sensible reality itself and the representative medium by which it could be signified both rely, in the end, on the same foundation: mathematics. As Alberti understood it, the mathematics that undergirded good drawing was the same thing that supported the natural order.[24]

Much has been made of Alberti's reliance on the notion of nature as the model of the artist, the teacher of the artist, perhaps even as the goal of the artist. But, at heart, the reason nature is the best guide to the artist, according to his book, is because it embodies so perfectly the geometric ratios; in a sense, nature is mathematics incarnate. Thus the depths of nature can be plumbed by the same method as the truest artistic expressions: through the application and understanding of mathematical proportions.[25]

It is in this sense, as artist re-creates creation based on the same principles on which creation is founded, that the artist moves from artisan to scholar, from a person merely plying a trade to a person actively engaged in the production of knowledge. That, in the end, was Alberti's vision: the artist as scientist, who pulls the veil of mystery from the visible world to reveal its workings.[26] All was to be based on proper understanding of place in space.

23. Ibid., 20–24.

24. In describing the intent of the three books in his dedication to Brunelleschi, Alberti indicated that the first book would be "entirely mathematical, show[ing] how this noble and beautiful art arises from roots within Nature herself" (On Painting, unnumbered paragraph that precedes book 1, paragraph 1, to Brunelleschi). Later, he said, "As Nature clearly and openly reveals all these proportions, so the zealous painter will find great profit from investigating them in Nature for himself" (On Painting, 36).

25. Again, nature is important because, as Gadol reads it in not only On Painting but also in several of Alberti's works, nature is viewed geometrically, and ratios order all sensible reality (Gadol, "Leon Battista Alberti," 293–94).

26. Indeed, Gadol argues that the method Alberti detailed helped lead to the development of the modern mind: "Focusing upon position rather than quality, determining the ideal proportions among sensible things rather than their spiritual worth as the approach [to] God, who transcends all sensory experience [perspective], provides the corner-stone of modern art and

In this type of representation, therefore, what one sees is the development of artistic modes of expression that were able to reflect the reality of the thing represented by participation in the principles that made the reality itself possible. The import of this way of thinking, it seems to me, was to collapse the difference between sign and thing signified so that the relationship between the two became a type of literal one-to-one correspondence.

Was this the intent of Alberti? It would seem so, at least in terms of a drive toward the artistically literal, because as Alberti moved away from form—circumscription and so forth based on mathematical principles—and wrote of content or meaning in the representational process, that too, it turns out, was put under the control of the artist. The representation was to be composed in such a way as to create a narrative, a story; in other words, technique was put at the service of form, yes, but it also served content. And form and content worked together, according to Alberti, to exhibit the "meaning" of the picture. This "historia," as it was termed, was understood as nothing other than the appropriate meaning directed by the signs. In other words, ideally, the representation was so composed that it signified the story/point/meaning that the painting had.[27] If one takes literalness to mean a type of univalency, then at this point, theoretically in any case, art in technique and meaning became literal.

---

science. *Prospettiva* is the discipline which provides the logical motif by which the Renaissance brought about the systematic revolution that characterizes the modern mind" (ibid., 385). Also quite helpful is the chapter titled "The 'Symbolic Form' of the Italian Renaissance," in Edgerton, *Linear Perspective*, 153–65. Aside from speaking of how the new perspective probably helped advance science even more than art (163–64), comments that run through this chapter on printing and verbal communication are also highly suggestive for the aims of this chapter.

27. Edgerton well describes the purpose of the "historia": through *historia*, desirable qualities are to be taught (and the purpose is, according to Edgerton's reading of Alberti, didactic through and through, see Edgerton, *Linear Perspective*, 31). This teaching, however, was to be accomplished primarily through evoking proper emotions (on this, see Cecil Grayson, introduction to *On Painting*, 14). According to Alberti, this was accomplished as follows: "A 'historia' will move spectators when the men painted in the picture outwardly demonstrate their own feelings as clearly as possible. Nature provides . . . that we mourn with the mourners, laugh with those who laugh, and grieve with the grief-stricken. Yet these feelings are known by the movements of the body. . . . I like there to be someone in the 'historia' who tells the spectators what is going on, and either beckons them with his hand to look, or with ferocious expression and forbidding glance challenges them not to come near, . . . or points to some danger or remarkable thing in the picture, or by his gestures invites you to laugh or weep with them" (*On Painting*, 41, 42). Carolyn Wilde observes, "Thus although Alberti was establishing general conditions for the construction of pictorial space, his system sets new limits, not only to the sorts of things which can be depicted, and to the manner of their depiction, but also to the meanings which those things have" (Wilde, "Introduction: Alberti and the Formation of Modern Art Theory," in *A Companion to Art Theory*, ed. Paul Smith and Carolyn Wilde [Oxford: Blackwell, 2002], 12).

Leonardo da Vinci: Signification and Knowledge

Leonardo da Vinci's *Last Supper* graces one of the walls of the refectory of the convent of Santa Maria delle Grazie in Milan. A work that took almost three years, da Vinci finished the work in the late 1490s (1497/98). One of the accomplishments of the painting is its illusion of depth: three-dimensional life has been captured on a two-dimensional surface. This effect was achieved by the application of linear perspective,[28] sometimes referred to as single-point perspective, and the *Last Supper* represents the culmination of Leonardo's work in the application of linear perspective to regular geometrical man-made shapes.[29] (After this he moved to human contours, experimenting with perspectives of light, colors, shading, and so forth. But though the spatial context became less controlled by linear perspective, that perspective still undergirds his work in the human figures he created.)

The idea of linear perspective is closely identified with the art of the Renaissance and with the aforementioned Alberti.[30] It was understood as the geometric explanation for the vanishing point—at the time called the centric point from a frontal perspective—the point where parallel lines over distance seem to converge. Think of standing on a railroad track and seeing the tracks converge in the distance. This becomes the basis for the development of the sense of depth needed to make paintings seem realistic.

There is a vast literature, containing vehement disagreements, on the development of linear perspective.[31] Some suggest that this perspective mirrors reality; others argue that it is purely a symbolic form expressing the worldview of the times in which it became dominant. A usual course of approach is to trace the following development: Early in the fourteenth century Giotto di Bondone (ca. 1267–1337) became aware that the problem of linear perspective

28. Linear perspective is about organization of space; as Wilde says, "Linear perspective in painting depends on establishing a theoretical vantage point from which the variable qualities of things, their appearance under perspective, can be systematically organized, so as to appear visually consistent" (Wilde, "Introduction," 9).

29. On this, see Kim Veltman in collaboration with Kenneth D. Keele, *Linear Perspective and the Visual Dimensions of Science and Art*, Studies on Leonardo da Vinci 1 (Munich: Deutscher Kunstverlag, 1986), 338.

30. For a brief assessment of Alberti's place in the history of art, see Wilde, "Introduction," 5.

31. For Alberti's development of linear perspective, see Wilde, "Introduction," 8–10. Scholars have greatly debated whether Alberti "invented" linear perspective or simply wrote down what others had discovered in his own time or recovered something found in the works of ancient Greek and Roman artists; yet no one denies the vast influence of *On Painting* on Renaissance art and its development. For some of these discussions, see Erwin Panofsky, *Renaissance and Renascences in Western Art* (Uppsala: Almqvist & Wiksells, 1960), 123; and Edgerton, *Linear Perspective*, 3–7.

was there to be solved. The work of Fillipo Brunelleschi (1377–1446) in Florence during the early 1430s represented the first practical application of it. In 1435 Alberti wrote a treatise, the earliest extant, on linear perspective and its application. Then much of this work received important contributions—theoretical, practical, and experimental—from Leonardo da Vinci. And there was a process of systematic study and reflection in what came to be known as academic art or school art, which continued through the seventeenth century.[32] There also are antecedents in the Classical Period of ancient Greece (480–300 BCE), and important shifts and developments in the Middle Ages. Though these are important, for our purposes we want to focus on the fact that these influences, shifts, and so forth converge in a unique way in the fifteenth century so that by the beginning of the sixteenth this revolution of perspective is well under way and sweeping Europe.

To condense a great deal of material,[33] let us explore the basics involved in producing the type of linear perspective found in Leonardo's *Last Supper* and what results from having produced such a work. The production of linear perspective has, first of all, to do with mathematics, especially geometry. Planes, lines, and points are involved in creating the spatial environment; what is more, ratio becomes important. Formulas had to be developed that governed how, for example, people separated by depth of distance in the picture could be realistically drawn.

The work also included the development or adaptation of instruments to help capture a realistic look. Leonardo used mirrors, reticulated nets, frames, and so forth to help guide the appropriate creation of proportion or to help judge whether the depth of an object had been truly captured.

Observation became important, observing things as they truly appeared in the natural world. Those artists who led the revolution in perspective aimed to render the natural world in their art in as realistic a manner as possible. For Leonardo, this meant understanding what exactly he was drawing; surface

32. The person who, it seems to me, has done the most research on the question of linear perspective is Kim Veltman. Some of his work, as in note 29 above, is available in print; other materials (a huge amount, really) is available on the Internet. For a history of the development of linear perspective (what I have provided in the text is a skeletal and abbreviated outline), see Kim H. Veltman, "The Sources and Literature of Linear Perspective," vol. 3, "Literature on Perspective," www.sumscorp.com/perspective/Vol3/title.html, which takes one to the table of contents. In Web format, it is easiest to click on the chapter title desired, and then one may click on the section within that chapter. So, citing chapter and section, one may find his account of the history of linear perspective at 1.2; 1.9; and passim throughout chap. 1.

33. Veltman, *Linear Perspective and the Visual Dimensions*, 338, esp. where Veltman says, "In his early work [Leonardo] explores the potentials of vanishing points and receding lines characteristic of linear perspective when applied to regular geometrical man-made shapes. These interests culminate in the *Last Supper* (1495–1497)."

knowledge was not enough. Therefore, for example, one should be able to draw down through an object—a person, let us say—through clothes, skin, muscle, bones, and then back out again. Or as Kim Veltman has pointed out: "Linear perspective, because it involves a systematic organization of space, introduces a means of representing convincingly the various levels or layers in . . . organic forms. . . . In short, the perspectival rendering of internal organic forms, Leonardo achieves uniquely by the technique of transparency."[34] In other words, when Leonardo spoke of observation, he did not mean it in any simple manner: there is more to it, so to speak, than meets the eye.

This led Leonardo to engage in the creation of models—halfway houses, if you like, between the thing being depicted (the natural) and the illusion being created (the picture). Thus for the best representation of the reality of the natural, as Leonardo understood it, one had to engage in the construction of the artificial, realizing that both are based on mathematical constructs.

This perspective moves one toward Leonardo's conviction that, for the truest representation of the natural world, there could be no practice without science. He considered experience important, but it had to be directed by theory and the theory had to be mathematical, with all the advantages of mathematics: an artificial language conveying to the mind the truest sense of the world as it is, and in the same exact manner each time its symbols are used. This involved a principle of reversibility, so that one can move from end back to the beginning (true in mathematics and linear perspective and a basic scientific concept). It also called for an assurance of repeatability, the hallmark of experimental method, documenting the hows, the method, of work in order to repeat it.[35]

These basics that relate to linear perspective then built toward a view of representation that is held not only by Leonardo but became generally held also by the developing scientific community. Leonardo was certain that mathematical language was superior to normal verbal language, that the signs of the former better represented things than the signs of the latter. What is more, the painting, the visual statement, was superior to the verbal statement because, if undertaken appropriately, the painting reflected the same mathematical and especially geometric laws that undergird nature and the natural world.[36]

34. Ibid., 202.
35. Ibid., 368–69.
36. Ibid., 368. Because of its link to mathematics, there developed an emphasis on particulars in a way previously not exhibited in art or art theory. A number of things that Veltman suggests in his essay play into understanding what has happened to signification, as I propose and discuss below. Linear perspective and its basis caused people to pay more attention to the verbal description of particulars (375); perspective "prompted new combinations of literal visualization and visual literalism" (377); "in the North there was a greater interest in the veracity

In this sense, Leonardo anticipated, for example, Galileo, who stated, "Philosophy is written in this grand book, the universe, which stands continually open to our gaze. But the book cannot be understood unless one first learns to comprehend the language and read the letters in which it is composed. It is written in the language of mathematics, and its characters are triangles, circles and other geometric figures without which it is humanly impossible to understand a single word of it."[37]

If, as articulated here, the universe is composed in the language of mathematics and the signification that opens up that universe is a literal one, then it is easy to see how one could slide into the position that the best method of signification, which opens up the cosmos and its reality, is the language of real knowledge of the way things are. In other words, the system of signification that leads to such knowledge is actually the language of truth. In this sense, Leonardo understood the artist to be a scientist in the strongest sense of the word: his "language" has circumscribed a body of knowledge that appears self-validating in terms of truth, because it is a language that is reversible, repeatable, and observable in the effects that it predicts.

Linear Perspective, Signification, and the Development of the Scientific Worldview

A fellow named Nicholaus Steno published his *Prodromus* in 1669. It marked the beginning of geology as a science of evolution, wherein the principles of relative age dating were laid out. Such dating, however, was based on understanding proper spatial relationships.[38]

Geologist Gary Rosenberg has argued that this grasp of spatial relationships, particularly in nature, was what set the West off toward its dominance

---

of verbal images, as reflected in Luther's emphasis on literal interpretation of the scriptures" (377). The connection between trends in art and art theory and the use of language is pursued further in a later work by Veltman (see Veltman, "Literature on Perspective," esp. 1.8; 1.16; and passim). Moreover, Leonardo's approach to art is seen not only as mathematical and scientific but also as embodying the modern mind: "For modern scholarship, Leonardo's scientific ideal of painting is a distinctly *modern* ideal: it instances the scientific habit of mind that motivates all his researches and that makes him one of the forerunners of the Enlightenment" (Robert Williams, "The Spiritual Exercises of Leonardo da Vinci," in Smith and Wilde, *Companion to Art Theory*, 75).

37. Quoted from Stillman Drake, *Discoveries and Opinions of Galileo* (New York: Doubleday Anchor Books, 1957), 237–38.

38. Nicolaus Steno, *De solido intra solidum naturaliter contento dissertationis prodromus* [Forerunner to a Dissertation on a Solid Body Contained Naturally within a Solid] (Florence: Stellae, 1669); an English translation can be found in *The Prodromus of Nicolaus Steno's "Dissertation concerning a Solid Body Enclosed by Process of Nature within a Solid,"* trans. John Garrett Winter (New York: Hafner, 1968).

in science.[39] Though the Chinese far outstripped the West in terms of technical achievements for a long time, it was the West's grasp on proper spatialization of nature that led to the fundamentals of the scientific outlook being developed in Western countries. In other words, this geologist declares, the West captured space in three dimensions while the East remained two-dimensional in its representations of nature. In particular, Rosenberg points to Renaissance art and its development of linear perspective, along with other techniques, that put the West on the path of true science.

His argument is that the words Steno used to develop certain principles of stratigraphy were the verbal expression of an artistic technique found in Leonardo da Vinci, especially as exhibited in his drawing of some hills in Tuscany. The visual preceded the verbal, though only in geologic terms. Leonardo himself articulated the basic scientific principle when he spoke of how art and science were two sides of the same coin, because he saw in both the use of mathematical principles to lay bare the truth of reality. The reason one can use mathematical principles to create linear expression—the means by which the three-dimensional is laid out in a two-dimensional framework—is partly because nature has been created according to mathematical principles—obviously and especially geometry. Rosenberg thus sees a strong connection between how space is represented and how one is then able to study it scientifically.[40] Others have suggested this connection between linear perspective and the development of science,[41] but Rosenberg is the first to apply it specifically to the creation of the geological sciences.

I find Rosenberg's ideas fascinating, but I think he has missed something more basic and perhaps also more diffuse: the change that he sees taking place in Western culture could be less causative than symptomatic. Perhaps rather than speaking of cause and effect, as Rosenberg does, we can simply recognize some basic shifts in signification, that those shifts have practical effects in the world, which then play back to strengthen the shift, which then have even more practical effects in the world (as reinforcing feedback). So, rather than cause and effect, let us say that the shift is in a sense both cause and effect, or if you like, a helix figure of interaction between culture and language. This process

39. Gary Rosenberg, "An Artistic Perspective on the Continuity of Space and the Origin of Modern Geologic Thought," *Earth Sciences History* 20, no. 2 (2001): 127–55.

40. Thus one of the main points of Rosenberg's article is that the development of perspective was crucial to the development of the scientific mind-set in Europe, and it also explains, therefore, why science rose in the West—where linear perspective in art developed—rather than in China, which until the sixteenth and seventeenth centuries was ahead of the West technologically.

41. Probably the best argued book on the topic of linear perspective and the rise of science is Samuel Y. Edgerton, *The Heritage of Giotto's Geometry: Art and Science on the Eve of the Scientific Revolution* (Ithaca, NY: Cornell University Press, 1991).

works toward a world in which what is seen as the "best" working of a sign becomes singularly authoritative and tied to the notion of truth.

What I am arguing—quite tentatively, as I explore my thesis through a variety of writings and expressions—is that signification itself became linear, where the sign—the best sign—was seen as a literal sign, a sign that reflected exactly a reality and in only one way. This happened in art during the Renaissance, where the visual sign was viewed as a true mirror of natural reality. The literal nature of the sign—one sign, one exact meaning, with a loss of anything resembling true metaphoric fluidity—is certainly essential to things such as mathematics and science. But one also sees this trend in language—spoken and written signification.

There are, then, impulses at work in the culture of the sixteenth century that pushed signification toward the literal. It did not happen completely and all at once. Yet the trend does, indeed, seem to be lodged there, and it began to affect the articulation of doctrine in the sixteenth century.

Social Context, Language, and the Shift to the Literal: Observations on Calvin and Beza

Some literalizing process was afoot in the sixteenth century. One may want to think of the artistic movement as giving impetus and vision to the scientific, or one may simply see a propitious confluence of artistic theory, scientific development, advances in mathematics, and so forth. Whichever view one takes, it still may be the case that this shift toward the literal in signification is one way (among others) to come to grips with developments in the Reformed tradition and can serve as one lens (among several) by which to view what happened in the sixteenth century and later.

And that is the point, at least initially: to provide a way to examine the place of Beza and others who come after Calvin within the context of their time and culture. In some of the older historiography there has been a tendency to view Beza's religious thought as the initial decline of Calvin's theology.[42] Once Calvin's image was repaired, at least among specialists, there was a tendency to transfer the negative stereotypes of Calvin to those who followed him: a "save Calvin from the Calvinists" kind of group, who sought to save the good name of the founder by passing off the bad assessments of him to his successors.[43] R. Scott Clark warns us against golden-age historiography, looking at

42. See note 7 above.
43. See Basil Hall, "Calvin against the Calvinists," in *John Calvin*, ed. G. E. Duffield (Appleford: Sutton Courtenay, 1966), 19–37. This tendency in the literature seems to follow a general

Calvin's time as a summit of sorts, after which there was inevitable decline.[44] For historiographical reasons, Richard Muller has certainly also questioned a host of authors who seem to embrace this perspective and replaces such a perspective with a more positive and historically contextualized look at the Reformed Scholastics.[45] And indeed, it seems to be an appealing way to "save" Calvin from a point of view that one finds even in the last writings of Heiko Oberman, at least as he wrote about the excesses of Reformed Scholasticism.[46]

The other option to avoid is to think of Beza and later Reformed Scholasticism simply as the natural fulfillment of the Calvinist agenda. Here the historical model is not one of golden age and declension but of the organic model so well articulated in the nineteenth century by John Henry Cardinal Newman in his *Essay on the Development of Doctrine*, wherein doctrine is a seed that naturally grows and develops.[47] If the danger of the golden-age

---

trend to protect a founder of a movement from the perceived excesses/problems/shortcomings of the followers when this founder is compared with other important founding figures in religious traditions. To stay close to home, one sees it later in the Reformed tradition in the treatment of Jonathan Edwards's followers, where, once again, those who came after him are accused of fundamentally altering the intentions of the "master." The most obvious example of this impulse is Joseph Haroutunian's *Piety versus Moralism: The Passing of the New England Theology* (New York: Henry Holt, 1932). Here readers find that Beza and other followers of Calvin are excoriated in the same manner as are the New Divinity divines who came after Edwards.

44. Carl R. Trueman and R. Scott Clark, ed., *Protestant Scholasticism: Essays in Reassessment* (Carlisle, UK: Paternoster, 1999), xv–xvii.

45. For his warning against golden-age historiography, see Richard A. Muller, *Christ and the Decree: Christology and Predestination in Reformed Theology from Calvin to Perkins*, paperback ed. (Grand Rapids: Baker Academic, 1988), 180. For his evaluation of the history of scholarship on the question of continuity between Calvin and his followers on especially the question of predestination, see 1–13. For his broader argument about the need for studying Scholasticism on its own terms rather than seeing it as a decline from the founding reformers, see Richard A. Muller, *Post-Reformation Reformed Dogmatics*, vol. 1, *Prolegomena to Theology* (Grand Rapids: Baker Academic, 1987), esp. 13–41.

46. See Oberman, *Two Reformations*, 136, 140, 141–42.

47. John Henry Newman, *An Essay on the Development of Christian Doctrine* (1845; repr., Notre Dame, IN: University of Notre Dame Press, 1989). Though I would not want to say that Richard Muller's work falls into this category, at times it seems to border on it. He argues that, historically, one must look at both the continuities and discontinuities of doctrine; yet he seems to highlight the continuities of the substance of Calvin's doctrines with what becomes Reformed Scholasticism while casting the discontinuities as simply a matter of method and form: "Much of the literature assumes a discontinuity between the thought of the Reformers and their orthodox successors without recognizing that a change in form and method does not necessarily indicate an alteration of substance" (Muller, *Post-Reformation Reformed Dogmatics*, 1:20). "Protestant orthodox theology is different from the theology of the Reformation—more so in form than in substance—but it is this very difference that marks its historical and doctrinal importance in the life of the church" (ibid., 1:311). Though Muller does not use the organic metaphors, it is not too difficult here to read him in terms of nineteenth-century organicism (an acorn is different from

historian is that the continuities of thought are ignored for the sake of mapping out a declension, then in the development model there is the danger of ignoring the real differences that appear for the sake of emphasizing "true" continuity.

Both approaches, it seems to me, take doctrine out of its social context, wherein there are both continuities and developments, changes and indeed losses, but more to the point, where there is an environment that changes over time and calls forth, at least for those who want to speak authoritatively within that culture, conformity to certain paradigms. It seems to me that *one way* (but certainly not the only way) to think of Calvin, Beza, and their relationship (and that of later Reformed Scholastics) is to explore the place they occupied in relation to a shifting paradigm of signification.

In his book *The Real Jesus*, Luke Timothy Johnson makes a comment about the Protestant Reformation, especially embodied in the work of Martin Luther, that is rather revealing. He implies that current movements in the historical-critical approach to the Bible that take the Bible out of its social situation within the church and place it outside the church into a hostile society that seeks to undermine its message are fundamentally Luther's fault (because of Luther's emphasis on a "right reading" of Scripture in combination with the individualism that, Johnson assumes, runs throughout Luther's theology). Though one may not agree with Johnson's historical summation about Luther's role and its effects on the history of biblical criticism, he does stress something of importance, if read aright: "[Luther's] approach to the New Testament . . . was deeply if unconsciously affected by the intellectual climate of the Renaissance."[48]

Johnson's words, "intellectual climate of the Renaissance," may be helpful if taken in the sense that they mean more than a simply conscious turn of the intellect—if "Renaissance" is seen as a movement that itself is product as well as producer of a paradigm shift in signification. Taken within this context, one can assume that developments in art are part of a larger development for the whole of Western Europe at this time, first perhaps among the literate, but then trickling down to the masses. Then one

---

an oak, though more in form than in substance). This is not to indict Muller's vantage point: indeed, I find it quite helpful at times. His point may well be valid when one considers theology in and of itself, yet I suggest that at some level a change in form actually leads to a change in how the substance is appropriated. As we have seen with a few of the Renaissance-era artists and their work and its interpretation, ordering something in a new way does have some effect on how knowledge is understood. For discussion of this and tips on where to look for more detailed analyses, see Veltman, "Literature on Perspective," 1.14; 1.16.

48. Luke Timothy Johnson, *The Real Jesus: The Misguided Quest for the Historical Jesus and the Truth of the Traditional Gospels* (San Francisco: HarperSanFrancisco, 1996), 68.

could as easily say that the Renaissance created the social space (or better yet, say that what is termed "Renaissance" is a way of signifying that new social space) in which the literal approach to Scripture would be necessary for one to speak authoritatively concerning religious matters. Again, if by "literal" one means a one-to-one correspondence between sign and thing signified, not only visual signs but also verbal signs are part of this shifting trajectory of signification. It seems that such a shift is apparent even to some within the sixteenth century itself. When Montaigne asked at what time people started "weighing and measuring words so exactly,"[49] he was asking about the weight of significance that individual words were, more and more, required to bear.

In some ways, Calvin served as a hinge figure, historically. He could be quite literal; on the other hand, he was also aware that, at times, the type of precision required in literal representation was not what was most moving. What we see in Calvin, in other words, is an embodiment of what I consider to be the dual thrust of the humanist movement: the notion of "good letters" along with the development of technical expertise in textual criticism. There was the mentality cultivated by the best of the Greco-Roman literature (and the biblical and patristic mentality for Christian humanists), on the one hand, and there was the expertise of textual recovery and translation, on the other. Calvin could work as a textual critic; this is something he learned from humanist scholars. On the other hand, he respected the breadth of language, and he especially recognized the rhetorical aspect of language, which for Calvin meant that language had to contain some flexibility when it came to the question of meaning. Two quick examples should suffice for illustrative purposes.

Example one: At times Calvin allowed the same word to mean two different things, thus providing space for the richness of a type of signification that is not bound to a one-to-one correspondence between sign and thing signified. One sees this in the way he dealt with 1 Corinthians 11, where Paul speaks of discerning the body. Calvin said that, *in this context*, "body" could mean both the true body of Christ and also the church as the body of Christ, whereas both Luther and Zwingli demanded that the word "body," in the 1 Corinthians 11:29 context, could mean only one thing, with Luther focusing on it as the true body of Christ and Zwingli on the church as the body of Christ.[50]

49. Michel de Montaigne, *The Complete Essays of Montaigne*, trans. Donald M. Frame (Stanford, CA: Stanford University Press, 1958), 757.

50. For Calvin's statement about the dual meaning of "body," see CNTC 9:264 (CO 49:501). For an analysis of how all three Reformers approach the notion of "discerning the body" in 1 Cor. 11, see chap. 9 above.

This instance reflects a more general stance of Calvin's, which serves as example two. In his "True Partaking of the Flesh and Blood of Christ," Calvin wrote of how, sometimes, the inexact metaphor carried the meaning better than a precise definition, at least in terms of reaching the hearts and minds of a congregation: "Although a figurative expression is not so distinct, it gives a more elegant and significant expression than if the thing were said simply, and without figure. Hence figures are called the eyes of speech, not that they explain the matter more easily than simple ordinary language, but because they attract attention by their elegance and arouse the mind by their lustre, and by their lively similitude better penetrate the soul."[51]

While not wanting to say that those who came after Calvin did not maintain an interest in rhetoric, I suggest that, for a variety of reasons, there developed an increased interest in exactly the more technical aspects of the humanist movement—especially in regard to establishing precise definitions, which tended to literalize the verbal sign (it certainly circumscribed it). One perhaps even sees the instincts of this move at work before Calvin began his work, for example, in the group that Erasmus wrote about in *Dialogus Ciceronianus*.[52] Here, rather than take Cicero as a rhetorical model for moving and effective speech, there was a group (and particularly a person) portrayed who would limit the use of Latin to its Ciceronian incarnation, using only words as Cicero would have used them. Again, there was a circumscription at work here to fence in language, its expression, and meaning.

What accompanies the trend in shifting paradigms of signification, exhibited in art and science and in certain thrusts of humanistic learning? In *Sanctifying Signs*, David Aers makes a persuasive case for the way Christian tradition was molded by how the sanctifying signs (in this case, both visual and verbal in relation to the Eucharist and to poverty) were controlled and tightly defined. Aers is writing about late medieval England, and he shows how the control of signification was tied to social control. Indeed, when the correct interpretation of the eucharistic sign became the controlling factor in the proclamation of a theological position as either orthodox or heretical,

51. John Calvin, "True Partaking of the Flesh and Blood of Christ," in *Selected Works of John Calvin: Tracts and Letters*, vol. 2, *Tracts*, part 2, ed. and trans. Henry Beveridge (Edinburgh: Calvin Translation Society, 1849; repr., Grand Rapids: Baker Books, 1983), 567 (CO 9:514), with translation slightly altered.

52. An English translation of this can be found in Desiderius Erasmus, *Ciceronianus, or, A Dialogue on the Best Style of Speaking*, trans. Izora Scott with introduction by Paul Monroe (New York: AMS Press, 1972).

with the consequences being execution for those found to be heretical, then the need for precision became extreme.[53]

It is no great leap, therefore, to the later time of the Reformation. Doctrine became more and more a basis for social control and punishment.[54] So, in addition to the intellectual shifts, which resulted in an increased emphasis on the literal, there were the wars of religion and persecution. Thus pressures came to bear on the doctrinal process that required precision. There was more: In an age of uncertainty, a topic of Susan Schreiner's research,[55] the need for authority also put pressure on language over and above the shift already taking place. If authority was needed as a foundation for certainty, then the authority that appeared most certain was most effective. And in an age coming increasingly to rely on the textual, the definition of words took on heightened meaning. The meaning that seemed surest was simplest, the meaning most related to the literal words of the text (so that an imposed "interpretation" seemed to be removed from the process).

There was also the change in location that had begun to take place in the Reformed tradition, adding to the weight of all the above factors in flattening out signification. As has been pointed out by numerous scholars, Scholasticism had to do with theology being done in the schools, whether they were medieval or early modern.[56] There was the concern for precision in language in the medieval schools: for example, when Thomas spoke of

53. David Aers, *Sanctifying Signs: Making Christian Tradition in Late Medieval England* (Notre Dame, IN: University of Notre Dame Press, 2004), esp. 27, though much of the book is implicitly related to this point.

54. This is not to say that there had not been earlier persecutions; there obviously had been. Indeed, it has been argued that the path to greater tolerance came through the Reformation. Yet whereas the force of persecution and extreme intolerance had been focused on groups outside Western Christendom and on small groups and individuals within, during the Reformation large state powers were involved in the struggles along with the apparatuses of various church authorities, part of which focused around matters of definition of doctrine and true Christianity, with civil penalties meted out to those who did not conform (the Council of Dort [1619] is one example among dozens). For one point of view on this situation, see Diarmaid MacCulloch, *The Reformation: A History* (New York: Viking, 2003), 645–56.

55. Susan Schreiner, "'The Spiritual Man Judges All Things': Calvin and Exegetical Debate about Certainty in the Reformation," in *Biblical Interpretation in the Era of the Reformation*, ed. Richard A. Muller and John L. Thompson (Grand Rapids: Eerdmans, 1996), 189–215. Though her essay does not present anything like the argument I make here, she does end her essay by speaking about how, within the context of martyrdom and execution, "certainty was the fundamental theological locus of the sixteenth century" (215).

56. David C. Steinmetz gives a fine introduction to Calvin's relationship to medieval Scholasticism: "The Scholastic Calvin," in Trueman and Clark, *Protestant Scholasticism*, 16–30. R. Scott Clark gives a quite helpful summary of some of the literature on Reformed Scholasticism and its contours: "The Authority of Reason in the Later Reformation: Scholasticism in Caspar Olevian and Antoine de La Faye," in Trueman and Clark, *Protestant Scholasticism*, 111–18.

the body of Christ in the host, he was quite specific that "body" meant "the whole body of Christ, that is, the bones and nerves and all the rest."[57] And one might trace the collapse of sign and thing signified—a literalizing process—to developments in medieval Catholic thought (again, see David Aer's acute observations here).[58] Thus there was a difference in cultural space that put the two school settings, medieval and early modern, into two quite different situations.

The change had to do with the shift in what constituted the culturally regnant form of language, and what use of language was recognized as best conveying truth. Though perhaps one sees the start of the process in medieval reflections on transubstantiation, it was the reinforcement of achievements in Renaissance art, architecture, and science that had begun to show the advantages of a literal method of signification. There was demonstrable power in the symbols; the type of language one finds in mathematics that supports work in both art and science exhibits a power to create wondrous things. As Zwingli worked with his own literal language, he might have insisted that "is" could mean only "represent" (one-to-one correspondence) from imbibing the growing spirit of the times in this regard (a sign can only legitimately mean one thing). Yet he missed the point when he tried to invoke an analogy from the art world, that no one would suggest that the representation of a person in a painting was actually that person.

What Zwingli missed was this: from the point of view of someone like Leonardo da Vinci, what is most truly represented in the best portraiture, what is best signified, is not the person per se but the mathematical qualities that serve as the basis for that person's form. In a sense, the picture, if done well, has really captured the essence of what makes for "form" in that person, for both person and portraiture are simply embodiments of the more foundational geometric principles at the heart of reality: thus the same reality is there in both, and thus, in a sense, sign and thing signified are actually collapsed.

The significance of my proposed theory is this: more and more, as the sixteenth century progressed, Beza and others who are thought of as followers of Calvin had to speak in the coin of the realm if they were to purchase any type of authority for their beliefs. Hence, what some see as a declension, or the development of an unnecessary rationalism, or growing entanglement in Aristotelian philosophy—all such was less a divergence and more an attempt to

57. See Thomas Aquinas, *Summa theologiae* (London: Blackfriars, 1964–81), 3.76.1, ad. 2: "Totum corpus Christi, id est ossa et nervi et alia huiusmodi."
58. The concern runs through much of the book, but see, for example, Aers, *Sanctifying Signs*, 17, 24, 25, 56–58.

address the culture in ways it valued through a medium it valued. And this was about method rather than content: many, obviously, will reject what became associated with the Reformed movement: its predestinarian affirmations. Yet the method of its presentation—in a precise, logical, literal-type language—represented, if you will, the only way of advocating its positions that would pass muster in a linguistic environment that required an almost mathematical approach in terms of signification.

What is more, Beza faced an even more severe problem than perhaps some who came after him—at least one might be led to think so if one extrapolates from the insights of Walter Ong. In *The Presence of the Word*, Ong argues that, beginning in the fifteenth century, the "word" became spatialized in a way it had not before because of the moveable-type press. There was a shift in which the visual began to take precedence over the aural in the use of words. Ong states: "The struggle, in which the disputatious oral approach to existence and knowledge lost much of its hold, was a struggle between hearing and seeing. Seeing won. With the shift in the sensorium by print, the large-scale campaign for the 'clear and distinct' soon began."[59] If seeing letters on a page, with the accompanying possibilities of literalism (by the letter) apparent by the very form in which language was presented, by writing rather than hearing—if this represented a shift in the way knowledge was won, think what an impression must have been made, not by a page of words, but by a printed table, something even more graphic.

Richard Muller has made a tremendous contribution to the study of Beza, and he has been particularly adept at putting Beza's famous *Tabula praedestinationis* into its larger theological context, helping to clear away several centuries of misunderstanding about the table and its meaning.[60] That said, however, the visual impact of the table was (and perhaps is) such that, one could say, it became a sign for the theology of Beza, however unfair or unnuanced this may be. If the trend of the sixteenth century was toward a literalization of signs, visual and verbal, then this combination sign, one that put words into a visually striking table, created a type of one-to-one correspondence between man and doctrine that, though perhaps unintentional and unfailingly unfair to the range and concerns of Beza's thought, came to serve as sign of the entire Reformed tradition.

59. Walter J. Ong, *The Presence of the Word: Some Prolegomena for Cultural and Religious History* (New Haven: Yale University Press, 1967; Minneapolis: University of Minnesota Press, 1981), 221.
60. See Richard A. Muller, "The Use and Abuse of a Document: Beza's *Tabula praedestinationis*, the Bolsec Controversy, and the Origins of Reformed Orthodoxy," in Trueman and Clark, *Protestant Scholasticism*, 33–61; and Muller, *Christ and the Decree*, 79–83.

Conclusion: Hardened Words, Hardened Hearts

We spoke earlier of how Jacob Burckhardt deemed Leon Battista Alberti the first "universal genius" of the Renaissance and that we would come back to him for his assessment of Calvin. It is quite bleak. Burckhardt asserts that "it was a misfortune for France that its chances for reformation came entirely into Calvin's hands." Burckhardt associates Calvin with predestination (as though Luther never uttered the word) and with the death of Servetus. Particularly for the latter, "it has been necessary to erect whole bastions of palliation around Calvin's behavior in Geneva." Burckhardt asserts that "the real Geneva had the greatest possible antipathy for him." Why? Simple, according to Burckhardt: "The tyranny of one single individual who makes his subjectivity the universal law and not only enslaves or expels all other convictions, including very good *Protestant* ones, but also every day insults everyone in the most innocent matters of taste, has never been carried further." And so, "Geneva endured him, the greatest pessimist, the stranger."[61]

Such an assessment lacks historical balance, yet it is typical. And one does not have to have read Western civilization textbooks to gain such an image of Calvin. The nineteenth century is full of popular novels that also associate Calvinists with predestination and persecution. Sometimes they run from the humorous, such as Harriet Beecher Stowe's *Old Towne Folks*, in which all level-headed New Englanders know to avoid the logic traps of the Calvinists; to obvious frontal attacks on the tradition, such as Leo Judd's *Margaret*, in which Christ himself appears to let the dour and controlling Calvinist know that the free-will–loving child Margaret is actually his true child.[62]

Hard words are now associated with Calvin and Beza: hard in the sense that they are rigid, meant as literal representations of the men and their doctrine, devoid of nuance or concern for context. And so we see how the trend in signification toward the literal during the fifteenth and sixteenth centuries has continued, at least in this regard (and others, I would argue: the culturally regnant language is still one, I believe, that relies most heavily on one-to-one correspondence between sign and thing signified, talk of postmodernism to the contrary).

Such a situation makes it difficult to cut through the stereotypes of Calvin and Beza: they are represented by the literal signs of predestination and persecution, and these hard words make for hard hearts (and intellects). They have

---

61. This paragraph, and the quotes contained therein, come from Jacob Burckhardt, *Judgments on History and Historians*, trans. Harry Zohn (Boston: Beacon, 1958), 131, 134–35.
62. For fuller analysis of these novels, see Davis, "Rhetorical War and Reflex."

become words that are part of our language and symbol system.[63] And if Calvin can occasionally slip through the vice-grip of stone-rigid representation, it is an uphill battle to free Beza and the rest of the Protestant Scholastics. My hope is that, in examining the shift in language and in understanding the import of such a shift, we can better understand Calvin and Beza and the whole range of the Reformed tradition in their respective contexts. Thereby we may have a means by which to undercut stereotypes that have resulted from that shift, stereotypes that stand in the way of real historical understanding.

63. There is no doubt that, in the minds of many, predestination is linked with religious persecution and that the broader Reformed tradition (in the United States, what is understood as the "Puritan" tradition) is primarily linked to the notion of predestination. For an analysis of this, see Davis, "Images of Intolerance." The use of Calvin as a symbol for negative things is surprisingly far ranging, as this chapter shows (on this, one should consult as well Marilynne Robinson, *The Death of Adam: Essays on Modern Thought* [1998; repr., New York: Picador, 2005], 12–24, 174–226). In addition, to see what sort of information is routinely given out for Calvin in high school history courses today, one can check the many Web sites that carry the Advanced Placement European History course outlines, one of which gives the following outline for John Calvin:

John Calvin (1509–64), *Institutes of the Christian Religion* (1536)
    Calvinism: predestination, the "elect," Puritan or Protestant work ethic
    Most militant and uncompromising of all Protestants
    Calvin established a theocracy in Geneva
    Michael Servetus (1511–53): Unitarian beliefs; burned at stake

See www.homestead.com/chaffeyaphistory/files/Euro_Notes_Terms_Concepts.htm. See also, Nathan Barber, *Peterson's AP European History*, one of the standard guides, found at www .petersons.com/pdf/ap_european_history_print.pdf, page 107.

INDEX